AN INTRODUCTION TO ENGLISH
HISTORICAL DEMOGRAPHY

Cambridge Group for the History of
Population and Social Structure
Publication No. 1

AN INTRODUCTION TO ENGLISH HISTORICAL DEMOGRAPHY

From the Sixteenth to the Nineteenth Century

D. E. C. EVERSLEY, PETER LASLETT

AND E. A. WRIGLEY

with contributions by

W. A. ARMSTRONG AND LYNDA OVENALL

EDITOR: E. A. WRIGLEY

Basic Books, Inc., Publishers
New York

CONTENTS

Preface   *Louis Henry*   vii

Editorial Note   *E. A. Wrigley*   x

1   Introduction: The Numerical Study
of English Society   *Peter Laslett*   1

2   Population History and Local History
     D. E. C. Eversley   14

3   Exploitation of Anglican Parish Registers by
Aggregative Analysis   *D. E. C. Eversley*   44

4   Family Reconstitution   *E. A. Wrigley*   96

5   The Study of Social Structure from Listings
of Inhabitants   *Peter Laslett*   160

6   Social Structure from the Early Census Returns
     W. A. Armstrong   209

Bibliography   *Lynda Ovenall*   238

Appendixes   264

Index   277

PREFACE

THE almost simultaneous publication of the *Introduction to English Historical Demography* and of the *Nouveau manuel de dépouillement et d'exploitation de l'état civil ancien* is a clear demonstration of the progress of historical demography. Works of this type are not written unless there are people who want to use them. This progress is evident in other ways also; in the amount of first-class research on the demography of the pre-statistical past which has been brought to a successful conclusion in the last fifteen years; in the appearance of historical demography at historical and demographic congresses; in the holding of meetings devoted entirely to this aspect of demography and history; in the creation of a society concerned solely with historical demography and of commissions of historical demography within historical and demographic organisations.

Only fifteen or twenty years ago this progress could scarcely have been foreseen. All the advanced countries had founded important statistical departments to record population numbers and movements. Apart from this there seemed to be scope only for amateur work of slight importance. Moreover, it was not thought possible to obtain good results except by a judicious combination of material drawn from two sources, the census on the one hand and the registration of vital statistics on the other.

Things have changed greatly since then. The success of other methods, in historical demography especially, has shown that this over-restrictive view was mistaken. Furthermore, even in current demography, that is the demography of advanced, contemporary populations, the classical methods no longer appear the best adapted to all problems. Sample studies are becoming increasingly important and, as a result, it is possible to use them instead of both the census and vital statistics or their equivalents. Making use of a single source of material is therefore no longer a characteristic of historical demography alone. Again, it is becoming recognised that using the classical sources of information, vital statistics and the census, which are anonymous, is not enough and that a nominative exploitation of either the one, or the other, or of them both, is sometimes necessary. This is already done, for example, in the study of mortality by socio-professional category in the United States and France; in British Columbia, H. B. Newcombe is attempting, primarily for genetic purposes, to bring together information about a single person collected by various organisations for different ends. In other words, the reconstitution of families, which has played an important part in the progress of historical demography is closely linked with some of the methods recently made use of by current demography. With this in mind it will seem less paradoxical that historical demography should have obtained some important results, especially in connection with fertility, before current demography.

This convergence of methods contributes, moreover, to the breaking down of the isolation of historical demography. This isolation will cease altogether when it becomes clear that all demography belongs, in large measure, to the historical sciences.

All these developments are such as to inspire historians and demographers working on the populations of the pre-statistical past with optimism. They might, however, have reason to fear that the state of the original documents which are available will create insurmountable difficulties.

Recent experience shows that these fears are often exaggerated. The parish registers of France are better than one might think, at least from 1740 onwards, and it is clear from reading this *Introduction* that English registers offer much greater possibilities than some scholars had at first believed. I am tempted to consider it a remarkable tribute to the success of nominative exploitation that it has found a way round the general absence of information about age at death in the burial registers, which is the worst deficiency of these registers. I am also tempted to conclude from this that, contrary to what is often supposed, nominative exploitation is indispensable for registers where ages (at death or, as in France, at marriage) are not given.

Preface

Difficulties do, however, still remain and the function of works like this *Introduction* lies precisely in teaching research workers how to overcome them. Nor is their usefulness limited to one country. The *Introduction* will interest French readers, to look no further, on several scores. It is very different from the French *manuels*, which are almost exclusively devoted to the techniques of analysing the registers and of family reconstitution, and many interesting developments are to be found in it which are not dealt with in the *manuels*. Moreover, it happens that some of the difficulties encountered in England in the eighteenth century are in general similar to those which occur in France in earlier periods. French research workers will be encouraged by this to work upon these earlier periods, for example the sixteenth century, and will find here a guide for their research. Finally, the *Introduction* devotes much space to methods of analysing lists of inhabitants and the basic documents of the early censuses. In a word this work is assured of a wide readership both in the United Kingdom and abroad.

Institut National d'Etudes   LOUIS HENRY
Démographiques, Paris
October, 1965

EDITORIAL NOTE

I T is prudent to begin with a disclaimer. This book was originally intended to serve several purposes: to describe the chief sources of information about the history of population and social structure in this country; to give brief accounts of the techniques which may be used in analysing the information; to try to establish common principles of working wherever possible; and to provide a full bibliography which should concentrate particularly on periodical literature since this is often the hardest to track down. Its title was to have been *A Manual of English Historical Demography*. But to have been as authoritative as such a title suggests would have meant a long delay in publication while the implications of work currently in progress were digested and a complete coverage of topics was achieved. Meanwhile more years would have passed during which work without uniformity of method or benefit of acquaintance with recent advances in technique would have continued.

The authors thought it impossible to reconcile fully the two desiderata of definitive treatment and early publication, and deemed the latter the more important consideration. This book therefore reflects rather a recognition of the *need* to provide guidance on sources and method, to ensure uniformity of presentation, and to compile a bibliography, than a full achievement of these aims. Indeed the pendulum swung far to the other extreme once a change of policy was agreed, for the manuscript was delivered to the publishers only six months after the book was first discussed. I hope that a second edition of this work substantially revised and supplemented will appear in, say, five years time and that this edition will fulfil the original conception. It would be foolish not to insist that parts of this edition will rapidly become outdated. In the meantime the authors hope that historians of all persuasions will find much in this work that will prove useful to them.

As a result of the decision to publish early, some types of source material (for example, the Hearth Tax returns) are dealt with only *en passant*. Some methods described are still in their infancy and will develop rapidly in the next few years. This is particularly true of the techniques adumbrated in chapter 5 on the analysis of listings of the inhabitants of communities, but it is true of all the chapters in some measure. Each chapter is now designed to show where rapid advance is taking place, how results are obtained, what materials are used, and what are the strengths and limitations of the techniques described.

Within the limits set by the need to secure uniformity in technical matters, each author has developed those aspects of his subject which seem to him most interesting and rewarding. Certainly the differences in personality and academic interests between the authors show through very clearly in their contributions, but I have felt this an advantage rather than a drawback since it provides an immediate illustration of the significance of historical demography to a very broad field of learning and scholarship.

The period covered by this book was determined mainly by the nature of the source materials used for historical demography. Recent advances in techniques of using parish register material pioneered in France have meant that the transition from the period of church-kept to the era of state-kept records now appears much less important than once it did. We do not move in 1801 (the first census) or in 1837 (the first vital statistics) from darkness into light in population history. The dark ages of population history ended in 1538, not in 1837. Yet the three centuries between these two dates form a natural whole in historical demography because throughout the period ecclesiastical documents are the source of the bulk of our knowledge. The year 1538 when parish registers were first kept in England provides a clear-cut beginning to the period. The census of 1841 may serve to mark its end. This census was the first to be taken after the state had begun to collect vital statistics and the published census volumes were for the first time based on information taken down separately for every individual in the country. This was recorded in enumerators' books which still exist and can be consulted at the Public Record Office. The last chapter of the book shows one method of bridging the transition from church-kept to state-kept records by using the enumerators' books to extract information very similar to that which can be gleaned from ecclesiastical sources for earlier periods by methods described in the penultimate chapter. But, even though the mid-nineteenth century is a less firmly marked division in demographic history than 1538, it is a convenient point at which to make a break since the demographic history of the last hundred years depends on different sources and requires different methods. It would form an excellent subject for a companion volume to this and I hope it will prove feasible to collect material for such a volume in due course.

This book could not have been produced so quickly and might not have been produced at all if it had not been for the generosity of the Calouste Gulbenkian Foundation in making a substantial grant to establish the Cambridge Group for the History of Population and Social Structure. Both Mr Laslett and I have been much helped by this support. Similarly the research which lies behind Dr Eversley's two chapters was made possible in large part by a grant from the Houblon-Norman Fund administered by the Bank of England. This enabled him to take study-leave during the academic year 1963–4.

E. A. Wrigley

INTRODUCTION:
THE NUMERICAL STUDY OF
ENGLISH SOCIETY

'AN abstract law of population', said Karl Marx in a famous passage, 'exists for plants and animals only.' He was writing after three generations of fierce dispute over the abstract law of human population put forward by Robert Malthus at the very close of the eighteenth century. But curiosity about the size of populations and the principles on which they change goes back much further than the time of Malthus, and nowhere further than in England. A hundred years or so before *An Essay on Population* was published, the first speculative attempts at the science of demography, as we now think of it, were being propounded under the attractive title *Political Arithmetic*.

Not that the writings of John Graunt, William Petty and Gregory King, who did most to create that short-lived enthusiasm of the early English natural scientists, could be called entirely scientific, on Marx's standards or on ours. Their view of the nature of social development amongst human populations and the scale of time which necessarily limited it, was still governed by the Christian Revelation. King's first principle about the 'origination and increase of the people of England' was as follows:

'That if the World was repeopled from 8 persons after the Flood and that England was peopled originally by two persons, or by a number not exceeding 20 persons, such first peopling was about the year of the World 2200 or 2300, viz. 600 years after the Flood.'

Gregory King has not been the only historical demographer to make questionable or even fanciful assumptions. His apparent simplemindedness will serve as an illustration of the curious tendency on the part of those who have interested themselves in this subject to air their particular foibles, to adhere to some unlikely proposition long after its implausibility should have become obvious. We cannot be certain that the methods and principles contained in this introductory volume will all turn out to be free of such faults. But our object is to present the beginnings of a technique which will in the end ensure that the numerical study of past English society is as objective as criticism can make it. A whole intellectual transformation has had to go forward since King's time to allow us to look at society and long-term social change in a numerical fashion. Not only has there had to be change in the attitude to history and to religious authority, but also a completely different view of human biological development, not to speak of advances in counting itself, in statistics. Meanwhile the evidence we use, the parish registers above all, but also the rudimentary censuses, the taxation lists, the head-counts made for so many different purposes, remains unchanged. The men who drew up these documents shared every one of Gregory King's intellectual preoccupations and his limitations, but scarcely any of them can have had his sharpness of insight and comparative modernity of outlook.

Part of the fascination of this subject is to try to compensate for this obliqueness of vision and its consequences for the evidence we have to use. All historical demography before the beginnings of official statistics has to be based on material gathered by men who neither had our purposes in mind, nor could have been made to see their importance if someone had tried to explain them. In England this means that no national totals of population are available before 1801 and very, very few local ones before that date. No vital statistics are available for forty years thereafter, and decades of time had still to pass before such figures were to be completely acceptable to the demographer. In spite of the early dawn of the arithmetical attitude in England, therefore, English social scientists have little advantage over others in respect of data about past population and social structure. The collection of data remains not just one, but rather the most exacting and important of their activities.

Even the evidence which we do have for the centuries covered by our volume is inferior to that for France over some, though by no means all, of our chosen period. Perhaps the superiority of French to English parish registration has been somewhat exaggerated. Certainly it is of the first importance that all three series in the register, baptisms, marriages and burials, should exist in our country in some parishes from as far back as the fourth decade of the sixteenth century. In France the burial registers are frequently defective until late in the seventeenth century, and this inhibits detailed work. Generally speaking the earliest English registers seem to have been well kept. This should enable us to examine the behaviour of populations much further back beyond the point at which industrialisation began than ever the French will be able to do. But when all this is said and done, it remains a somewhat mysterious thing that the English parish priest seems on the whole to have been much less responsible as registrar than the French curé. It argues for a very different relationship between church and community, a difference which also manifests itself in the tendency in some English parishes not to use the parish church for certain of the ceremonies, but to go elsewhere.

When we try to recreate the atmosphere in which the records we use came into being, the source of our difficulties is made plain. If we think of the educated priest, or the literate parish clerk scrawling out the words and figures in the appointed book after the baby had been borne from the font, or the body laid on the floor of the grave, with the puzzled faces of the illiterate peasants crowding round him, we can see at once how far our purposes were from his mind. If he failed in his task at the time, because it was cold, or the sun had set and he had no light, or because he had something else to do, then it might lie upon his conscience, if he was a conscientious man. He might go back and do the job another day. Or he might not. His neglect of his duty went against the orders of his superiors and we may believe that he would also feel it as a breach of faith with his parishioners. But whether or not a sense of duty in the mind of a priest, duty to his order or duty to his flock, was sufficient to keep him at his task of registration consistently enough to earn our praise so long after he is dead, it is impossible to imagine that he could ever have anticipated being judged on our criteria.

These few details of the nature and the origin of the material which can alone be used in the numerical study of English society

3

before the coming of statistics must surely make it clear that this study is now, always has been, and always must be a matter of approximation. The whole of this volume, even the interlude in which Mr Armstrong addresses us from the relatively ordered and certain atmosphere of the early years of the census, is to some extent an exercise of the historical imagination. But because this has to be the case, as it is with so much of the rest of the activity of historians, it does not mean that the results are so unlikely to represent the truth that they can be disregarded. Nor does it mean that this particular discipline is without significance for history and for social science in general. Quite the contrary. We hope that the studies described here will demonstrate three quite different propositions.

The first is that a great deal of new information has now become available, of interest to historians, sociologists, economists and even to biologists and students of literature. In fact we venture to think that the techniques which are now being developed and applied for the first time consistently to English material and which we shall be describing, answer questions which have hitherto been regarded as unanswerable, beyond the pale of knowable fact. Who could have supposed only a decade ago, that the age-specific fertility of any community of French peasantry who died as long ago as the year 1700 would become a part of established knowledge? And who, until even more recently, would have supposed that it might be possible to obtain this information for English peasants dying a whole century earlier? For this is what will happen if the parish registers of Colyton in Devon yield as rich a harvest as that reaped from the registers of Crulai in Normandy by Gautier and Henry in France.

'Age-specific fertility' may seem a strange term to many historians, especially to local historians or to those with an even less specific interest in the English past, the general readers of historical literature. But a glance at Dr Wrigley's and Dr Eversley's chapters will show that it is only one amongst a whole series of new terms which we hope will come to have a place in the universe of historical discourse. And for each term there is a corresponding statistic. Infant mortality, that favourite measuring-rod of welfare, should soon become a commonplace of accurate estimation rather than a matter of fragmentary and somewhat wishful guesswork. Expectation of life at birth; the chances of a woman being pregnant at the time of her marriage; the rate of illegitimacy; the size of families; the lesser (or greater) liability of gentlemen to die than craftsmen and peasants; movement of individuals from place to place about the country; perhaps, ultimately, their movement from position to position on the scale of social differences in England, the best graduated of all societies: all these and more are on the way to demonstration.

Age-specific fertility means the number of children borne in relation to a woman's age, and this varies, being higher in the mid-twenties than in the mid-thirties, or indeed in the late teens, and very much higher than in the mid-forties. When Louis Henry at the *Institut National d'Etudes Démographiques* began his classic study of pre-industrial French demography he was chiefly concerned with the question of how many children women would bear if no contraceptives were used, if women married at the time of their lives when they could expect to have the greatest number of children and went on having them as long as they were fertile. His curiosity went far beyond the straightforward question 'How many children can a woman of a certain age be expected to produce?' But the knowledge he set out to acquire was of a kind which social scientists would always have liked to have had, and knowledge which historians had always thought beyond their reach.

He used the method known as the reconstitution of families, which he had already used to study the families of the great – the aristocracy and the wealthy bourgeois families of Geneva – and adapted it to the analysis of the records of the villagers preserved in the parish registers. A great deal more came to light than a measure of natural fecundity and these other pieces of evidence also bear the mark of knowledge which is valuable, because it sets up a comparative standard for very familiar features of our own lives and is always also in a sense knowledge about ourselves. To take another example, there is the matter of the age at marriage. The age at marriage which was usual amongst our peasant ancestors, will always tell us something about our own lives as husbands and wives because we can begin to compare ourselves with them. Who would have expected not so very long ago to be in a position to know that a high proportion of ordinary Englishmen, the peasants and the craftsmen, the labourers and the paupers, in the time of Elizabeth, or Anne, or of the first three Georges, got married in their late twenties and even in their early thirties? There must always be a great interest in learning how large was the number of children which an Elizabethan or a Georgian English countryman could expect to have, given that his wife was also older than might have been supposed, often older than himself.

All of this could certainly be used to show that demographic history does indeed illuminate change in the whole structure of society, even if no one would now expect of it what Marx said was impossible, that it could be made to yield one single abstract law of development. But this belongs to our third proposition, which will be that this numerical study must soon become important to everyone seriously interested in social change. Let us now turn to the second general claim, that work of this kind requires a new relationship between specialist and non-specialist, professional and amateur, the university department and the record office, the research institute and the evening class. Not only is the numerical study of society fast becoming a new activity for those pursuing the study of the past, and its relationship with the present, it is doing so in part because it has to be organised in a novel way.

This is a study which has to be done collaboratively, yet the work of each collaborator is an end in itself as well as a contribution to the whole. Undertakings on this scale, except amongst natural scientists, usually have as their object some huge multivolume work: a dictionary of biography, a history of parliament, an encyclopaedia. Though they may be exhaustive, such enterprises can never be final and the individual parts of it are seldom self-contained. They tend to fit together in the manner of the pieces in a jig-saw, and only the man who assembles them all together ever sees the completed picture, which when it is at last entire, is too vast ever to be appreciated as a whole.

The collaborative work which has already been started and which will finally piece together much of the past history of the population of England as far back as records will permit, does, of course, have some common features with earlier joint ventures. Not all of the archivists, the local historians, the amateurs pure and simple, who in the autumn of 1964 began

6

filling up forms sent from Cambridge by the Group for the History of Population and Social Structure will interest themselves in the entire enterprise. Recording baptisms, marriages and burials month by month, by harvest year and civil year, recording bastards, twins, and so on, for one particular parish may seem to those who volunteer to do it a rewarding end in itself quite apart from the numerical study of social development. Meanwhile the historical demographer with his calculating machines, his punched cards and his computer is dependent on this unrewarded work as no other historian or social scientist has ever been before him. Every casual comment of his correspondents, about the weather in a particular year, about a certain type of disease, a flood, loss of cattle or of crops, taken from a note scrawled so many years ago by an anxious parish clerk, may be as important to him as a set of figures in themselves. This is a job in fact which everyone can do, everyone interested in English society and its history, and a job which never will be done unless large numbers of people do it all together.

Even though the local historian may not be familiar with the full range of interest of the demographic historian, he is well aware of what he gains from the systematic study of his registers, the search for possible listings of inhabitants, and so on. There is a great overlap between his local interests and purposes and the general aims of a national research project. Much of the work he might carry out in any case in a slightly different form. He may not be concerned with sociological laws or demographic principles, but he is keenly sensitive to the lives of individual people and the registers tell him about them at the most important moments of their lives. Moreover, once the task of counting for each parish is done, it need never be done again. As the sets of filled-in forms pile up, knowledge grows cumulatively greater. When the whole is at last available, it need not result in a set of volumes as unwieldy as the *Dictionary of National Biography*. Much of this precious new knowledge might be presented in a short book. It is knowledge which no expert could acquire by himself or even with a staff of research assistants. The records of ten thousand English parishes are too bulky and scattered for this to be possible. Nor could a central body ever acquire the wealth of local knowledge possessed by

7

local historians up and down the length and breadth of England.

But this is not the end of the collaborative character of this work. The demographic history of England is certainly an end in itself; it is a body of knowledge worth assembling and extending for its own sake. But it is very, very much more worth having if it can be seen in comparison with the demographic history of France, of Spain, of Germany, or of Western Europe as a whole. If it is important to try to determine by numerical means all that can be told of social development in one country, how much more valuable would it be to work it out for several?

We may cite an example of this since it is essential to our subject. The divergence of social attitude and social structure between the society of the English Colonies in America and of Englishmen who stayed at home is one of the great themes of comparative culture, especially during the years which are covered by this introduction, from the mid-sixteenth to the early nineteenth century. Throughout this whole period it is thought that the nascent colonial societies must have been in sexual unbalance, more men than women, more bridegrooms than brides, whilst in Europe and England the sexes were much more nearly in balance. Psychologists and sociologists have already begun to wonder whether the differences between the New World and the Old may not have part of their origin in this important difference of emotional experience and attitude. Would it not be valuable to have systematic knowledge of the evidence? Will there not come a time when the demographic history of colonial and nineteenth-century America begins in turn to shed its light upon the social structural history of European countries?

Local as it is, therefore, the history of population and social structure is in its essence also an international, comparative and institutional study. Those willing to contribute to it, professional or amateur, will be contributing to the advancement of knowledge as the natural scientists do, with no regard for language or for frontiers.

Intellectual history or the study of political science, which have been my chief intellectual preoccupations, may seem to be a long way from the calculation of the mean age at marriage of the peasantry and the nobility, or the exact effect on the intergenesic interval (interval between births) of the death of a

8

new-born baby. But the relationship is logical enough and just such as it should be in the contemporary intellectual world.

History is defined as the records of peoples who write and since its very beginnings western Europeans have done their thinking and played their politics by means of the written and then also the printed word. But until the generation of our own immediate fathers only a minority could read and write, so that only a minority could have any part of political or intellectual life. It is a fact, therefore, that during the period covered by this volume and for the whole of the preceding time too, politics went forward and thoughts were discussed by the few who were literate in the presence and on behalf of those who were not. European intellectual and social history throughout most of its course was indeed a question of two cultures, a literate culture and an oral one. The first was the culture of a small group which could only be understood within that group, the second the culture of the whole in which of course the literate minority had its share. It is therefore an overriding condition of the study of both intellectual and political activity that the relative proportion of the literate and illiterate should be known, or estimated. Questions of who could read and write, who owned books, who knew enough and had the confidence to write books, and who wrote so badly and read so slowly that they could at best follow their superiors from afar, are therefore questions of principle for historians of thought and for political scientists too. They are inescapably numerical questions.

We hope soon to collect at Cambridge evidence on literacy from all over the country with the help of local historians and others interested in the work, just as demographic evidence is being assembled now. But the numerical questions asked by political sociologists in our own day concern many other features of groups and individuals than the ability to read. In order to understand social and political behaviour nowadays we study other aspects of the social characteristics of groups and of the individual personality; class, status, occupation – then age, sex, marital condition, religion, colour, and so on. These again are all numerical questions too. These have always been important questions. They have always been determinants of the behaviour we call political and intellectual. They can be examined and in some cases measured. Therefore when any opportunity to examine such evidence presents itself it must be seized with both hands. The beginnings of such a technique are sketched out in my later chapter in this book devoted to the analysis of social structure from listings of inhabitants for a period going back as far as the last year of the sixteenth century. The numerical study of English society is accordingly of unexpected significance to intellectual and political historians, even if they have only recently come to recognise that this may be the case.

The whole of this introduction is intended to make it clear that demography even when defined in its most limited sense, totals of population and their tendencies to change, birth rates, death rates, marriage rates, fertility, expectation of life, illegitimacy, age at marriage and all the rest, is central to this same indispensable, numerical study. Just as the census is essential to the understanding of political change in recent times, so we hope to build up a body of knowledge of equal importance for the understanding of political change in the past. A time may come when we shall know enough about the technique of a numerical study of society in the past, and have enough material at our disposal to be able to make a chronological junction between the preliminary studies described here as going forward for the period from the sixteenth to the nineteenth centuries and political sociology as it extends itself backwards in time from the twentieth century. It is important that these studies should be prosecuted not simply for our country in isolation but comparatively with other countries.

But these are pioneering sentiments rather than a prospectus already prepared. Let us turn from intellectual history and political science which were chosen because on the face of it they seemed least likely to fall under our third principle about the numerical study of society. This was, it will be remembered, that those interested in social change of any sort must now reckon with its conclusions, even its earliest and most tentative ones.

It goes without saying that social history or economic history could be used to demonstrate our case. Economic historians have always been interested in population and social structure and have long been accustomed to the construction of models and to statistical method. A fuller knowledge of the history of fertility and mortality in England before and during the Industrial Revolution would add immensely to our understanding of that period of fundamental social and economic change. The link between economic and demographic history is very intimate, and the connection goes both ways. The historians and demographers of France have given us a lead in the study of environment and its effect on vital statistics which may end by helping to solve the problem of the part which they played in the process of industrialisation everywhere.

The familial and emotional life of our ancestors is our subject here, even more than their intellectual and political life, their public appearances. Their literature must therefore concern us, and in the literature of these centuries much hangs on the play of birth, marriage and death. Lear was a widower who lived too long, and had only daughters to succeed him. Hamlet was a victim of the speed with which his dead and outraged father was replaced with a despicable substitute by his mother, no sooner in fact that most of the peasant women whom we meet in the records replaced their dead husbands, if they could. The intention of the dramatist becomes clearer, if we know how familiar to his audience was the situation he creates. Perhaps it may be thought that facts like these lose their literary quality, their classic appeal, if they are expressed in numbers. But why should this be so? If literature deals in fundamentals, demography may do so too.

Social change in these centuries has preoccupied the general historian more than in any other period of our past. For the last generation or two the discussion has gone on in terms of the rise of a class, the middle class, and the disturbances and changes which it brought about looked upon as social structural in their cause and significance. The limitations of this view have become apparent for all to see in recent years, and one of the most distinguished of its exponents has come at last to the view that urbanisation, the growth of the cities and especially of London, must be brought in too, especially if we are to understand the religion and the science of the time. The new Master of Balliol has recently remarked that science is not a product of Protestantism or Puritanism but that both science and Protestantism sprang from the shift from the values of an agrarian to those of an urban society. We may end this brief survey of the numerical study of English society by putting these claims into something like numerical terms, not perhaps for quite the purpose which Christopher Hill had in mind but for social change of the overall, general kind. What does it mean to say that at bottom social change can be thought of as urbanisation, and that the transformation of England was due in part at least to the growth of London? What does it mean when it is spelt out as the historical demographer might spell it out, for the benefit of the social, the intellectual, the scientific, the general historian?

It is indeed true that the development of London into the largest city in the world (perhaps as early as the time of Cromwell) is a fact of massive importance in social and demographic history throughout the three centuries with which we deal in this volume. The dislocation in the lives of thousands of peasants and craftsmen who left their little towns and small villages to go to settle in this enormous urban complex may have been an important source of new attitudes and changed values, as well as of doubt and loneliness. But to assert the importance of urbanisation is a beginning, not an end.

Once we try to understand how considerable this effect really was, how many people had to move to keep London perpetually expanding, how much their life in London differed from the life of the countryside, we begin to see that this explanation is no simple one, no final, easy resting place. We have to know, for example, how much of the increase could have come from London itself, which means knowing how many children Londoners had; how many children survived their early years; at what age they could expect to get married and how long they could expect to live after marriage. As for increase due to immigration, we must know the age of the newcomers; how large were their families; of what sex they were; how quickly the disasters of the plague could have been repaired by this influx and so how far these terrible occurrences could be said to intensify migration and urbanisation. And in order to gauge this whole complex of events with any accuracy we have to know what proportion the population of London bore to the population of the whole country. Above all we must find out whether there were times when London was increasing, whilst elsewhere in the country population was falling. If ever that was the case, then all the effects upon the whole society which

12

have been listed must have been multiplied and intensified.

A process of this far-reaching character, complex and intricate, yet in principle subject to measurement in all its details, goes beyond the resources of traditional historical method. It is not necessary that every historian should become familiar with the slide rule, or logarithmic tables, or the language of computers. But he should acquaint himself with the sort of questions which can now be asked and answered in studies of this kind, and know what types of historical material can be subjected to analysis in this way. Rough and ready as it is, this preliminary work will have served its purpose if it helps to bring about this end.

Peter Laslett

2

POPULATION HISTORY AND
LOCAL HISTORY

POPULATION history, as it is described in this volume, consists essentially of a series of connected and methodologically unified studies of one aspect of local history. The object is to discover the mechanisms which lie behind the complex observed relationships between economy, social structure and population movements. It is true that such movements are apparent in national statistics, but it is clear that the mechanism can only be observed at the level at which it operates – that of the individual, his family and the immediate community in which he lives and works. National movements do play a part – for instance, it was for long believed that the Speenhamland system was the cause of large families, and recent studies suggest that the French provision of generous family allowances and other concessions introduced during the last thirty years influenced individual decision sufficiently to produce far-reaching secular changes in the birth rate. Similarly, widespread climatic catastrophes, national and international epidemics, legislation for the protection of the health and welfare of the individual, as well as significant movements in real incomes, will all tend to affect every individual in the community. But in the lives of ordinary people, these national or international factors either play a very subordinate part compared with the immediate local influences, or they make their appearance, not as a precise fraction of a national average, but as a force whose strength is peculiar to each locality, not only because of general circumstances, but because its effectiveness depends on its combination with other general or local factors. In other words, the circumstances of each individual and each local community are in a sense unique, and though it is possible to group these as a matter of convenience into broad categories, any drastic national averaging of experience tends to hide the local realities behind the generalisations.

To give a few examples within the British Isles: the arctic winters and flooded summers of eighteenth century annals often went unnoticed in western Scotland or East Anglia; the cholera of 1831/2 was fatal in only a few areas, at least on any considerable scale; the Speenhamland system become operative in different areas at various times and failed to penetrate some counties; customs of inheritance of agricultural holdings were entirely different in West Wales, Cumberland and Nottinghamshire.[1] Whilst the general expectation of life probably rose very considerably between 1760 and 1840, there were decades when it dropped sharply in industrialising towns.

The understanding of the demographic process, the inter-relationships between employment opportunities and marriage, between nutrition and fertility, or between water supplies and death rates, depends, therefore, on intensive studies at local community level. In this respect, demographic history differs from general history. If one follows the discussions on the scope of local history in relation to national history one realises that there the justification for local studies is slightly different: it is not claimed that national movements are the aggregates or averages of local ones, but that local events, on the one hand, are worth studying because they loomed large in the consciousness of ordinary people, and on the other hand, because they may provide illuminating glosses on the national chronicle.[2] In political, ecclesiastical or constitutional history, the events at national level constituted complete happenings in themselves, however much historians may seek to explain them in terms of influences which may be derived from local pressures (e.g. in the history of the 1832 Reform Bill, or the debate on Home Rule).[3] In traditional economic history, there are also national movements, which, whilst statistically representing aggregates of local events, nevertheless may be said to be meaningful in the national context because the local microcosm reproduces the national generalisations. Thus the enclosure movement, or the repeal of the corn laws, or the legalisation of trade unions,

15

though provoked by individual reactions to environment, and providing fascinating local variants, nevertheless form part of a coherent national story where the local tale makes the general account more vivid.

Population history is in a somewhat different category. Here, with few exceptions, the local framework represents almost the total environment of the event, which becomes national only by a later statistical device, for its determinants cannot be measured (if at all) at more than village or, at most, regional level, and owe little or nothing to debate or action in the centres of administration or power. That hundreds of thousands of Irish folk came into Britain in the middle of the nineteenth century, or that middle class people began to practice birth control in the later decades, may be explained in terms of national catastrophes or general social changes, and under certain circumstances, these movements may be given fairly accurate global statistical expression. But these aggregates are averages of widely different local phenomena, each of them occuring at levels of significance determined at the local level. Only rarely, in fact, can we understand the general movement by clear reference to a general cause, and if we can, then the intensity of the movement still varies so much from area to area that the general explanation must be regarded as incomplete.

This is the primary difficulty which has been encountered in dealing with such widespread phenomena as the rise of population in Great Britain (and elsewhere) from the end of the seventeenth century onwards, with its great peaks of growth at uneven intervals, and with the decline of the birthrate since the end of the nineteenth century. That these changes occurred has long since been known, but if an explanation was attempted, it was generally of a fairly simple kind, at least until recently. Growth was said to be due to medicine, hygiene, better nutrition or higher real wages.[4]

When the rate of growth began to decline, this was often explained in terms not dissimilar to those used in the previous period. Only now a higher standard of living (expressed in terms of better food and clothing, housing, education and leisure) was cited as leading to changes in marriage habits and eventually to family limitation. Population still grew, because death rates fell, but total growth was less fast because birth rates fell also.

There is no point in rehearsing here either the fallacies propounded, or the various attempts which have been made, again in general terms, to criticise the erroneous assumptions made (works of both kinds may be found in the bibliography). One would rather say that each such student study ended with the demand that the generalisations should be tested by the production of case histories. This demand has been much strengthened in recent years by the appearance of carefully conceived and statistically sound local work in France, mainly under the guidance of M. Louis Henry, to whom every historical demographer is deeply indebted for the demonstration that valid conclusions can be drawn from the most painstaking reconstruction work based on the old registers, and that the labours involved, though huge, are not unlimited. The application of his methods to English conditions will form the substance of Dr Wrigley's chapter in this book.

For reasons which will be explained later, we do not feel, however, that these methods are the only ones which can be used, and we shall also demonstrate the feasibility of other types of statistical study. All the procedures described in this volume, however, are based on the belief that the local unit offers the best chance of resolving the historian's difficulty. This statement does not involve a claim that the study of the small unit constitutes the whole of what is required to answer the national question, either by itself, or in the aggregation of local averages. It is rather that at present beyond the national totals (often of doubtful validity), we have only a minute number of local studies, and these will need to be increased considerably before the next attempt is made to improve on the general account.

Although these studies should be local, no single parish, or even group of parishes was a self-sufficient entity. Movement, as has been shown in numerous studies of migration and some few of the constancy of local populations,[5] was on a considerable scale, and where the origin of marriage partners has been investigated, it has been shown conclusively that by the eighteenth century, if not earlier, marriages of quite ordinary folk took place on at least a county-wide basis, and some families in a

17

life-time might make several moves within a region, along rivers and sea-coasts and overseas. Even where people did not move themselves, they were subject to regional and national influences. Some of these we have mentioned. Wars, civil war and rebellion, mercenary and yeomanry service, as well as the peaceful needs of trade, caused a much larger part of the population to move outside the village community than the older historians realised. Even modest land-holders had to sue in London courts or had business at the Quarter Sessions. All coastal counties provided fishermen and sailors. The great regional fairs and markets involved many besides the professional traders and manufacturers. All this means that we must constantly consider the larger scene even when describing the demographic experience of a single village. Epidemics swept the country in the wake of the travellers – seaports tended to be affected most. Local food shortages and their relief depended on the system of communications. Opportunities for marriage, as far as they were connected with employment and land-holdings, were conditioned by the place of each community in the regional or national system of production and distribution.

Long before industrialisation, young people left home to become domestic or farm servants, and to be apprenticed to a craft or profession. The hiring of servants took place at markets and fairs which often had regional rather than local significance. In the maritime counties recruitment of sailors reached far inland. The wars of the eighteenth century led to the raising of increasing numbers of men for the regiments of the militia. Once a single member of the family moved, for any of these reasons, to a distant parish, other displacements might follow. A young man apprenticed in Exeter from an upland Devon parish might return home with a bride from the coastal area, or a village girl might follow him; or he might acquire a settlement in the city, and a younger brother or even a more distant relation might follow in turn.

In other words, it was not a completely immobile population at any period and one of the objects of our study is to discover the local differences and periodic fluctuations in mobility, and thus to link the parish history with the national scene. In postulating this, we are not reversing the argument from which we started – that for the individual in the village, the factors which determine life and death can only be measured properly in his immediate environment. But we are saying that insofar as national or regional influences intrude into people's lives (as they did to an increasing extent), their incidence, and their relative strength, defies mensuration on the very large scale. This applies, amongst other things, to the well-known emigration debates: whether 'push' or 'pull' factors were more important. Both types were operative, but only the local study can say which was decisive in a particular case. Emigration tended to be so localised in its incidence that the state of cultivation, harvest, systems of tenure, or even the movement of fish shoals seem of the greatest significance.[6]

Given the necessity for detailed local research, we then face the question of method. A good deal of work has already been done in the last few years, both here and abroad, but there has been a serious lack of standardisation, with the result that though each individual piece of research has been useful on its own merits, we have been hampered by the lack of comparability. Recent contacts between scholars in various countries have shown that internationally this lack of comparability is even worse, and yet there is a universal desire to make the results of research widely available and useful for eventual studies at continental levels.[7]

Before we deal with the different methods which may be used for local studies, we face a number of general problems which, to a greater or lesser extent, obtrude themselves into every type of local quantitative work, and whilst there cannot be, in the nature of things, a clear set of rules to fit every case, we attempt to set out the kind of considerations the research workers must bear in mind. The important prerequisite in each case is not so much that the procedure should be absolutely standardised to conform with all the desiderata set out, but that the investigator should be aware of what is desirable. If local conditions force him to adopt in part a different framework or method, he should be aware of this and fully set out his reasons for adopting his own variations of the standard procedure so that comparability may at least be maintained for a large part of the study.[8]

THE CHOICE OF SELF-CONTAINED SUB-GROUPS

The biologist wishing to measure the characteristics of an animal population chooses, as far as he can, a totally closed population – rabbits in an enclosure, fruit-flies in glass jars. Human beings are seldom found under such conditions, at least in modern history. Island communities may under certain circumstances lead isolated existences for several generations, but literate recording and trading societies have, almost by definition, contacts with other communities and an increasingly high degree of mobility. British rural societies even before the agricultural revolution of the eighteenth century did not consist as is often believed, of self-sufficient manorial or parochial settlements, immobile and inbred. Even the common labourer exercised a greater freedom of choice in his settlement than is often understood. There were, indeed, attempts to restrict movement, long before the Settlement Act of 1662, but it is very doubtful how far legislation ever succeeded in restraining internal migration.[9] As a result, we find that one of a number of different limitations is imposed on our studies. Either, by means of reconstitution, we deal only with those families who remain in one parish or within a very small group of parishes within which we can treat every entry of baptism, burial and marriage, or we count, by aggregation, all events which took place in one or more parishes. In the first case, we can never be certain that those who remain, and can therefore be analysed, are a good sample of all families. Whether we assume, as was formerly believed, that migrants were mostly idle vagabonds, people who could or would not do an honest day's work, or whether we believe, as many observers did in the nineteenth century, that the most energetic and able-bodied migrated or even emigrated in search of work,[10] we cannot be certain that the stable element is also a normal or average population. This is more likely to be a problem where we are dealing with the relatively few cases (before 1800) of long-distance migration than with the short movements which, as we have tried to show, were part of the normal pattern of life. But those who went away to become sailors, to settle overseas, to join the militia, or even to be transported to Botany Bay, may well have been a tougher breed than those who stayed. Genetically, there is the serious question whether those who remained members of relatively small communities and inter-married, often to the point of close in-breeding, exhibited the same characteristics as those who migrated and married at a great distance. (It would probably be difficult to find, in sixteenth and seventeenth-century England, examples of completely closed communities, though there is a presumption that they did exist in the upland and borderland areas of the Celtic fringes of Britain.)[11]

If, on the other hand, we are dealing with the population of a place *in toto*, without reference to their family relationships, and calculate, on the model to be described below, their life experience as a rate based on total population, we run into difficulties of another kind, whether or not the information is in fact complete even with respect to the particular locality studies. If emigration has taken place, mortality is exaggerated if the young were removed and the old remained behind. If immigration occurred, especially of young people of active working age, marriage and fertility rates may be over-stated. This we cannot check unless we revert to the nominal analysis of the families involved.

Thirdly, if we are fortunate enough to find a place which, on an entire or sample analysis, suggests that its population was relatively immobile, and neither emigration nor immigration on a serious scale took place (or balanced out), then we may well be able to carry out either the reconstitution of a large proportion of all families mentioned, or obtain reasonably balanced results by aggregation. But in that case (at least in the context of the British economy from the seventeenth century onwards) we should be dealing with a locality which might in itself be unrepresentative of the country as a whole, because of the implied isolation from the main currents of national economic life. For that reason it might not be a good place to demonstrate the secular changes which took place, at least in so far as they have any connection with economic and social structure.

It follows from these limitations of single places, that we will be much better placed when analysing groups of settlements. As all studies so far made in this field have shown, great as mobility may have been, a very high proportion of it operated over relatively short distances. Generally speaking, marriages between persons resident in the same parish, and those involving a partner from an adjoining parish or one within a five-mile radius, account for 75–80 per cent of all marriages, and if we extend the radius to fifteen miles, we are likely to include all except an insignificant fraction of places of origin of partners. Now admittedly the movement of marriage partners is not the whole movement, but it is a fairly good indicator of what took place. Had people habitually moved across county or regional borders, a higher proportion of marriages between persons described as originating from distant places should indicate this. This is what we find at times of exceptional disturbances. Thus, during the French wars we find numerous entries in areas where militiamen were quartered which testify to the loosening of the normal restrictions during those periods.[12]

But we have the later evidence of places of origin as revealed by the mid-nineteenth century census reports, on which the work of Redford[13] was based, to confirm our suspicion that long-distance movement was exceptional, as far as most areas were concerned. There are notable exceptions, such as many coastal areas, London, and places along the main internal lines of communication. We may accept the contention, then, that unless there are strong local reasons for supposing that long-distance movement was frequent, each parish belonged to a group within which a very high proportion of all movement was contained. If settlement is evenly dispersed over a large area lacking natural barriers to movement, we may find a slightly different type of relationship. Each area has still its natural centre (usually a market town) and movement will be to and through this town, so that there would still tend to be a pattern of marriage which is distinctly centripetal. But at the fringes, distinctions will be blurred, and on the boundary, there will be an equilibrium of attractive forces. This system is well known from studies of modern shopping habits, social and commercial provision in rural areas, and communication patterns.[14] But a study of settlements in the British Isles shows the frequency with which we do encounter noticeable obstacles, compared with, for instance, the Central or Western European landscape. From London northwards we encounter the Chilterns and the Cotswolds before we reach the Pennines. Only on the east–west axis is there relatively unobstructed movement between the Welsh border and the North Sea, but the area is

22

notoriously poor in transverse communications. Disregarding the truly isolated island or quasi-island settlement areas, then, we find the map of the British Isles full of features which mark off settled areas from each other. Quite moderate hill ranges of no more than 800 ft elevation, rivers, bridged or fordable only at long intervals, marshy tracts and forests, all form natural barriers to movement. Beasts could not be driven across them easily, or food brought to market without hardship. Barriers of this kind sometimes mark also a change in soil type, and different forms of agriculture lead to different settlement patterns and social relationships. Coal outcrops produce isolated industrial settlements within an otherwise agricultural tract.[15] Topographical breaks may form a language barrier like the 'Landsker' which separates English-speaking Pembroke-shire from the Welsh-speaking upland areas: to the south, the 'Englishry', fertile, maritime, later often adhering to the Church; to the north, Welsh-speaking, barren or pasture land, Nonconformist and out of touch with the rest of the world – these are crude characterisations, but they produced a real enough barrier to settlement.[16]

It is impossible to give a general rule for identifying such areas. Often they survive with a topographical description emphasising their separateness – the Isle of Thanet, the Vale of Evesham; or they possess a generic name which singles them out from the rest of their counties – the South Hams, the Felden, the Forest of Dean, and so on.[17] The suggestion we make here is that it is such areas which will prove to contain within themselves the greater part of all short-distance migra-tory movements, and form a suitable framework for work in historical demography. They possess the additional advantage that since they exhibit common internal economic characteristics they increase the possibility of a meaningful comparative study which will eventually crystallise local and special factors from amongst the national and universal phenomena.

There are some possible aids to the identification of such areas. They seldom correspond to a single modern administra-tive unit. On the other hand, the ancient divisions of administra-tion, the hundreds, wapentakes (in former Danish areas) and wards (in Northumberland), sometimes constitute manageable and meaningful groupings, especially in rural areas.[18] The 'hundred' refers to the number of hides in the unit, and as each hide was thought capable of supporting a peasant family, the whole constituted originally a collection of about 100 families – at a time when the whole population of England was probably little over a million. By the time of the first census, the population of the rural hundred was, typically, somewhere between 3,000 and 5,000, or, let us say 800 – 1,000 households. Since the population of the whole country was round about ten million, and since much of that increase was in urban areas, the concept of the hundred having increased six-fold since Domesday times or earlier is not too fanciful, and provides us with the convenience that much information relating to nineteenth century population (for instance, the summaries of baptisms, burials and marriages in the census of 1801 and until 1831) was given, outside boroughs and certain special areas, only for the hundreds, etc. Though, of course, originally compiled from answers from individual parishes, this gives a useful basis of comparison with modern counts within the same units.[19] It must be stressed, however, that these ancient divisions had in most cases become almost totally irrelevant to the economic and social conditions even of the seventeenth century, and that it is mainly because the origins of market towns and nucleated parishes sometimes go back to the older concepts, that it is worthwhile ascertaining the ancient boundaries.

The hundreds are not difficult to identify from the older census reports, and works like Samuel Lewis' *Topographical Dictionary*[20] give a fairly reliable outline of the boundaries of hundreds and boroughs. But they are by no means the only logical way of grouping villages together, and in many cases, by the eighteenth century, quite unsuitable for a group analysis (some of the wapentakes and hundreds in Yorkshire and Lancashire had over 100,000 inhabitants early in the nineteenth century, a single parish like Bethnal Green had over 60,000 souls in it, and so on – clearly one must use one's judgment). In some areas (East Anglia, Kent and Sussex) the hundreds are grouped into larger units (e.g. in Sussex into rapes) and in some cases these may be found more convenient though they are usually much larger.

However carefully the area for study is chosen, there still remains the problem of residual migration. The usual method employed is to work forward from a base year in which population is known (or can be estimated with some degree of certainty) or backward from a similar landmark at a later date, or a combination of these two methods, deducting or adding as the case may be, baptisms and burials, and explaining the resulting excess or deficiency by migration.[21] It will be noted that this method only applies where two counts at fixed points in the time scale are available, such as a Hearth Tax return and a census, or two census years. The difficulty of course is that one cannot be certain how much of the resulting discrepancy is in fact due to deficiencies of the sources and how much to net migration. If, for instance, we have a parish with an estimated population of 1,000 in 1670, and if the 4,200 baptisms and 3,200 burials in the following 140 years are compared with an 1811 population of 2,500, it is possible that there was a net inward movement of 500 people into the parish, or that 500 baptisms were never registered, or any combination of these two factors (it is not conceivable that burials were invented, but there are cases of parishes acting as receiving areas for burials from neighbouring parishes where burial grounds were full). Beyond this point, only analysis by reconstitution can give any clearer answer in detail. But it is worth noting that even short of complete analysis by this method, a check on family names can often give useful clues.[22] In a community which remains stationary, but where some movement in and out takes place, the number of family names disappearing from the register is just about matched by the new ones emerging, whether one indexes every name in the register or merely takes a sample (in larger parishes) every tenth year. Where immigration takes place, however, the new names outweigh the old ones which disappear, and the margin by which they do so gives some comparative measure of immigration, and the same is true in reverse. This method needs further investigation, however, and no quantitative guide is available. It should be noted in passing that it is in any case inapplicable where, as in Wales, a large part of the population shares eight or twelve surnames.

It is useful, however, to observe the population trends after 1801. Where, as in most industrial areas and in the regions immediately adjoining them, growth is above the national rates for the thirty years after 1801, and if the economic expansion which then took place has its origins in the eighteenth century, there can be a strong presumption in favour of immigration, though undoubtedly such regions also had faster natural growth. Unfortunately it is precisely these areas which also have the worst deficiencies amongst the baptisms, both because of the relative strength of Nonconformity in many cases, and because of the failure of the church to enforce baptism amongst the newcomers, especially when parishes grew to unmanageable proportions.

REGIONAL STUDIES

The research worker faced with a choice of areas each possessing reasonably good sets of registers (by tests to be described later) is often faced with the apparent lack of criteria which would help to settle which are the most valuable areas to exploit. Perhaps the first thing one should note, when consulting our bibliography, is the uneven distribution of existing detailed work in historical demography. Allowing for the fact that the list is probably incomplete, and that a very large number of analyses still await publication,[23] the fact remains that there is nothing like an even coverage of our national archives. The first and most obvious need is to begin work in those economic regions which remain quite untouched, to establish a basis of comparability.[24] The choice of a region for study must in the first place depend on the primary long-term interests of the investigator. Apart from charting the course of population change in our national history, most of the recent work in this field has been orientated towards the solution of certain problems connected with the pattern of social and economic change. This is likely to remain a first priority for some time. The most important area studies, then, will be those which are likely to throw some light on the controversial issues: the consequences of enclosure on population;[25] the effects of wars, the origins of the industrial labour force, especially in labour intensive sectors such as mining, textiles and pottery;[26] the consequences of industrialisation for the standard of living of the population (as measured by, amongst other things, mortality rates); and so on. In view of the great difficulties connected with the study of the population of large cities, there is a good case for concentrating on those regions where industrialisation may be viewed on a relatively small scale, in spite of the fact that this cuts out some of the more extreme effects of concentration associated precisely with overcrowded centres of very rapid growth like Liverpool. For agrarian problems there is little difficulty: not only do rural registers tend to be much better, but there is sufficient information about agricultural tenure and technology to define homogeneous areas (e.g. the Wiltshire Downs, the Fens or the Fylde). Industrial isolates, however, do also occur, such as the Coalbrookdale coalfield, the Furness Region, the Scottish highland iron districts and so on.[27] It is within such regions that we obtain the best opportunity for a study of groups of related parishes with a common type of economic development and containing within them a sufficient proportion of short-distance migration to offer good opportunities for both aggregation and reconstitution.

SUB-GROUPS: OLIGARCHIES, SECTS AND OCCUPATIONS

Attempts to study the demographic experience of special groups within the general population go back to the period when various general theories of population change were being evolved, and the detailed studies were required to prove (or disprove) the existence of special characteristics of aristocracies, intellectuals or protestants. The literature of this field is large and need not concern us here, except that works such as those of Bailey and Day, Chatcauncuf and Fahlbeck[28] are in a true sense precursors of recent work which has set the trend in the modern investigation of sub-groups.[29] The advantage of such work (leaving aside its value in theoretical controversies) lies in the fact that the universe to be studied is finite and has left detailed records capable of statistical analysis. Members of families are more rarely lost without trace through migration. Names tend to be identifiable beyond doubt. Legal requirements of land-holding and inheritance ensured more scrupulous record keeping than for the population at large. Similarly, certain religious sects and privileged (or even persecuted) minorities kept records which enable us to identify their members easily.

In Germany and Holland Mennonite genealogies have

27

provided basic material for population studies. In England and Ireland an investigation of the Quakers from the seventeenth to the nineteenth century has been begun.[30] Such work has the advantage that it may describe certain closed populations with greater accuracy and completeness than is possible in the case of the generality of the people. But this does raise the question of how far such sub-groups are in fact useful for comparative purposes. It is likely, from the start, that at any rate the oligarchies, and quite possibly the narrowly recruited minorities (such as the Quakers) were less subject to the direct effects of famine or shortage of work, either because they were not 'at risk' or because a highly organised system of mutual security insulated them against the general shocks. Nor would their propensity to marry be subject to the same pressures as that of the population at large. Mortality from those epidemics which were known to be 'no respectors of persons' should affect all groups equally, but in practice they never do, if only because mortality from a virus of given deadliness is still less in well-nourished and well cared-for people, and possibly in those who have, in some indefinable way, a greater will to live, than in the mass of the common people. Abortion rates, and later on, the spread of contraceptive knowledge and devices, would not have equal significance amongst these different groups. Mortality from war service, duelling or travelling accidents would affect the arms-bearing classes more than ordinary mortals. All this does not constitute a reason against undertaking studies of this type, but it draws attention to the fact that again we must promote comparative studies whereby we either compare similar social groups within one country over a period of time, or else choose equivalent social strata elsewhere. This in itself is often difficult, since the rules which created the particular degree of inbreeding and self-recruitment in the orbit of the *Almanac de Gotha*, the Geneva *bourgeoisie*, or the Society of Friends are scarcely the same. It is in fact likely that these special groups will share the general trends in, for instance, the development of mortality with the population as a whole, inasmuch as they are subject to similar environmental conditions. But this vague concept has little to do with what interests us most in this connection: that is, how people respond to changes in economic opportunities, food supplies, public sanitary measures and so on. It will therefore be necessary to devise a method of measuring the comparative mortality of the select groups on one hand and the ordinary population on the other, whenever this is possible. In the last 150 years the tendency has been for mortality, fertility and nuptiality rates to converge – this is especially true of infant mortality where all social groups are approaching what now appears to be an irreducible minimum. But until the end of the nineteenth century, for instance, there was still a formidable gap between social classes in this respect, and even in present-day England it is not unusual to encounter infant mortality rates of ten per thousand related births in a healthy suburb, compared with over fifty in a central slum area.

Where such studies are related to denominational groups, the differences of behaviour may be built into the system. Catholics were opposed to birth control, Quakers eschewed spirit-drinking, some sects practised polygamy and others lived in rural communities which looked after their children and encouraged large families. These aspects of their behaviour do not invalidate such research, but they do suggest a more systematic description of the groups or areas chosen for intensive analysis than is at present customary.

SOME SPECIAL PROBLEMS OF TIME-SCALES AND DIVISIONS INTO PERIODS

Although the subject has been dealt with elsewhere in general terms[31] it is worth drawing attention to questions of time scale and divisions in this context. One of the most striking features of existing studies is the fact that it is so often impossible to compare events in different localities for similar periods. There are many instances where events affected greater or smaller tracts of Europe simultaneously. The 'great winters' of 1709/10 and 1740/41, the cholera in 1831/2 or the influenza epidemic in 1919 are all epochs of continental significance. Natural catastrophes, rainy seasons, harvest failures due to disease, civil and international wars all tend to be noticeable over large areas. High grain prices may favour enclosure over many English counties in the same year, a canal boom sets public works in motion all over the country. But it is often impossible to compare like with like. It is important to arrange demographic information in such a way that it is possible to trace the connection between these events, which are not found by the orthodox division of chronology, and the demographic statistics, which normally are.

When we look in fact at the time structure of demographic analyses they range from monthly or seasonal accounts to the tables of Henry and Gautier in their Crulai study,[32] where certain values are recorded only over several generations without a breakdown for identifiable shorter epochs. Some advice on possible practice when using aggregative methods and reconstitution is printed below, but it is essential in any case to keep in mind the need for a meaningful chronology. Once again, we have to see the demographic analysis largely as related to the time-scale of social and economic history, rather than in terms of centuries and decades, let alone reigns. The official end of the reign of Charles I, coinciding roughly with the end of the fifth decade of the seventeenth century, happens also to mark the end of a period of active civil war and the beginning of the Commonwealth administration, with noticeable effects on the parish registers of England. In every sense '1649' is a landmark. But more often this is not the case. It is customary, in graphic representations of time series, to point arrows at noticeable breaks in continuity which are, in some way, supposed to 'explain' the change of direction. But in the field of population statistics, it is well known that the echoes of past events are often stronger than the sharp impact of a contemporary crisis. Apart from the inevitable lag of births behind conception, the decision to marry or to postpone marriage often follows a considerable time behind the event which affected it, and deaths are often the result of malnutrition many months after the agricultural crisis which caused it.

We need not dwell here on the countless other combinations of circumstances which can affect population changes. The point of the demonstration is merely that immense care must be taken over the collection and storage of data, so that it is possible afterwards to re-combine them in any way required to test their relation to other series. From the point of view of a conveniently neutral representation, the quinquennial or decadal aggregation of data starting with the beginning of the first year of each decade or quinquennium (e.g. 1701–10 or 1701–5) is preferable, provided always that the calendar year begins on 1 January. Where it does not, special problems arise which will be dealt with below in the chapter on aggregation. Longer periods should always be multiples of the shorter unit employed in sub-totals. Quarter-centuries should be broken down into quinquennia. As far as possible the beginning and end of such periods should be made to coincide with the centuries.

In practice, however, it will be found that there is constant need to rearrange the data in other ways. In price histories, we are familiar with the concept of the harvest year.[33] Unfortunately, this has only limited application as far as our field of studies is concerned. If we take the conventional beginning of the harvest year we may use this consistently over a long period of time regardless of when the harvest was actually completed and supplies reached the market. In fact, however, we know that prices (and decisions dependent on them) could change at various periods according to the time when the prospects were known – the upward move especially might come with an early blight, a summer drought or an autumn flood. In the true sense, the food price year is that which runs from one point when the prospect is assessed, to the next, which may be a period from nine to fifteen months in length. This does not matter with long-term averages of the kind we normally use in economic history or even within a short cyclical movement, but when gauging the response of population to food supplies and so on there does not seem to be any special merit in choosing a year from Michaelmas to Michaelmas, or Easter to Easter, rather than the calendar year.[34]

If the original data are collected by months, they can then be re-grouped into three-monthly periods (seasonally or in the normal quarters) which will reflect the short term influences. These three-monthly units can also be aggregated later into any multiple which is found convenient. In small-scale surveys, it seems sufficient to keep the original working sheets for this purpose, though for larger operations the punched card is probably much more convenient. If, for instance, it is decided to assess the magnitude of the phenomenon now known as the 'post-war bulge' it may be necessary to add up all births or baptisms for a standard period from the end of a war plus nine months and divide them by the number of marriages which took place from the month in which peace was declared to the end of that standard period less nine months. This is relatively easy if we can take aggregates already made on a quinquennial or decadal basis and then add or subtract the number of three-monthly periods necessary to make up the required period.

Beyond this basic precaution, the researcher is free to adopt his own ingenious devices for measuring factors in which he is interested. We need not here discuss the propriety of using the techniques of social statistics in general to resolve particular difficulties in population history. Where gaps occur in the records, interpolation is often used in a variety of ways (and extrapolation backwards in some cases) to complete the series for one or two parishes in a group whose records do not begin till sometime after the rest, but which can be brought in to produce useful totals in this way.[35] Whether in any individual case it is more appropriate to use as the basis of interpolation the experience of a particular register before and after the gap, or the contemporary experience of other registers in the group, or a combination of the two, cannot be determined by recourse to a set of rules peculiar to our field. It is enough to point out that more meaningful results can often be obtained by using a larger number of partly defective registers than a smaller number of perfect ones. There remains, however, the problem of how one may recognise whether registers are in fact partially defective – complete gaps are easy enough to spot, and to amend, but short-term under-registration undoubtedly does occur and is hard to remedy because it can seldom be defined quantitatively.

SOME ASPECTS OF STATISTICAL INTER-RELATIONSHIPS AND INTERPRETATION[36]

The remarks which follow are, like much else in this chapter, addressed to the historians who venture for the first time into a field which the professional demographer knows to be full of special pitfalls of a statistical nature. That this is necessary is shown by the loose use of terms like birth-rate, fertility, mortality or natural increase, in most standard historical texts as well as many scholarly monographs on local history. The particular instances which are printed here do not form an exhaustive catalogue of difficulties, but they should be sufficient to warn those who jump to conclusions from insufficient evidence. Most of them apply only to the aggregative method, though in some cases they may also be relevant in the interpretation of series derived from reconstitution. What is said here is not in any sense a substitute for some training in demography. But by drawing attention to some of the commoner pitfalls of logic which are encountered in work published in this field, others may be preserved to some extent from errors of interpretation which would mar otherwise valuable investigations.

There is not, except in a purely statistical sense, such a thing as a birth rate, or marriage rate, for a given size of total population which can provide useful information on the nature of the process of change at the level of the individual family. An age and sex structure such as that of Finland and of the USSR at the end of the war produces an unusually small number of potentially fertile couples. Such situations must have been common in the past, and only an age-specific birth rate for women coupled with a measure of availability of men in the same age-groups can give a satisfactory indication of the real level of fertility. The significance of this is shown, for example, in Friberg's study of Dalarna and in Bourgeois-Pichat's detailed investigation into the age structure of the French population where it is made clear that a decline in fertility produced an increase in aged dependants, at a time when increases in the length of education and training added to the number of dependent children and delayed the start of married life.[37] If mortality falls at the same time for infants and old people, the active age group will be still further burdened and fertility may fall further, both in real terms, and even more so when measured by a crude statistical device, since births will be spread over a larger total population. Under such conditions it is clearly only the measurements of age-specific fertility that can assess the significance of the change. Similarly, where the sex structure is in any way abnormal it may be highly important and should be studied in detail (normality here meaning at any rate rough equality of sexes in the marriageable age groups). An example of this is the early history of the United States of America with its male surplus, as opposed to the striking female surpluses of the European areas from which the immigrants

33

came.[38] If the sex structure is omitted from analysis, the effects of crises and wars will often be under-estimated.[39]

In other words, each statement about population movements needs to be related to those 'at risk' and in terms of the total situation as it faces the individuals we describe. The age at marriage is in part dependent on sex structure and the expectation of life. If marriage is dependent on succession to an agricultural holding or business of a parent, these factors may become institutionalised.[40] Marriage *rates*, as such, will tend to fall when mortality falls, or fertility rises, because the total population becomes relatively larger. This is part of a natural cycle. Thus we find a close association of high marriage rates, low marriage age, and high mortality in Sweden, followed later by lower marriage rates, higher marriage age, and lower mortality.[41] It is clear that the problem of interrelationships is basically different in a fairly primitive society with uncontrolled mortality and fertility from what it is in modern times with general low mortality and the possibility of birth control. The automatic responses to crises or periods of prolonged misery, or else to high prosperity, give way to a more complex system where the deliberate reactions to the actual or expected economic situation play a much larger role than those engendered by the immediate family situation. Inheritance, primogeniture, dowries, vows, burgess rights, apprenticeship regulations – these are the typical determinants of the response of nuptiality to changes in mortality or fertility. Later, unemployment, family allowances, school fees or agricultural subsidies are much more likely to affect the deliberation of those about to found families.

The question then arises again: how can we best give statistical expression to this network of relationships? Ideally, the answer lies in the 'profile' which we can give to each cohort of individuals born or married in a certain period. If we investigate, let us say, all couples married in a particular valley in the period 1751–60, we can describe them in terms of their ages at marriage, their previous nuptiality, the marriages themselves as a proportion of all possible marriages in that age group in the area, or the proportion surviving from birth to the age of marriage. We can follow their marriages in terms of the number, sex and spacing of children, the early life-expectation of these children and the likelihood of their own survival to marriageable age. We can estimate the length of the effective union within the marriage, and calculate the chances and effects of any remarriage of a partner in the event of the death of one spouse.[42] Now in this way, we should describe a particular set of people in an entirely unambiguous way, and we could distinguish them from other people who lived before or after them, or in other areas. Moreover, if the local records are sufficiently good we can describe simultaneously the climate and harvests of the locality, changes in tenure or agrarian technology, the course of prices, labourers' wages and rents, the passing of wars, revolts or epidemics.

If industrial areas are involved, we may be able to outline changes in methods, quantities produced, and trade crises. We can add, in many cases, parallel statistics at national level – rates of interest, volume of international trade, taxes collected or excise duties imposed. In this way, we obtain a set of data which should help us to provide some sort of rational explanation for population behaviour. If we collect sufficient numbers of case histories, in cohort form, there is a possibility of testing these explanations rigorously by means of correlation and regression techniques. Each situation has to be seen as a complex system of simultaneous equations, so that it is not possible, from a single example, to establish whether fertility declines as real wages rise, as opposed to other possible causes, such as for instance reduced infant mortality, more miscarriages through increased gin consumption or changes in systems of tenure. But if we have a large number of cases of declining fertility, associated with the possible causal factors at varying levels of intensity, it is (at least in theory) possible to produce a model. This may never prove possible, but it is worth bearing in mind that from a scientific point of view this would be the ultimate aim of such an inquiry.

In actual fact, we should be unlikely to leave the material in the complex and unwieldy form suggested by this multiplicity of series and equations. We should devise certain 'type' populations in their context, much as the modern demographer has his models which simplify the characteristics of age structure and reproduction, and notations such as the net reproduction rate which are themselves combinations of a number of series. It is likely, however, that some new tools will have to be forged for this purpose. We know what is meant by a 'stable' population. But a population may increase at a compound rate of one and a half per cent per annum by reason of many different combinations of mortality and fertility. Some writers take the view that this is not an important question – that it is immaterial, for instance, whether the saving of life is at the infant or the adult level, but this is clearly not so as soon as we view this growth in its economic context.[43] There should be different notations for a population which shows this natural increase of fifteen per thousand according to whether the respective birth and death rates involved are forty-five and thirty, or twenty-five and ten, and so on. The expectation of life at birth, at marriageable age, and at sixty, are very different in their significance for the long-term trends of growth. In other words, a given combination of relative rates may produce entirely different patterns of movement over a generation. If one expresses mortality in terms of survival through the period of fertility of males and females, one arrives at one good index of long-term effects.[44] In the case of fertility, the best-known measure has been the net reproduction rate, but it may well be that one of the devices now used to gauge short-term changes in family size (the measurement of the probability of an nth plus one child following an nth child)[45] might also be applied to cohorts in historical demography to pin-point changes in behaviour more accurately than is possible by reference to whole generations.

We must also be aware of the general limitations of the static analysis, at least as far as linking population and economic changes is concerned. Even if we know age and sex structure at a given point of time with some degree of accuracy, this does not in itself provide us with sufficient explanations of the process of change, though it may help us to include or exclude certain categories of explanation. Census-type statistics mainly serve their purpose as a basis for the calculation of vital rates from current registration statistics. Naturally, if the census includes questions that enable us to determine the number of married couples, unmarried adults, widows and children per family, we can draw more conclusions about movements between census inquiries. For this we require the original household schedules, and where these have survived the structure which may be derived from them does yield some clues to change.[46]

The existence of isolated sets of reports, or defective registration series, brings us to the question of methods to allow for imperfections, corrections to make deficient series comparable, and the extent of information which may be derived from poor records. Here again practice differs widely. It may be true that the exact method of compensating for gaps is not of dramatic consequence in some of these cases – it can be shown, for instance, that the inflation of baptism and burial rates by a variety of factors to allow for under-registration does not really affect the shape of the curves to any large extent, provided that the relative corrections for different classes of event are not in opposite directions and within the same general order of magnitude.[47] But there should be some convention whereby published statistics which have been subject to correction should be accompanied by the original series, and the grounds for the correction stated, since the crude series will often reveal important facts which the correction masks, and the reasons for the alteration will normally in themselves throw light on prevailing social conditions. Only too often we find that published work includes interpolations to bridge gaps which admittedly improves the long series but glosses over the reasons for the gap.

CONCLUSION

We have raised many of the difficulties which tend to occur when one is working with the raw materials of historical demography in rather summary form since it is not possible to give examples of all the obstacles one may encounter. Comparatively few registers have so far been exploited, and it is likely that as additional sources are opened up, new hazards will arise. Conversely, as the experience of the last few years has shown, new types of documents are also coming to light, and these may facilitate the work.

Those who intend to work in this field must in fact equip themselves to meet the individual opportunities and difficulties presented in their chosen area. The rules which we have worked out in the chapters which follow are intended to deal with a 'normal' case – but each parish does in fact in some ways deviate from the normal. To this extent, everyone must make their own rules to meet the special peculiarities of their territory, in so far as the standard rules cannot be applied. However, the over-riding requirements still apply, and it is worth re-stating these so as not to leave any doubts:

1. Never throw information away. Although you may not be personally interested, for instance, in the proportion of those buried as paupers (with a 'P' against their name in eighteenth-century registers), somebody else will be. Record them even if you do not publish them.

2. Arrange your material in standard divisions by area, and period, so as to make it comparable with the work of others, irrespective of the groups of parishes or years into which you may choose to aggregate your facts for your own purposes.

3. If you need to supply missing facts by guessing (in other words, by interpolation or extrapolation), the fact that this has been done must clearly be stated. The same applies to any corrections to statistics inferred from evidence about deficiencies. For instance, if all baptisms have been 'inflated' by ten per cent this must be recorded, and both the corrected and the uncorrected series stated side by side.

4. It is part of the process of interpretation to make use of contemporary social, economic, and political information. Thus, wherever possible, demographic series for a locality should be accompanied by an outline chronology in relation to the area studied, as well as any series of statistics which have a bearing on the lives of the people studied. Examples:

Date of enclosure of each manor or parish,

Dates of turnpikes, canals or railways, reaching the locality.

Local repercussions of national events – Civil War, the '45 rebellion, raising or quartering of militia, outbreaks of Luddism.

Wheat price series from nearest market.

Local wage rates (including assessments where these survive).

Assizes of Bread. Records of local harvests. Weather records. Known epidemics whether recorded in registers or collected nationally.[48]

D. E. C. Eversley

NOTES

1 The *Reports* to the Board of Agriculture inspired by Arthur Young and Sir John Sinclair and published from 1793 onwards, usually contain an explanation of the local system of tenure etc. Some of the regional differences are briefly summarised in Lord Ernle's *English Farming Past and Present* (6th ed. London 1961), 226 ff. See also Richard Heath's *The English Peasant* (London, 1893) and H. Rider Haggard's *Rural England*, 2 vols. (London 1902). For a comparison between English, Welsh, and other European systems, see Frederic Seebohm, *The English Village Community* (London 1883). For a longer list of local reports and evaluations, see O. R. McGregor's introduction to Ernle, 6th ed., above, xcl ff.

2 See H. P. R. Finberg, 'Local History', in *Approaches to History, A Symposium* (ed. Finberg: London 1962).

3 See for instance the local accounts in *Chartist Studies* (ed. A. Briggs: London 1959).

4 Some of the traditional statements of these explanations will be found in G. T. Griffith, *Population Movements of the Age of Malthus* (Cambridge 1926). For the progress of the debate since that time, see *Population in History* (ed. D. V. Glass and D. E. C. Eversley: London 1965), Chapters 7, and 9 to 16.

5 Cf. the section on internal migration and settlement in the bibliography at the end of this book (esp. Buckatzsch). This movement is particularly striking in England, but it is also encountered elsewhere. Cf. E. Gautier and L. Henry, *La Population de Crulai*, I.N.E.D., Cahier 33 (1958), 79 ff.

6 For these influences Scandinavian work is illuminating. See K. M. Drake's unpublished Ph.D. thesis, *Marriage and Population Growth in Norway* (Cambridge 1964). Also his mimeographed paper for Section VII, Third International Economic History Conference (Münich 1965), and that of E. Jutikkala.

7 In recent years, attempts have been begun to standardise work in historical demography internationally. Two organisations, the Congress of Historical Sciences, and the International Union for the Scientific Study of Population, have set up Commissions on Historical Demography. Working rules are slowly being evolved which, it is hoped, will produce material which is comparable in the statistical measures adopted and in presentation. Some of the rules already agreed unofficially are incorporated in the next chapters of this volume.

8 Some general problems of methodology have been described in the author's 'Population, Economy and Society' in *Population in History* (ed. Glass and Eversley), 23 ff.

9 P. H. Styles, 'The Evolution of the Law of Settlement', *Univ. of Birm. Hist. Journal*, ix (1963), 37, 39, 43, 63.

10 S. & B. Webb, *The History of Trade Unionism*, 2nd ed. (London 1896), 184.

11 The subject does not seem to have been studied systematically in Britain, where there has been heavy concentration on urban sociology. For some survivals of older types of community see C. M. Arensberg & S. T. Kimball, *Family and Community in Ireland* (Cambridge, Mass., 1940); and W. M. Williams, *Gosforth, The Sociology of an English Village* (London 1956).

12 It is true that the description 'of this parish' often found in registers may be misleading if we are dealing with a former migrant who had by the time of marriage obtained a settlement and there may have been other reasons why the true origin was not stated. See Chapter 3, below, page 64.

13 A. Redford, *Labour Migration in England, 1800–1850*, 2nd ed. (ed. Chaloner: London 1964). See also W. A. Armstrong's chapter, below.

14 H. E. Bracey, *Social Provision in Rural Wiltshire* (London 1952). P. Sargant Florence, *Economics and Sociology of Industry* (London 1964), ch. 3.

15 Typical in this respect are the North Somerset, Kent and Coalbrookdale (Shropshire) coalfields.

16 On the coastal western side, the 'Landsker' is in practice a moderate barrier to intermarriage before 1800, but where it runs along the slopes of the Prescelly mountains, the obstacle becomes almost absolute (author's unpublished researches on Pembrokeshire parishes).

17 For the South Hams, see J. Saville, *Rural Depopulation in England and Wales, 1851–1951* (London 1957). The population history of the Warwickshire Felden is in J. M. Martin: *Warwickshire and the Parliamentary Enclosure Movement*, unpub. Ph.D. thesis (Birmingham 1965).

18 For a description of these divisions and references to other sources, see S. & B. Webb, *English Local Government*, new ed. (London 1963), 1, *The Parish and the County*, 284 ff. They point out the large differences in the extent of the Hundred: up to a few hundred square miles in Lancashire, but only two in some Southern counties, such as Dorset. This is true, but the great majority of them were of more manageable size for our purposes.

Later on the 900 ancient subdivisions were transformed into 675 Petty Sessional Divisions, but since these do not correspond with the early census returns, they are, perhaps, no more useful than some of the Hundreds. See also, Interdepartmental Committee on Social and Economic Research, Guides to Official Sources, no. 2, *Census Reports of Great Britain, 1801–1931* (H.M.S.O. 1951), Section VII, pp. 95–97.

19 See also: Census 1851, pt. I, vol. I (i), lxii ff., for Hundreds, etc., and *ibid.*, lxxix, for Poor Law Unions.

20 S. Lewis, *A Topographical Dictionary of England*, in several editions from 1831. The later editions include very clear maps of the administrative divisions. He also published separate volumes dealing with Wales, Scotland and Ireland.

21 See Chapter 3, below.

22 See E. J. Buckatzsch, 'The Constancy of Local Populations and Migration in England before 1800', *Pop. Stud.*, v (1951), 62–9. There is a very useful analysis of the constancy of names in a parish register in V. H. T. Skipp, *Discovering Bickenhill* (Birm. Univ. Dept. Extra-Mural Studies 1963), 40–2. This work also contains an analysis of origins of marriage partners, with the now familiar result that between 1683 and 1746 there were many marriages involving persons from a distance, but later such marriages became very rare.

23 The largest number of unpublished parish register analyses is in the hands of Mr. J. T. Krause of Rutgers University, New Jersey.

24 Few counties appear to have been left completely unexplored, but in comparison with one or two which have received some detailed attention (e.g., Nottinghamshire, Cumberland, Lincolnshire, Warwickshire and parts of Yorkshire), most of the British Isles awaits exploration. See bibliography.

25 The classic work on this is still E. C. K. Gonner, *Common Land and Enclosure* (London 1912), though his figures for individual counties have often been superseded. Cf. also Martin, *Warwickshire and the Parliamentary Enclosure Movement*.

26 H. C. Pentland, 'Population and Labour Supply in England in the Eighteenth Century', mimeographed paper, Third International Economic History Conference, Section VII (Münich 1965). Also J. D. Chambers, 'Enclosure and Labour supply in the Industrial Revolution', *Econ. Hist. Rev.*, v (1953), 219–43.

27 See S. Sogner, 'Aspects of the Demographic Situation in Seventeen Parishes in Shropshire, 1711–60. An Exercise based on Parish Registers', *Pop. Stud.*, xvii (1963), 126–46. Also J. D. Marshall, *Furness and the Industrial Revolution* (Barrow-in-

Furness 1958), and 'The Lancashire Rural Labourer in the Early Nineteenth Century', *Transactions of the Lancashire and Cheshire Antiquarian Society*, vol. 71, 1961.

28 For these authors, see D. E. C. Eversley, *Social Theories of Fertility and the Malthusian Debate* (Oxford, 1959), ch. 2, 53.

29 See chapters 5 and 14 by S. Peller and T. H. Hollingsworth in *Population in History* (ed. Glass and Eversley). Also Hollingsworth 'The Demography of the British Peerage', supplement to *Pop. Stud.*, xviii (1964), and L. Henry, *Anciennes familles genevoises*, I.N.E.D. Cahier 26 (1956).

30 By the present author. Preliminary results of an Irish pilot study to be published later in this series.

31 D. E. C. Eversley, 'Population, Economy and Society' in *Population in History* (ed. Glass and Eversley), 28 ff.

32 See fn. 5 above.

33 The year is established with reference to bread or grain prices at Michaelmas. Cf. the series in T. S. Ashton, *Economic Fluctuations in England, 1700–1800* (Oxford 1959), 181. But as may be seen in A. D. Gayer, W. W. Rostow and A. J. Schwartz, *Growth and Fluctuations of the British Economy, 1790–1850* (Oxford 1953), II, 659 ff., there are all kinds of seasonal patterns other than harvests to be taken into account when constructing price and activity indices, so that a single measure taking only food into account is inadequate. In earlier periods, no doubt, bread would be the chief determinant of living standards, but by no means the only one.

34 In any case, the comparison of one year's prices with one year's vital statistics is likely to be misleading, and in, for instance, quinquennial averages, the question of when the reference year begins is even less important – always provided we are consistent in our choices. For a particularly careful and illuminating presentation of demographic information in relation to agricultural production and crises, see P. Goubert, *Beauvais et le Beauvaisis de 1600 à 1730*, S.E.V.P.E.N. (1960), vol. I, 30–84, esp. 45–59 and vol. II (Tables, etc.), 71, graph 52.

35 Cf. J. Kovacsics, 'The Rectification of Demographical Data by the Aid of Extrapolation and Interpolation'. *Proceedings, International Population Conference, Ottawa, 1963* (Liège 1964). Also K. Dux, 'Estimation of the numbers of the population by the superimposition of trend functions', *Proc. of Colloquium on Historical Demography* (Budapest 1965).

36 Good demographic textbooks include P. R. Cox, *Demography*, 3rd ed. (Cambridge 1959); B. Benjamin, *Elements of Vital*

Statistics (London 1959); A. J. Jaffe, *Handbook of Statistical Methods for Demographers* (Washington 1951); H. H. Wolfenden, *Population Statistics and their Compilation*, 2nd ed. (Chicago 1954).

37 N. and I. Friberg, *Dalarnas befolkening pa 1600-talet* with English summaries (Stockholm 1953); J. Bourgeois-Pichat, 'The General Development of the Population of France since the Eighteenth Century' in *Population in History* (ed. Glass and Eversley), 474 ff. For the general significance of age structure see H. Leibenstein 'The Impact of Population Growth on "Non-economic" determinants of economic growth', U.N. World Population Conference (Belgrade 1965), paper no. A.9/1/E/95.

38 See J. Potter, 'The Growth of Population in America 1700–1860', in *Population in History* (ed. Glass and Eversley), 680–85. For the American population, since no current registration statistics were available, the ratio of children 0–4 years per 1,000 women 15–49 has proved very useful, even for refined measurements of differential fertility. See the authors quoted by Potter (T'ien, Yasuba).

39 E. Jutikkala, 'Finland's Population Movement in the Eighteenth Century' in *Population in History* (ed. Glass and Eversley), ch. 23, Table I, 555–557.

40 G. C. Homans, *English Villagers of the Thirteenth Century* (Cambridge, Mass., 1942), Book II, esp. ch. 11.

41 G. Utterström, 'Two Essays on Population in Eighteenth Century Scandinavia' in *Population in History* (ed. Glass and Eversley), 526 ff.

42 Gautier and Henry, *Crulai*, 85 ff.

43 See Eversley, 'Population, Economy and Society', in *Population in History*, 52–57. For the meaning of the term 'stable' population, see A. H. Hawley, 'Population Composition', in *The Study of Population* (ed. P. Hauser and O. D. Duncan: Chicago 1959), 370 ff.

44 T. H. Hollingsworth, 'A Demographic Study of the British Ducal Families' in *Population in History* (ed. Glass and Eversley), 309.

45 See Clyde V. Kiser, 'Population Research', in *Review of Sociology, Analysis of a Decade* (ed. J. B. Cutler: New York 1957), ch. 3, 63–64. See also C. Westoff, R. Potter and P. Sagi, *The Third Child* (Princeton 1963).

46 See chapters 5 and 6 below.

47 See below, chapter 3.

48 C. Creighton, *History of Epidemics in Britain*, new ed., with introductions and bibliography by Eversley, Underwood and Ovenall (London 1965) is still the best reference work for this purpose. Often it is possible to find out whether, for instance, a smallpox epidemic occurred in a certain area in a particular year.

3

EXPLOITATION OF ANGLICAN PARISH REGISTERS BY AGGREGATIVE ANALYSIS

AGGREGATION OR RECONSTITUTION?

FROM the point of view of accuracy and certainty, the investigation of the history of local populations by the reconstitution (or nominal) method cannot be excelled. Nevertheless, it is unlikely that all future work will be done by this method, even if studies now in progress and the establishment of a national sampling procedure should greatly reduce its cost in time and money.

The reason for this is to be found in the nature of the Anglican registers. First of all, areas of very great mobility or heavy incidence of Nonconformity are even less suitable for the reconstitution than the aggregation method, because the effectiveness of the former depends even more on being able to complete the records of a high proportion of all families, whereas, as we shall try to show, aggregation does yield a pattern of fluctuations which is valuable even if it relates to unconnected individuals. Secondly, as has already been mentioned, reconstitution becomes very difficult in areas where only a few family and first names are found, e.g. in Wales, parts of Scotland, and even some English districts. Thirdly, and most importantly, we can see little prospect in the short run of finding the resources to complete a large number of reconstitution studies, while at the same time it is of great importance to analyse population movements in many different regions as quickly as possible. Aggregation, in fact, can often be a prelude to reconstitution, for with this comparatively rapid system of analysis, it is possible to pinpoint those areas and periods of population history which saw the most striking changes, and

44

these will later repay the more detailed study which can alone give final answers to certain questions, notably those connected with the age at marriage and the fluctuations in marital fertility.

There are, however, positive advantages which commend the simpler method in some cases, and they are not in every case to be attributed to the fact that it does NOT suffer from the difficulties of reconstitution. In the first place, less information is actually wasted. In reconstitution, odd entries belonging to no recognisable unit are recorded, but do not enter into the ultimate averages, if no supporting information can be found, e.g. a death is of no use unless the age of the person can be traced, and a birth loses its significance in isolation from a family pattern of fertility. In aggregation, however, these isolated events (which may, in a highly mobile area, be the majority of all entries), do stand out in their significance, especially for large-scale migration movements, for epidemics and famines, the fluctuations of illegitimacy and other specialised fields of inquiry. The most important advantage, however, lies in the comparative ease and speed with which registers can be scanned to extract a great deal of significant information, and, as indicated, to single out those periods and areas where a much more thorough analysis is desirable.

The material and the choice of area

It is not intended here to provide an introduction to parish registers in general. For this purpose, J. C. Cox's *Parish Registers of England* still remains invaluable and little has come to light about their nature which was not known to Cox.[1] The remarks made here are intended merely to give some supplementary guidance for those seeking demographic information. Even a superficial glance at a selection of original registers shows that there are wide variations in quality, and the first task is to learn to distinguish those which are likely to be useful for our purpose from those which, though possibly interesting in other ways, are unlikely to yield results for either of the methods described here.

The first issue is simply one of completeness. An official inquiry was undertaken in 1831 into the state of the Anglican registers as they were then in existence, and the results are published in an abstract forming part of the 1831 Census publications and the original answers from clergy are also still in existence but the printed version is the quickest preliminary check as to whether any registers were missing 130 years ago.[2] These lists are frequently unreliable in detail – many registers have disappeared since that time, and a few have come to light, but there is no exhaustive modern inventory. Therefore the first task in each case is to check with the incumbent of a selected parish where the registers and any copies are kept. At the time of writing, the custody of the ancient registers is rapidly being transferred to the care of county archivists or librarians where there are no archivists, and these officers usually have the fullest knowledge both of originals and transcripts.

There are now in existence several thousand typed or printed transcripts of the old parish registers. A list of its own holdings was last issued in 1963 by the Society of Genealogists[3] which has in its possession not only the largest collection of such transcripts but also the most up-to-date information on the progress of further work. A list of the principal local printed series of transcripts is found in our bibliography.[4]

If it is decided to work from transcripts, it must be borne in mind that these are not always full or reliable. Those undertaken by the reputable societies are normally highly accurate and full, but many lesser works exist, often consisting of the minimum shortened entries and omitting vital information, e.g. residence of parents in the case of baptism, occupation, and certainly in very many cases everything except the names of the parties in marriages.[5] Therefore it is important where a transcript is used to consult the original.Unless the transcript can be relied upon in every detail, it is as well (if working from the original is impracticable) to obtain a photostat or microfilm of this, so that it may be compared when required with the typed or printed version.

Then there are the so-called Bishops' Transcripts as a result of early legislation which were supposed to provide a check on the local clergy.[6] Their defects have been fully discussed by Cox, but nevertheless they have their uses. First of all we have found some cases in different parts of the country where the Bishop's Transcript spans the period for which the original register has been lost, and in this case it may be better than nothing, especially where a group of parishes is involved.[7] But in most cases it is obvious that such transcripts can only contain less, rather than more entries than the original. They are useful when it is desired to undertake a rough preliminary count to check the general credibility of a register (see below), or rather a large number of registers, because they tend to be concentrated in regional depositories. Originally they were usually kept in the diocesan registry, but recently in many cases they have been transferred to county archives or record offices. In the case of Wales they are in the National Library of Aberystwyth, and defective as they are, they save much tedious journeying around inaccessible rural parishes in the Principality. Researchers should in any case look at them if a serious study of an area is made. Like the worst of the modern transcripts, they often contain less full information in respect of each entry. Printed transcripts do, incidentally, often have one very great advantage over the original: they are carefully indexed. As will be shown below, this is an advantage even where full reconstitution is not attempted, especially for establishing age at marriage and infant mortality. Other things being equal, therefore, one is inclined to choose a printed rather than an unprinted register, and an indexed one rather than an unindexed one.

'Other things being equal . . .' – that is the difficulty. How can one test whether a register is worth attempting or not? Continuity is clearly the first requirement. This can only be established by a year-by-year scrutiny of the register. Apart from the fact that half of the ten thousand registers listed in the Parish Register Abstract of 1833 do not begin before 1600, and one seventh only after 1700, there are serious gaps in the great majority of them during the period of the Commonwealth. Some of them have no entries, others have entries performed by the 'parish registers', officials specially appointed for this purpose, and contain entries of births rather than baptisms, a valuable variant where it is done conscientiously.[8] This period therefore needs checking in every register before a start is made. But there are other gaps, less obvious, caused not only by the loss of entire books, but also by the often cunningly performed removal of particular pages, and by absentee clergy. This last omission is often hard to trace, especially in small parishes, where nothing happened in one or all three categories of entry (especially marriage) for a year or two at a time. As a general rule, however, we do not meet baptism rates at an average of less than twenty per thousand over a quinquennium, nor burial rates below that figure, or marriage rates below five per thousand, except where there have been omissions, and this rough check can be quickly made in a patchy looking register.[9] If, by tests to be described below, we guess the village to have contained 250 inhabitants in about 1700, and it has grown to 500 by 1801, but successive years yield no marriages and only half a dozen baptisms, we know the register is likely to be defective. On the other hand a parish of 100 souls can, and often does, fail to record a marriage for five years at a time, so that the rough test rules should not be applied to the very smallest villages. Special considerations also apply to parishes in close proximity to others (e.g. in towns of no more than 3,000 inhabitants which may possess up to five parish churches) where it is often found that one or other of them is seldom or never used for sacraments, especially where it lacked space for extension of burial grounds. This, however, tends to be an urban rather than a rural problem.

One special difficulty arises out of the different systems of parochial organisation which one finds in different parts of the country. Many large parishes were not subdivided into autonomous units, in response to the shifting distribution of the population, until the second half of the nineteenth century. But, for the convenience of the parishioners, chapelries existed – in some cases up to a dozen or twenty of them within one parish, and, apart from services, they were used mainly for baptisms, whereas marriages took place in the mother church and, usually, burials also (though in some industrial districts this was not the case). There the registers only make sense if one takes the registers of all the places of worship in the parish together. The chapelries were usually very small, with only a few hundred inhabitants, but there are important exceptions in the case of places which were growing rapidly in the eighteenth century. Thus, by 1831 the chapelry of Aberystwyth in Monmouthshire (not to be confused with the more famous place in Cardiganshire) had over 4,000 inhabitants, and Bilston in Staffordshire, had nearly 15,000. In Lancashire the problem of chapelries is particularly acute. There are also, in most counties, a number of 'extra-parochial' places (often seats of the gentry), which may slip through the net, with separate registers, although their numerical significance is small.

If a preliminary check has led to the view that the register is substantially continuous and contains no obvious gaps, it is still worth pursuing the entries by the style of the handwriting. Changes of incumbent may produce serious discontinuities. Sometimes there is evidence that all entries were written up subsequently, one assumes from rough notes kept by the priest, or even from memory, and these can usually be distinguished by a remarkable uniformity of entry. Entries made at the time, even if the handwriting is the same, show some variations of ink and style which may be a guarantee of authenticity. Another problem is that of very old incumbents. Since it is not unusual to have the same vicar for fifty years, and cases of seventy years are known it is possible that the quality of entries deteriorates in the later years of the incumbency.[10]

We now assume that the register has passed the first tests sketched. What guarantee do we have that it relates to the whole or the greatest part of the population?

Nonconformity[11]

Two factors militate against completeness: general laxity towards religious observances (often coupled with rapid population increase, urbanisation and increased difficulties in reaching a church) and the spread of Nonconformity. The first of these is not hard to trace – it is common to practically all the rapidly growing areas of industrial Britain, and it makes it almost impossible to perform valid statistical operations in such areas precisely at the time when detailed observation is most required.[12]

Nonconformity, however, is not peculiar to industrial areas, and very uneven in its incidence. Where it is widespread, and leads to complete defection from the church, it invalidates registers very quickly. How do we know how strong Nonconformity was and whether it affects registers?

The first step is to consult a good general history of the county concerned. The best guides are those provided in the relevant volumes of the *Victoria History of the Counties of England*,[13] where these exist, and, in the topographical sections, under the entry of the villages in detail. The *V.C.H.* generally gives the date of the establishment of the chapels of the different

49

denominations, or at least the dates of the buildings. This usually tells us whether the place had dissenters of the first generation of 1662 – Congregationalists, Quakers, Unitarians Independents, Baptists, or only the later Nonconformists, mainly Methodists, who rarely had separate places of worship (as opposed to Meeting Rooms) before 1780.

If the parish had an established community of dissenters before the third quarter of the eighteenth century, it is necessary to find out how numerous this was. This may be checked in various ways. The size of any surviving place of worship is unlikely to be reliable, since it was probably rebuilt several times since the original construction. Burial grounds should be inspected – the presence of many tombstones of an early date is a sure sign of the significance of the community. Their absence is no guarantee of the contrary. Nonconformist registers survive, however, and should be consulted.[14] Some of them are published and those of the Society of Friends are transcribed and arranged chronologically and alphabetically, but only by quarterly Meetings (i.e. usually stretching over one large or several smaller counties).[15] For the Quakers, and for the others, the list of original registers should be consulted.[16] The registers themselves are now mostly at the Public Record Office, and, if one survives, it must be consulted to see how numerous the entries are compared with the Anglican ones. The fact that a register exists is no guarantee that it reflects the full extent of Nonconformity. There is plenty of evidence in the parish that Nonconformists did bury their dead in churchyards, that the births of their unbaptised children were recorded in the church register (for legal reasons, it is supposed), and certainly, with the exception of the Quakers, most Nonconformists seem to have married in the church. That there were no fundamental objections to this, and that the church was regarded as an almost neutral institution, is evidenced by the fact that even Nonconformist ministers were buried in Anglican graveyards.[17]

If there were no chapels before 1800 (there were very few districts with none after that date) no surviving registers, and no mention of dissenters in the church books, the case is straightforward enough. Conversely, there are strongly affected areas. The persecuted minorities of the pre-1688 period tended to cluster, for safety, in certain areas – for instance in the Chilterns and the area immediately to the north and east. How then do we measure their effect on the church registers? The best test is obviously a straightforward percentage calculation based on the extant Nonconformist and Anglican registers. We need to remember that not every village had its Baptist or Quaker chapel or meeting house, even in the strongholds, and that figures for one chapel need to be spread over the whole area served by a particular place of worship.[18] If that is done, it will usually be found that the effect is very small, and that what looked like very large registers became insignificant when compared with the Anglican aggregates. It is difficult to make a general rule, but unless the number of baptisms, or burials, for all Nonconformist groups together in any one collection of parishes, comes to over ten per cent of the corresponding church registers, there seems little cause for concern. It is not, after all, a question of totals, but of relative movements, and unless we assume that the Nonconformists represent an entirely different type of population from the Anglicans, we may omit them – or, of course, add their totals into the parochial figures, provided we can allocate them correctly. This, however, is not possible unless each chapel serves one village alone, or the chapel register gives the exact home of the people recorded.

A much greater difficulty exists where we have evidence, for instance, of a Baptist congregation which, did not bring its children to church for christening, but buried their dead in the churchyard and solemnised their marriage in the church. This could lead to serious underestimates of fertility if the Baptist group was over ten per cent of the total population.

An entirely different problem is presented by the Methodist revival and the breaking away of the Methodist Connexion in its various branches from the Anglican church. Until 1780 (or thereabouts, depending on local circumstances) the Methodists usually used the Anglican sacraments, though they had their own places of worship. They can be ignored so long as they did not begin to solemnise marriages (for which a licence was required), open burial grounds, or christen their children.

Some notion of the extent of Nonconformity may be gained from the Abstracts published by the Registrar-General after 1837. Thus, he reported in 1843[19] that in 1841, of 122,496 marriages, 114,371 were according to the rites of the established church. Of the 8,125 not so performed, 5,882 were in registered places of worship and just over 2,000 in registrars' offices. By 1850,[20] eighty-six per cent of all marriages were still being held in Anglican churches, and of those which were not, only just over half were in registered places of worship. Only 9,626 took place in Nonconformist chapels. These figures refer to the period when the discriminations against Nonconformists and Catholics had largely disappeared, and civil marriage had been established, and they argue convincingly for the idea that down to 1800 at any rate, the official church statistics must have comprised all but a small fraction of the population.

It might be argued against this use of the marriage customs of the nineteenth century that in any case Nonconformists used Anglican churches for the marriage ceremony even where there was a strong local community. This was certainly the view of those who, after civil registration began, were charged with the task of listing the old registers.[21] We prefer to use the post-1837 evidence as one of several indicators of the prevalence of Non-conformity in an area, rather than as a basis of numerical corrections of the original registers.[22]

Again, the legislation of the nineteenth century gives some idea of the territorial distribution of Nonconformity. Under the acts of 6 and 7 William IV c. 85 and 1 Vic. c. 22, there were licensed 3,106 places of worship by 1850. But their distribution in England and Wales was very uneven. Some counties either had absolutely very few because they were small (two in Anglesey, four in Rutland), or relatively few because Non-conformity was not strong (thirty-five in Hertfordshire, forty-three in Worcestershire). Others had relatively many more; thus Carmarthenshire had 64; Lancashire, with 313, had most, Yorkshire came next with 286, then Middlesex with 173. The precise distibution of these places can still be ascertained, and it is advisable to check on this point when working on parish registers.

Another index of the strength of Nonconformity, or the laxity of parents, may be had by comparing, after 1837, the number of registered births in a registration district with the number of recorded baptisms in church registers. In country areas, a low ratio of baptisms probably means that Non-conformists were strong; in town areas, laxity is the more probable answer. Since burials in country areas continued mostly in churchyards, these do not provide such a good index in relation to registered deaths.

As a general rule, any area which returns fewer than ten per cent of all marriages in 1840 as having taken place in a registered place of worship (other than an Anglican Church) is unlikely to have been a stronghold of Nonconformity, and its records may therefore be used with some confidence on that score.

Since, as has been widely argued[23] English registers tend to be less and less useful after 1780 in any case (and we support that contention), it may be asserted that the activities of the Methodists and other later Nonconformist sects need hardly trouble us, unless, as we have said, there is strong evidence in the shape of buildings, burial grounds or registers, that a significant community existed. This did happen, especially in Wales, and in some English mining districts, but if it did, it can hardly be missed even by the most casual reading of local history. One must beware of the habit of worried local clergy exaggerating the dissenters' menace – there are many examples in church registers of complaints that the paucity of entries is due to Methodist or other activity. These assertions should not be accepted without further proof.[24] The dissenters provided a convenient scapegoat for priests who (especially during the evangelical revival in the church itself) felt obliged to explain away the empty pews and disregard for the sacraments.

We need to stress the fact that although the date 1780 is mentioned by Krause and others as marking the beginning of an accelerated decline in the reliability of registers as a whole, this does not mean that there is any uniformity about the process. Many registers continue to be very trustworthy long after this date, and indeed we have seen series, especially in rural parishes in strong Anglican areas, where there is no apparent break in continuity down to the present day. Clearly each register must be examined on its merits.

Jews and Roman Catholics form, in most districts, such an insignificant part of the total that they, again, may be largely disregarded, but it should be remembered that there are clusters of settlements, e.g. Catholics in the Highlands and Jews in London who may be of local significance – but this fact will usually be elicited from local histories beforehand.

A guide to plausibility

Supposing now that we have chosen our area for study (in accordance with the general ideas expressed in our methodological chapter) and that the register has passed the preliminary tests of continuity, completeness and relative freedom from Nonconformist influence. It is then still possible that for local reasons it does not present a true picture of the population. There may be many reasons for this. Absenteeism may occur intermittently. A strict local incumbent may drive intending couples to marry elsewhere where fewer questions are asked, especially before 1754. We have evidence of local vagaries, such as the absolute refusal of parishioners to use a particular church for either baptism or burial – due to superstitions of one kind or another. It is therefore necessary to begin operations by a very rough check on the plausibility of the register.

What follows must be held to apply to the unit chosen for study. Individual parishes, especially where there were fewer than 500 inhabitants, and also where there were a number of parish churches in close proximity to each other, would rarely pass these tests. But where, as we have recommended for the aggregative method, a group of related parishes is under scrutiny, the considerations put forward here should be borne in mind: if the registers do not conform to the standards suggested, great care is required in utilising them for statistical purposes.

We know, from work which has already been done, that there are fairly narrow limits within which vital rates operate in any particular era. For our purposes, we need not concern ourselves with upper limits, since we are unlikely to have fictitious entries. But what, in practice, are the lower limits to plausibility? Basically, rural areas never reached crude death rates below 15 per thousand, and urban areas 20 per thousand, until long after civil registration began. The birth rate, on the other hand, was very rarely below 30 per thousand. Where we have been able to establish the fertility of marriage beyond doubt, the number of live births per couple is rarely less than three and rarely more than five, taking into account all marriages, whatever their duration (marriages which lasted until the end of the fertile period frequently show averages above five).

54

But taking the general average, birth rates of not less than 30 per thousand would imply marriage rates, at the same period, of round about eight per thousand. At all events rates much below this, or above this, imply either under-registration or marriages, or of baptisms.[25] These figures cannot be applied to single years (when anything might happen) but they tend to be correct over periods of five years or more.[26]

These are sweeping statements and of course very special and temporary local conditions may militate against such rules. For instance, new areas of settlement peopled by young immigrants may temporarily achieve very low death rates and correspondingly high birth rates; conversely, deserted old areas (extreme case: Highland clearances) may produce exceedingly high death rates and low birth rates. These special factors are however complementary, so that it is permissible to use the notion of a combined birth and death rate. Unless the community is monastic or has a very imbalanced sex structure ('Klondyke' population) a death rate of under 20 should be accompanied by a birth rate of well over 30. Therefore, if the combined number of births and deaths is fewer than 50 per thousand, there is some presumption in favour of omission. As we shall describe later, there may be in any case good reasons for some general upward revaluation of all figures. Therefore, if a parish shows fewer than about 45 annual entries of baptisms and burials per 1,000 of the population, the figures need close scrutiny. But, of course, we may not know what the population was. In that case, it is useful to take the 1801 census as a rough guide, and to assume that the poulation doubled between 1700 and 1800.[27] If we then connect the two points by a straight line (an unlikely picture of what actually happened, but it will do for this rough test), we may have a start for our check. Take a parish of 1,000 people in 1801. We assume there were 500 in 1700, and therefore on our model 800 in 1760. If in that year there were 10 burials and 14 baptisms, we have a combined rate of 25/800 or 30 per thousand, or 33 per thousand with a correction of ten per cent. This would lead us to think that there was some under-registration. But we could now take away the linear growth assumption and remember that growth is likely to have been faster in the second half of the century, so that we would not postulate a population of 800 for 1760 but perhaps only 700. Our figures then begin

55

to look more plausible (34–8 per thousand). But we should still want to look for special reasons why the figures should be so low.

In fact we should not accept the totals for a single year, but at least five-yearly averages, since both by pure statistical accident (especially in small parishes) and by natural causes large short-term fluctuations occur – e.g. 'baby-boom' years are followed by others very deficient in births, and wholesale epidemics tend to be followed by very low death rates, on the 'weeding-out' principle (that is, the assumption that at times of exceptional mortality there will be many extra casualties amongst those with weak constitutions).

Other tests of plausibility can be devised, but the main rule is that the first rough count must be used to eliminate the patent absurdities, whatever they may be. A proportion of marriages to baptisms of 1:12 is as absurd under British conditions in our period as one of 1:1. If a parish shows such very abnormal age-structure as to make such rates a reality, it is clearly unsuitable for study in any case. In practice it will be found that groups of parishes very rarely exhibit extreme characteristics, at least outside towns.

Starting and finishing dates

Continuity and homogeneity of data are more important than very long runs. Most population histories begin with a date as remote in the past as any documentation will allow, but on closer scrutiny, the earlier periods are often of very doubtful quality. As far as the study of registers by our methods is concerned, there is often no point in going back to the earliest entries, because so often serious breaks occur for sufficiently long periods to make comparison difficult. We have already mentioned the Commonwealth period, and there were others. But it is certainly not true that the earliest registers are necessarily the worst. No general rule can be made and there are clearly cases where a sufficiently long and carefully executed series of entries provides a basis for comparison with later dates.

It is very frequently the case that the absolute number of entries is quite different at various stages of the registers. Usually the earliest periods are those which have the fewest entries – if we assume total national population growth to have been threefold or fourfold from the sixteenth to the end of the eighteenth century this would also apply to the average, and parishes which grew more rapidly would exhibit even greater differences. Conversely, where there was depopulation, or a falling-off of the resort to the church's sacraments, later figures might be smaller than earlier ones.

Now large figures and small figures are not always comparable. The smaller the absolute number of events, the larger the percentage error which will result from mere occasional carelessness, or from purely fortuitous events. For instance, where there were, on average, ten baptisms a year, the chance arrival of two immigrant families both producing twins soon afterwards will result in a nearly forty per cent increase of fertility in a parish of 300 souls; or a single boat capsized in a storm will double the death rate of a fishing village. These accidents tend to be reduced to their proper proportion where the community is larger, and there are more events.

Moreover, a graphic representation of a long period of time is difficult to interpret. If one uses straightforward arithmetic quantities, fluctuations which take place at times when the number of events was small will be entirely lost on a scale which admits the later, larger figures. If on the other hand, we use a logarithmic scale to make the curve more intelligible, the violent ups and downs of early years can be even more exaggerated, and yet they are unlikely to be very meaningful except in the sense that they demonstrate the irregularity of the movements of small numbers. Since the possibilities of error are even larger in these early series of very small numbers, no conclusions can be drawn, in any case, from any positive or negative growth rates indicated by them. If they are investigated, they should if possible be presented separately from the continuous series involving larger numbers which become usual at the later stages. As a general rule, no register or group of registers is worth exploiting statistically at a period where the annual average number of events is fewer than about 15 – 20, for the reasons we have just stated. Since quite a large part of the population lived in very small communities, this rule means in practice that if we wish to include such settlements in an aggregation, we must add sufficient parishes to make up a group satisfying the minimum size likely to yield reliable results (this principle is followed by modern statisticians, for instance, in the

57

analysis of 1 per cent or 10 per cent sample census data: where the method would yield very small figures for single administrative units, data are only printed for the next larger unit which would return statistics on which a greater degree of reliance can be placed).

A number of studies have been made in which a group of parishes are aggregated, but the series begin in, for instance, 1600 with only two parishes, and another one is added every ten years, until in 1700 we operate with a full complement of twelve parishes. Clearly in such cases, horizontal aggregation produces quite meaningless totals, and only where the numbers of the population are ascertained, and birth, death and marriage rates are calculated, can we produce worthwhile averages. Figure 3.1 illustrates this point.

Figure 3.1. Burials

	Norton	Weston	Easton	Southill	St Mary's	Total
1661–70	34					34
1671–80	26	16				42
1681–90	22	18	17			57
1691–1700	24	27	19	30	80	180
1701–10	39	29	30	41	86	215
1711–20	35	30	24	53	104	246
1721–30	47	51	32	51	115	296
1731–40	40	35	30	44	120	269

It shows that the only group totals which are comparable are those after 1691, unless we use backward extrapolation to supply the deficiency.

It is, however, also possible to calculate *rates* of growth by natural increase regardless of the number of parishes involved, though clearly their reliability increases with numbers. Similarly, where we can calculate infant mortality from the incidence of deaths under one year (see below 71–2 and 76) in relation to total births, we may use annual or decadal averages regardless of the number of parishes involved.

For instance, using the same group of parishes as before, we make up the example shown in figure 3.2. Great caution is required in such cases and it is far preferable to use series involving the same parishes throughout.

As regards terminal dates, we have already stated that we

	Norton		Weston		Easton		Southill		St Mary's		Totals		Infant Mortality per thousand baptisms
	Baptisms	Infant Burials	Baptisms	Infant Burials	Baptisms	Infant Burials	Baptisms	Infant Burials	Baptisms	Infant Burials	Baptisms	Infant Burials	
1661–70	30	5	—	—	—	—	—	—	—	—	30	5	167
1671–80	34	6	18	6	—	—	—	—	—	—	52	12	231
1681–90	26	6	25	5	22	4	—	—	—	—	73	15	205
1691–1700	35	12	30	7	30	5	35	5	—	—	120	29	242
1701–10	27	9	36	10	41	5	50	14	120	18	274	56	204
1711–20	39	6	40	11	27	8	60	12	132	21	298	58	195
1721–30	45	8	42	6	30	6	46	7	105	21	268	48	179
1731–40	52	8	48	13	46	9	55	13	146	21	347	64	184

Although we would say in this case that the earlier infant mortality rates are much less reliable than the later ones, they are still all comparable. The same would apply if we had figures for marriages and baptisms, with respect to marital fertility.

Figure 3.2 Baptisms and infant burials

must concur with Krause that many English parish registers after about 1780 become increasingly unreliable by any of the tests we can devise. This does not mean that they are useless, but far greater care is necessary in handling them after that date and without tests of plausibility they should never be accepted at their face value, especially in the vicinity of large centres of population. Where emigration occurs on a large scale, the resultant statistical complications are so numerous as to defy classification: death rates fall if young adults migrate and hence fewer births take place; or they rise if emigration leads to a rapid ageing of the population; birth rates fall in the first case and fall faster in the second; marriage rates may rise if emigration means increased economic opportunity and fall if the population ages, and so on. Therefore a rough test of the consistency of the data (see above 54–6) after 1780 is even more necessary than before. Clearly a parish will drop out of a group analysis where its figures begin to appear suspicious either because of migration, or the spread of Nonconformity, or general laxity. As with the starting date, there is no particular merit in prolonging series beyond a certain point of statistical reliability.

What we have outlined so far belongs to the preliminary stage of investigation. The student intending to perform work on registers will have tried to satisfy himself that the material is worthy of study. Although the procedures suggested may occupy several days, or even a few weeks of work, they will be found rewarding, for the next stages will take very much longer, and they are not worth the effort unless one may be reasonably sure that the material will stand up to scrutiny.

In practice, most registers will show whether they are worth even the preliminary effort as a result of a few hours' work. The collection of several smaller parishes into a group may require more prolonged tests. In the end local knowledge, and common sense, will often affect the final decision as to whether a piece of work is worth doing or not. Throughout, we need to ask ourselves whether the figures which emerge are plausible in the sense that their visible fluctuations accord with the limits of biological possibility, and whether they reflect what may already be known, in rough outline, of the history of the area under study.

With these general considerations in mind, we proceed to the next stage, that of recording and adding up the data from the registers.

THE STAGES OF AGGREGATION

Recording the data

We begin with a cardinal rule common to all this type of work – throw nothing away. There are clearly many categories which we could use in the recording forms advocated here which are unlikely to turn up in many registers, and even where they do, they may be rare. For instance, few registers give occupations for any length of time,[28] fewer still give ages at death,[29] or cause of death.[30] The civil state of the deceased is usually given in the case of widows, but much more rarely in other cases. Certificates of burial 'in woollen', or the 'P' marking the pauper burials, apply only in certain periods. Nevertheless, since we do not know when we start work what information is given regularly, or in statistically significant quantities, it is better to record everything which may be quantified. In any case such information, even in isolation, is often historically valuable as a gloss on the figures even where, statistically, it is insignificant.[31]

Baptisms – There hardly seems any need to explain that baptisms are not births. Only in Quaker registers is a birth a birth, beyond doubt. In other denominations births take place which are not recorded as baptisms at the time, and conversely, there are many baptisms which refer to births in previous periods, even earlier decades, or births which took place elsewhere.[32] Farr discussed the extent of under-registration, as did all subsequent workers in the field, culminating in Krause's virtual rejection of baptism as an indicator of births in the nineteenth century.[33] Even after civil registration began births were under-registered.[34] Some baptisms took place in private, either in well-to-do large households or as an emergency measure – these were sometimes entered in the parochial registers, but probably as often they were not, and sometimes both private and public baptism is entered for the same child. Stillbirths are very occasionally noted, and should be entered, but this happens so rarely that one presumes they were usually omitted. Even neo-natal deaths must have been ignored in many cases, especially if baptism never took place – one avoided questions by registering neither the beginning nor the end of a short life which had no interest to anyone except the parents. Many illegitimate births must have been ignored, because only strong religious convictions would lead one to baptise the child, and since we know that its expectation of life was even lower than that of legitimate children, we have here another large source of omissions. It is easy to see how the spread of the Baptist religion, illegitimacy, stillbirths, neo-natal deaths and private baptisms could lead to the 40 per cent under-registration which was demonstrated in the nineteenth century, and that the 15 per cent correction used by some writers is nothing but a lower limit to what is required. But in the nature of things we have no checks on our guesswork.

The information available on baptisms is usually the date of the ceremony (with very occasionally the actual date of birth added), the name of the father or both parents, and illegitimacy if that applied. In some cases the abode or occupation of the father is given. Almost invariably the child's name is followed by the words 'son' or 'daughter' (or their Latin equivalent). If twins are born, this is usually explicitly stated, so sometimes are posthumous births, and the fact of neo-natal deaths. Illegitimacy is expressed by a host of euphemisms or terms of disapproval. Strangers are often so distinguished, so are clergymen, the squirearchy and nobility, and other notables.

There are cases where two consecutive entries of baptisms of children from the same family do not refer to twins. Here usually one child had been born earlier but his baptism had for some reason been delayed. Where three children are baptised together, there is a strong presumption in favour of this kind of occurrence. From a statistical point of view, it is unlikely to matter which explanation is adopted (in view of the rarity of these cases), unless the incidence of twinning as such is being investigated.

Burials – The same remarks apply, in some ways, to burials as to baptisms, except that whereas many who were born alive never received baptism, none who died escaped burial. The only question is whether a person was buried in consecrated ground or whether there was failure to record the fact. Most students therefore think that in the absence of organised burial in secular or sectarian graveyards, Anglican burial registers tend to be much more complete than baptismal registers.

62

The usual information given apart from the name may be summarised as follows. Adult men: none. Adult women: if a wife, name of husband. If a widow: usually stated, but not universally. If a spinster: no additional information. Children: normally name of one or both parents. Age, cause of death, abode or occupation of father are much more rarely found. Burial in woollen, payment of taxes where appropriate, and pauper burials, are recorded at some periods, but scarcely ever give information of demographic value. They should be recorded, as also any catastrophes or epidemics which are featured, however rarely, in the space left for marginal remarks.

The printed register form, which came into use in 1813, allows for the age, condition and abode of the buried person to be stated, but although this improves the information for those who are recorded, the general deterioration of the registers after that date cancels most of the advantage derived from this amplification for statistical purposes. Our specimen forms printed below clearly become inapplicable after 1812.

Marriages – Unlike burials and baptisms, marriages were affected by Lord Hardwicke's Act of 1753, in that registration after that date becomes more comprehensive, takes place on a printed form, and supplies some additional information.[35] It is impossible to say what proportion of marriages before that date escaped parochial registration on account of the malpractices of the time – it was obviously higher in London, and amongst the wealthier classes, than amongst the ordinary country folk who stood to gain little from hedge ceremonies. The normal pressures of village life ensured better regulation than any Act of Parliament. Nevertheless, two improvements may be noted as a result of the Act: whereas previously, the normal information consists solely of the name of the married parties, we have, in most cases, after 1753, their place of settlement[36] and their civil condition. There survive in many parishes special books recording the reading of the banns. Where the marriage register is missing these may be used to supply the information, but apart from the obvious need to eschew the duplicating or triplicating of events, we can never be certain that the marriage actually took place, or indeed in which parish it took place, if the bride and bridegroom resided in different places, unless we find the corresponding marriage entry in another register. In other

63

words, although the Banns books may occasionally be used for genealogical purposes, and although they will establish in some cases a presumption that a marriage took place shortly afterwards (where this may help to ascertain the age at marriage of parents of children subsequently recorded), it is much safer to ignore the Banns books altogether, and rely solely on marriages so recorded in the registers.

The origin of the partners after 1753 (and before, where it is given) provides social data, as we shall explain. However, a word of caution is required. Research workers have noted that whereas in the seventeenth and eighteenth century 'mixed' marriages are common enough, up to fifty per cent of all of them being between persons of different parishes, much greater uniformity creeps in later until in the early nineteenth century there are often whole decades without, apparently, anyone from outside a small village being involved.[37] So far there is no definite explanation for this phenomenon, but it is obviously connected with the operation of the Poor and Settlement Laws.[38] The risks inherent in declaring one's origin to be somewhere else were so great that bridegrooms in particular pretended to a settlement at the place of marriage – a fiction the incumbent seems to have allowed so long as no-one became chargeable. But this is not a totally satisfactory explanation, and one can only say that after 1800, along with other aspects, the information on the origins of married parties, seems to become less reliable. In each case where it is proposed to use evidence on this subject it will be as well to devise some simple test for a sample of cases where both bride and bridegroom are described as being of local origin, by trying to trace back their baptism to registers twenty to thirty-five years before the date of marriage. If less than half those so described can be found, the term 'of this parish' is fairly clearly suspect, for even the high turnover rates of population sometimes found in areas of change would only in exceptional cases allow such a high proportion to immigrate in a generation. If the family names of the sample are not found, the presumption is even stronger that the person concerned came from elsewhere.

If a group of parishes is being investigated, an alphabetical index to marriages is a useful device. Much less labour is involved than in full reconstitution procedures, but at the cost of producing a brief card entry for perhaps ten per cent of all events in the register we may devise a number of quick checks which will be explained later.

Aggregation

In the last chapter on methods we have discussed the question of division into periods at some length. In practice, for the reasons set out there, we advocate that apart from the annual (calendar year) record, there should be aggregations into quinquennia or decennia, quarter or half centuries and whole centuries, and that each sub-period should begin with the start of the year 1, rather than 0, i.e. 1706, 1711, etc. This means, amongst other things, that we can count back to correspond with the later census years – though all the early censuses with the exception of the first, were taken as late as the end of May or the beginning of June. This way of counting also seems to be receiving some support at the international level.

The annual total will be derived from the monthly totals of the original sheets. One difficulty arises from the change from the Old Style to the New Style Calendar in 1752.[39] It will be remembered that the old year began on 25 March. Although there was in practice a great deal of confusion, the accepted style was to refer to any date down to 24 March as belonging to the previous year. With continuous registers, it is not usually difficult to ascertain where the break comes, and it is recommended that when the original entries are collected, a thick line should be drawn under the last event for December, and that this should mark the end of, for example, 1743. Even though the January, February and March entries may still be marked '1743' they should be allocated to 1744. One difficulty arises if there is an isolated entry referring to 'March 1743' for instance. Strictly speaking, up to 24 March this should mean 1744 new style, and from the 1753 onwards it should mean what it says. If there are other entries before and after and the register is tidily chronological, this is simple enough. But some people were in the habit of treating the whole of March as the first month of the new year, and after reform many people continued to use the old ways. Similarly, some people used 'March 1743/4' for the new year, and some did the same for January or February, and there were more of these after reform. Sometimes the stroke and the additional year, or the words 'O.S.' or 'N.S.' are added by later hands. The Quakers did not use the heathen months, but spoke of 'first', 'second', etc. month, and whilst 'first month' is always March until reform, exactly the same mixture of usages occur in their registers, and we have seen many Anglican registers using roman numerals for months, thus landing us in the same confusion. In other words, each register must be examined as to its usage at different periods.

Aggregation procedure

We reproduce here samples of the standard forms which we recommend.[40] Local variations may be necessary, but it will be helpful if at any rate the main totals are produced and tabled in the suggested form.

It is best to use ordinary spiral-leaf notebooks for the first counts, and then immediately transfer the totals to the year sheets at the end of each twelve-month period. Most people count in fives, using four strokes for each entry and then a fifth across to produce an easily recognisable group. If monthly divisions are used on the annual sheets, it may be possible to insert the strokes in each space, and add the number, but this tends to obscure the figures for later operations, and it is best to begin with rough books. Exactly the same headings as those for the annual forms are then used to produce summary forms for quinquennial and twenty-five year periods (there is normally no point in providing a special duplicated form for half centuries, centuries and longer periods – this information will be contained in the final tabulations contained in the report on the study).

The next stage is to add up events for the chosen group of parishes. For this purpose the normal form can be used, though care must be taken to alter the heading to show what is involved. It is important to undertake the adding up even at the monthly level, so as to bring out seasonal fluctuations clearly for the whole area.[41]

Then add to the straightforward record those derived monthly and annual data which require the original material as their basis. The two most important ones (in the sense of affecting materially any later analysis of the causes of change in population and their relation to economic and social conditions) are

BAPTISMS

Parish: | County: | Reg. Book No. | Starting:

Year:	Legitimate		Illegitimate		Totals				Sex not given 9	All Baptisms 10 (5+6+9)	Remarks
	Male 1	Female 2	Male 3	Female 4	Male 5 (1+3)	Female 6 (2+4)	Legit. 7 (1+2)	Illeg. 8 (3+4)			
January											
February											
March											
Jan. – March											
April											
May											
June											
April – June											
July											
August											
September											
July – Sept.											
October											
November											
December											
Oct. – Dec.											
Whole Year											

Total Private Baptisms	
Total baptisms not of infants (included in figures above)	
Still born (not included above)	

Figure 3.3a

67

Parish:		County:		Reg. Book No.		Starting:						MARRIAGES		

Year:	All Marriages	Bridegroom					Bride					Both of this parish.	Neither of this parish.	Remarks
		of this parish	adjoining parish	same county	else-where	widow-er	of this parish	adjoining parish	same county	else-where	widow			
	1	2	3	4	5	6	7	8	9	10	11	12	13	
January														
February														
March														
Jan. – March														
April														
May														
June														
April – June														
July														
August														
September														
July – Sept.														
October														
November														
December														
Oct. – Dec.														
Whole Year														

Total Marriages where:	Both partners of this parish
	Bridegroom only of this parish
	Bride only of this parish
	Neither partner of this parish
Marriage took place:	In Bridegroom's parish
	In Bride's parish

General Remarks

Figure 3.3b

68

BURIALS

| Parish: | County: | Reg. Book No. | Starting: |

Year:	Man 1	Wife 2	Widow 3	Spinster and other 4	All women 5	All Adults 6	Sons 7	Daughters 8	All Children 9	Infants M. 10	F. 11	sex not given 12	All Children 13 (9+12)	Strangers etc M. 14	F. 15	Paupers M. 16	F. 17	Total Deaths 18 (6+13)	Remarks
January																			
February																			
March																			
Jan – March																			
April																			
May																			
June																			
April – June																			
July																			
August																			
September																			
July – Sept.																			
October																			
November																			
December																			
Oct. – Dec.																			
Whole Year																			

Remarks

Figure 3.3c

69

Parish:		County:			Period: 1701 - 1725					
	Legit. M. F.		Illegit. M. F.		Totals				Sex not given	All Baptisms
					Male	Female	Legit.	Illeg.		
1701										
1702										
1703										
1704										
1705										
Total 1701 - 5										
Average 1701 - 5										
1706										
1707										
1708										
1709										
1710										
Total 1706 - 10										
Average 1706 - 10										
1711										
1712										
1713										
1714										
1715										
Total 1711 - 15										
Average 1711 - 15										
1716										
1717										
1718										
1719										
1720										
Total 1716 - 20										
Average 1716 - 20										
1721										
1722										
1723										
1724										
1725										
Total 1721 - 25										
Average 1721 - 25										
Total 1701 - 25										
Average 1701 - 25										

Figure 3.4

70

infant mortality and age at marriage. It would of course be even more interesting to determine mortality in general, but experience has shown that infant (or at least child) mortality can be determined relatively easily, whereas adult mortality measures can, in the absence of data about ages at death, only be derived from something akin to full reconstitution.

Infant mortality, in modern parlance, means deaths of children under twelve months. Strictly speaking, therefore, the correct way of measuring infant mortality is to go back over baptism records for twelve months from any burial entry marked 'son or daughter', and if the baptism of the child is found, to record this fact (in columns 10 and 11 of the burial forms) along with the total number of those described as being 'sons' or 'daughters' of someone and therefore presumably being unmarried children living at home. In earlier work we sometimes assumed that the appellation 'son (or daughter) of' was rarely used for people over about twenty. In fact, recent investigations suggest that the term was also used in some cases where an unmarried son or daughter lived at home, or even in the same parish as the parents, though never after the child had married, or had gone to live in another district. On the other hand, it is quite often the case that an unmarried child under the age of twenty, and even living at home, is buried without any indication of parentage. It seems safe enough to assume that these cases cancel each other out, or at least that we may treat the total percentage of burials recorded in the manner indicated as being an index of child mortality (we cannot, of course, use this method for anything more refined, such as a measure of life expectation).

In fact, children were often not baptised for some time after they were born, and experience shows that register dates are often unreliable within fairly wide limits, owing to the practice of recording events sometime after they took place. It is easier, and quicker, to look through all the baptism entries for the earlier part of the year in which burial took place, and the previous year, and provided this method is followed consistently, we obtain a rough measure of infant mortality which can be used over the whole period of the register though it cannot be compared with modern data. But if preferred, the strict twelve

71

months' period may be used, and this has the advantage that the results then bear comparison with those derived from reconstitution. Child deaths and infant deaths give useful series which may later be compared with those for total mortality.

Modern statistics demonstrate the very rapid falling off of mortality after the first four weeks of life. This improvement in the prospects of the child may not have been quite so striking in the days before accurate registration. Nevertheless, as in the case of child mortality in general, what we need is an index of the danger to the baby, and for these purposes, especially in view of the limitations of our material, the important point is to be consistent in the method used to find which child burials refer to children born in the immediately preceding 'year'. On the average, looking back through the register for the earlier part of the year of burial, and the whole of the previous year, will cover a period of eighteen months from baptism, and this fact, coupled with the possible delays before baptism was performed, may mean that we are dealing with deaths of children up to nearly two years. This is immaterial so long as the same method is used throughout. Certainly mortality between eighteen months and two years is very small indeed compared with the earliest months of life.

It is possible, though laborious, to say something about the age of marriage in the case of indexed printed registers (e.g. from those published by the Shropshire Parish Register Society where whole groups of parishes are printed, such as those of the Hundred of Ford). When one looks up the names of the partners in a marriage in the index two possibilities exist: either one immediately finds an unambiguous reference to the baptism of one or both of them in the records of twenty to thirty-five years earlier, or one does not. If there is only one baptism of a person of the right age group, this will furnish an age at marriage. If there is no entry of baptism in the parish in question, or one of a very small number of others close by, or if there is more than one entry of a baptism for the correct name, it will clearly become too laborious to search further. In this way one establishes a very restricted sample consisting of persons of not over-popular names, and of those who did not move away from their native parish before marriage. Often this will yield only a dozen ages at marriage per parish, unambiguously, in a decade. Nevertheless, this may be a useful index, especially when combined with evidence from several groups, and the attempt should be made with all printed indexed registers.

Alternatively, as already mentioned, one can make one's own card index of marriages and then check the baptisms of earlier periods against this index – but this is much more time consuming, and not as effective as full reconstitution.

A further 'derived' set of statistics concerns the origin of marriage partners.[42] A good contemporary topographical map of the area is valuable here, and a gazetteer wherever possible.[43] The localities of the area should be divided as in the forms into: the parish proper, the parishes next adjoining (or within the group if it is a group study), other parishes in the county, and 'elsewhere'. 'Elsewhere' may be further sub-divided, though not on the form, into: counties next adjoining, rest of England (or Wales as the case may be), rest of the British Isles, and abroad. The last categories are so rare in most registers as to defy statistical evaluation, but they may be recorded in the margin as a matter of interest. Some workers prefer concentric rings drawn from the home parish church, and record the origin of marriage partners by reference to the distance of their parish church from the one in which they married. Though accurate, this method has the disadvantage that owing to the large variations in accessibility, a category like '10–15 miles' tends to have very different meanings according to whether this is 12 miles by river barge to the other end of London (with luck an hour's journey for a few pence) or a day's walk over the Pennines. Equally, of course, some parishes are very large and some very small, so that the definition by parish location is not universally useful. Nevertheless, the pattern of settlement in parish clusters as such, and the tradition of the county, are strong enough to make the distinction advocated a useful one, if used with discretion. Sheffield and Sedbergh are both in the W. Riding, and 80 miles apart; but Bridgnorth and Sutton Coldfield, though not even in adjoining counties (Salop has no common frontier with Warwickshire) are 25 miles apart along a good highway. Clearly the local pattern must to some extent be the guide to the interpretation of the statistical result.[44]

73

Derived statistics

Before we turn to the calculation of rates, let us consider what may be discovered by relating the raw data to each other (leaving out for the present the question of corrections).

Most series produce figures for natural increase. This means quite simply the growth (or decline) of the population for any given area and period by the excess (or deficit) of births over deaths, baptisms over burials. It serves a useful purpose inasmuch as it tells us, if we can rely on the original data, whether the population is likely to be growing, stationary or declining. By presenting this in simple graph form[45] we obtain some sort of picture of the changing size of the gap, and whether it is produced by relatively faster (or slower) growth or decline of births (or deaths). Such graphs have the merit that in an easily understood form they tend to pin-point years of epidemics and catastrophes, the consequences of marriage booms (or periods of fewer marriages), and the impact of measures for controlling mortality. We need to realise, however, that this sort of measurement cannot produce any 'explanation' of population change, but simply serves to underline periods of change which will have to be investigated from another point of view.

A much more significant secondary calculation concerns marriages and baptisms. Strictly speaking again, marital fertility can only be measured by imputing births to particular marriages. But in a (theoretically) closed community the same result can also be calculated, at least for longer periods, by dividing all births by all marriages. And even for an open community, we may assume that over the years most births (or baptisms) belong to families then resident in the parish, which gives us again a rough measure of differences in local fertility, and differences over time.

On the other hand, marriages are much more difficult to pin down accurately, in the sense that far more people marry in a parish which is not the one in which they eventually settle. This is not a movement which cancels out as between parishes, for some parishes, as we have said, were much more popular for this purpose than others. Once again, it is most likely that within a group based on a recognisable centre these irregularities are reduced to a minimum.

74

A further difficulty lies in knowing how to define the period limits for the numerator and denominator in any period. At one extreme, the births which took place in 1750 are virtually unrelated to the marriages of that year. At the other extreme, practically all the births from 1701–1800 may be imputed to marriages contracted in that century – only a fraction of those at the beginning stem from eighteenth-century marriages. For shorter periods, therefore, we use the device of overlapping periods. If we pursue our quinquennial and decennial divisions, it is useful to adopt the idea of a half-overlapping decennial period. That is, baptisms taking place in 1726–45 are divided by the number of marriages contracted in 1721–40. Some births will have taken place in the families so created before 1726; some births after 1726 will be the product of marriages contracted before 1721; some births will still be taking place after 1745; some births in the period 1741–5 proceed from marriages contracted after 1740. The precise proportion of such births falling outside the periods chosen but attributable to marriages which took place within them cannot be known, but statistics of completed fertility both from the past and from present series suggest such a heavy concentration of births within the first fifteen years of married life, that the fraction will be heavily weighted by the occurrences inside the marriages *in existence* at the central period of the combined span of years (in this case 1731–5). This is, in the nature of the operation, an index of ✓ fertility rather than an exact measure, but as such it is superior to a system of dividing baptisms of a short period by the marriages of the same years. We are comparing long-term trends, and the fact that probably something like seventy-five per cent of all births and marriages in these two periods will be related, gives us a reasonable basis for a measure of change.

Good results can also be achieved by using running averages for rather shorter periods. If we start with all baptisms which took place in 1736–45, and divide those by the marriages of 1731–40, we obtain a ratio. This ratio is the first entry on a table, or it may be plotted on a graph. We obtain the next ratio in the following manner: to the total of births (in the numerator) we add those of 1746, and we deduct those of 1736. To the total of marriages (in the denominator) we add those of 1741, and deduct those of 1731. Then we divide again, and this is the second ratio. In this way a series can be obtained which will iron out the more haphazard fluctuations, and a long term trend is established. It will be understood that in the example quoted, the first ratio denotes the fertility for a notional year, which we can call '1738' or we can allot it to a period 1735–40.

Infant mortality rates are also calculated by relating raw data to each other, in this case by dividing total births or baptisms in a given period into the number of infant deaths in the same period and multiplying by 1,000. Strictly speaking again, if we take a whole decade, some of the deaths of children under a year old in the first year relate to births in the previous year, and some of the children born in the last year of the decade die outside it, but before they are twelve months old. Though logically important, this fact does not affect the measurement of infant mortality in our period.

Further derived statistics include the sex ratio (defined as being the number of boys born for every 100 girls), which can have important repercussions on growth rates, the sex distribution of total deaths (affording a clue to migration), the proportion of illegitimate children, and the infantile mortality rate and sex ratio of such deaths. In addition, any other data which can be derived from the entries where appropriate – civil condition, occupation, age at death, cause of death, or taxation entries such as those relating to the taxes of the end of the seventeenth century – may be tabulated.[46]

The calculation of rates – In order to compare the experience of nuptiality, mortality and fertility, in different areas, it is desirable to reduce all figures to rates per thousand of the population. This operation presents perhaps the greatest difficulties encountered in analysis by aggregation. Fortunately, as we shall show, it is not in fact necessary to know to a high degree of accuracy what the population was in a given year, but to establish marker or reference points which can be used to fix the approximate line of a population growth curve, to which the vital statistics may be referred to establish rates. The principal requirement is, of course, that the shape of this curve should not be solely determined by the birth and death figures themselves, since otherwise the argument may become circular. We require data about the size of the population, at least at some points, which are independent of the annual variables.

The census reports from 1801 onwards provide us with the best reference points. In the absence of migration, total population in any one year may be derived by subtracting births and adding in deaths for every year backwards from the census.[47] Provided registration has been adequate, we then obtain the basis on which rates may be calculated. Unfortunately, the assumption that no migration took place can seldom be made. The task, therefore, is to find a fixed reference point (or several such points) further back in history to increase the accuracy of rate calculations.

The best such reference point is another census, and the reader is referred to Mr Laslett's chapter for further details regarding the scope and occurrence of these local enumerations. But for the great majority of parishes it is unlikely that such documents will be found, and we therefore turn to the Hearth Tax as the most universal form of taxation, and the best clue to the size of the earlier populations.

We will not discuss here how this tax was levied – there are now very good historical descriptions which indicate both the scope and the limitations of the Hearth Tax lists.[48] For our purposes, it is enough to indicate that for most localities in England, and many in Wales, lists survive in the Public Record Office for more than one year of assessment. As a general rule, it is best to choose the fullest assessment available. As complete editions show, there is often as much as fifty per cent difference between counts of hearths within a twenty-year span. Sometimes exemptions (on grounds of poverty) are recorded, at other times they are missing, possibly because they were on a separate roll. The general rule is that households could not have been invented, but they could have been omitted, so that the longest list is also the best. We count for our purposes the number of entries in each parish, not the number of hearths, since one entry refers to one household. The exceptions mostly refer to one-hearth households, and are quite often those of paupers living on their own, but this cannot be taken for granted.

Once we have the number of households, we go on to convert these into total populations. The question of the multiplier has been fully discussed elsewhere and the result is that conventions have been established following closely on the model laid down by Gregory King.[49] But it must be remembered that national averages are not necessarily applicable to local circumstances. Since we are dealing in this chapter mostly with rural areas, we may rule out the multipliers above 5, and up to 8, which have been found applicable in urban areas. Probably most values will lie somewhere between four and five persons to each household, though the results of Mr Laslett's analysis may lead to a revision of this figure, and no definite recommendation will therefore be made here. But a statistical feature must be pointed out. Suppose we have a parish of 100 households in 1672, and 1,000 enumerated persons in 1801. If we use the lowest suggested multiplier for 1672 we have 400 persons: if we choose 5, there would have been 500. The total growth in one case will have been 150 per cent to 1801, and only 100 per cent in the other – which looks formidable. But the difference in the annual growth rates will not be so very great – on the lower population (derived from a multiplier of 4) the annual rate will be just over 7 per thousand per annum; on the higher starting population, it will be about 5·3 per thousand. If we take a medium multiplier of 4·5 persons per household, the rate becomes about 6·2 per thousand. In this case, the deviation in growth rates of the extreme assumptions from the medium one will be of the order of 15 per cent and since such a figure is probably well below the range of error of entries, we are not going to find that a difference either way in the reference figure of 10 per cent will affect our vital statistics very much. Or we can put this point in another way. For a given year, if the assumptions we have made produce a population of 600 plus or minus 60, the results on the rates will be as follows:

20 baptisms on 600 equal 33 per thousand
540   ,,   37   ,,   ,,
660   ,,   30   ,,   ,,

Similarly, if in the same year we observed 15 burials, the rates would be:

on   600   25 per thousand
540   27·7   ,,
660   22·8   ,,

Therefore the annual rate of natural increase (which is the really significant part of the whole exercise) will be:

on	600	8 per thousand
	540	9·3 ,,
	660	7·2 ,,

These differences are very small. In fact, the margin of error on the number of recorded events is likely to be much larger, and the combined effect of errors in baptisms and burials, and the size of the base population, may produce extreme limits of errors which are very wide apart indeed. But errors about the base population of the order mentioned cannot affect the direction of the movement of rates to a significant extent. We are not claiming that accuracy about the multiplier is unimportant in general (indeed a great deal hinges on household size), but merely that assumptions about the size of the initial population are not as important as is sometimes thought for the description of growth rates.

There are, however, additional marker points available to the student of local history. One of the most important is the so-called Compton census which has been only partially exploited,[50] as well as many other ecclesiastical inquiries of the eighteenth century into the state of church-going and the progress of Nonconformity. These are less reliable than the census or the Hearth Tax returns (partly because respondents were expected, or thought they were expected, to give a certain reply). Nevertheless no local inquiry should be pursued until a search has been made in the County Record Office for such local statistics. As with estimates based on the Hearth Tax returns, the exact location of a reference point is not so important as that there should be some long-term indications of the shape of the curve. If it is found that the acceptance of a population number for a given year leads to absurd values for average birth and death rates, it is obviously unsuitable; on the other hand the fact that the resultant rate is within the limits of plausibility does not guarantee the accuracy of the figure. A great deal of common sense is required in the use of such information.

Most other forms of evidence are even less reliable. Window Tax schedules may be dismissed, since this tax was a great deal less well administered than the Hearth Tax. Lists of freeholders entitled to vote at certain elections survive, but give little clue except as to the size of a particular class of landholder. One

79

possible source are the enclosure awards (as far as they were made before the first census). In some cases these contain lists of all landholders, large and small, including cottagers, with common rights, and may therefore be regarded as household lists. But since many of the entitled owners were absentees, and since there were usually squatters and other persons without even the smallest common rights, they may be misleading. Where the enclosure award or map gives the tenant as well as the owner, or where owners who are absentees can be identified from local histories, something may be salvaged.[51] It is difficult to lay down rules for the use of such information. An attempt should always be made to ascertain the total size of the population for at least the Hearth Tax period and an early census, and to fix as many intermediate points as possible.

Whether to take the census of 1801 or 1811 as a reference point depends on one's view of the accuracy of the first attempt 'to ascertain the numbers of the people'. The further we go into the nineteenth century, the better the census reports become, but the worse the registers. However, it might be as well to take the 1811 census as the terminal date, since after 1812 the new form of printed register began to be used, so that in any case rather different methods of aggregation become applicable after that date.

Since names and surnames were not recorded until 1841 there is no possibility of linking parish records with enumerated families until that date.[52] The enumerators' schedules until that time merely ascertain the number of people in each household, and although in 1821 an analysis of these schedules may provide a more detailed age and sex structure than is possible from published census records, and thus provide some age-specific birth and death rates, the additional information thus obtained seems hardly worth the effort. In exceptional cases, however, where the parochial record continues to be apparently complete (by the tests already stated) into the period of civil registration, the link up to 1841 may perhaps be accomplished, and certainly the stated ages (and birth-places) of the extant population is a useful check back to records of earlier periods. In general, however, migration and the shortcomings of most of the registers in the nineteenth century make this sort of work nugatory.

Basic tests of rates – Suppose we have now obtained our starting and finishing points for the run of parochial records. The next step is to aggregate the baptisms and burials as previously stated, and to see what will be the relationship of the difference between the two totals compared with the difference between the enumerated population at either end of the period. It is extremely unlikely in the 'raw' stage, that the sum will come out correctly, i.e. that

Population 1811 less Population 1670 =
Baptisms 1670 to 1811 — Burials 1670 to 1811

We now look for the cause of the discrepancy.

1 Natural increase *larger* from the registers than actual growth of parish.

This may be due (*a*) to under-registration of burials – therefore we check for Nonconformist and secular burial grounds (this is occasionally found even where baptisms are adequately registered, but not usually).

(*b*) to emigration, especially in counties adjoining areas of rapid growth. This can only be checked by looking at birth places of survivors in these areas in the 1841 or 1851 census, and by checking on the rate of disappearance of established names from the parish under investigation. Both these methods are laborious and give qualitative rather than quantitative information.

If burials are presumed to be complete, then emigration must be assumed to be the chief cause, but the distribution as between these two causes of the deficiency will usually be a matter of guesswork. Other indicators of emigration are: high marriage rates in relation to apparent rates of population growth; possibly large number of cases of first or second baptisms, with no subsequent traces of the name (this is relatively simple to check nominatively by following up any easily recognised name from the entry of marriage for five years, especially during the later stages of the eighteenth century).

2 Natural increase *smaller* than growth in aggregates. This will then be due conversely to:

(*a*) under-registration of baptisms (which is likely both in urban and Nonconformist areas).

(*b*) immigration.

81

Here again we first check for Nonconformist baptismal registers. If these do not exist, then we check on immigration. This may be done by looking at 1841 or 1851 census schedules for the older age groups – assuming there is no difference in the life expectation of natives and immigrants, it should normally be possible to ascertain the proportion of the population which immigrated during stated periods, at least back to about 1780. In this case it is possible, with some trouble, to ascertain the cause of the discrepancy at least at a fairly late stage.

It is always possible that the gap, either through failure to register or through migration, is a product only of the later period. This is why a check for an intermediate year is of the greatest importance.

If all the information we possess in a given area consists of a fairly reliable starting and finishing population, and annual natural increase (or decrease) rates, it is very difficult to give any general guidance as to the probable appearance of the real growth curve. We tend to assume, on the whole, that under-registration and immigration, which lead to the discrepancy between true total increase and recorded natural increase, are more important as we come to the end of the eighteenth and the beginning of the nineteenth century. Moreover, population increase accelerated during this later period. In other words, a graph showing growth should show a steep rise in the total population curve, and an increasing divergence between the curve calculated from baptism and burial figures and a 'true' curve.

Smooth growth curves are in practice unlikely. At any stage during the period under review, agreement between an actual and a computed population may be larger or smaller than shown in a graph based on even rates (see Appendix B). There may even be agreement at the end between the two figures, and yet divergence in the intervening period. The agreement may be accidental: under-registration of baptisms, for instance, may have been just cancelled out by emigration. Thus, the real population in 1811, in a certain parish, may have been 1,200. The computed population may also be 1,200 although a net 150 baptisms had gone unrecorded; but a net 150 people emigrated, so the end result tallied. In such a case we obtain correct totals for the wrong reason.

To sum up: the mere fact of the net balance of births and deaths apparently agreeing, or not agreeing, with information from census type sources, must not be taken in itself as an indication of the reliability, or unreliability, of parish register material. Rather, it is necessary to look carefully at each case for sources of discrepancies, and to test completeness by some of the methods already described.

Corrections

Acting purely on the assumption that there must be under-registration, Talbot Griffith, in 1926, applied a 10 per cent correction factor to burials and 15 per cent to baptisms, thus eliminating what he called the 'jump' between baptism and birth rates before and after civil registration (but without actually measuring the gap itself as later investigators did).[53] That there had to be a correction had been demonstrated by Brownlee ten years earlier. He also adduced proof (arithmetically) that the correction rates applied did not really matter as long as they were in the same relationship which Griffith used, i.e. larger corrections for baptisms than for burials, as common sense seemed to dictate[54] (by the same reasoning that we have just used to demonstrate the relative unimportance of small errors in the base population).

In actual fact these corrections had a long previous history, going back to Farr and even to Rickman. Full accounts of these attempts have been given by Krause and Glass[55] and it is not now in dispute that the gap between baptisms and births at the end of the ecclesiastical period of registration was very much greater than had been assumed by Griffith. It certainly was not constant throughout the eighteenth century as most of the earlier writers assumed.

The outcome of these discussions, so far as the present day research worker is concerned, is that whatever national rate may be adopted by various writers, there cannot be a single local rate of correction applicable for all events and for all areas. This can easily be seen by looking at the varying sizes of the gap to which we have referred. Moreover, applying correction factors to close the gap may be completely mistaken if the gap is in fact due to migration. In three of the English case studies by relatively crude methods a straightforward correction along Griffith lines produced fairly plausible results,[56] but this is no reason for adopting this method. When corrected and uncorrected rates are juxtaposed, the major movements which provide anything like a clue to the causes of population changes stand out equally from both sets of rates. The fluctuations of the eighteenth century are of much greater magnitude than could be eliminated by the difference made by a 15 per cent and a 10 per cent correction (i.e. if a 15 per cent baptism inflation and a 10 per cent burial inflation produced a larger or smaller natural increase rate than the one which actually occurred, the margin thus created would be much smaller than the difference in natural increase rates in 'good' and 'bad' years which are known to range from plus 15 to minus 10 per thousand).

Corrections may usually be made if there is strong positive local evidence of any kind on which to base them. If, for instance, Nonconformist baptisms or burials are separately recorded, but registers survive only for certain periods, it may be correct to make a corresponding allowance for all years under review. No general rule can be applied – except that in every case where corrections are made, both series must be shown, so that the significance of the correction may be gauged. The existence of a local cut-rate 'marriage shop' would lead to a correction for the marriage rate, if one could be certain of the local affiliation of the marriage partners (but Dale Abbey, for example, served a wide area, as did many reputable Nonconformist chapels and burial grounds).[57]

It is quite another matter to apply a general correction factor to a population curve, distributing all the factors which lead to a final under-registration in a hypothetical manner along the entire length of the curve (i.e. imputing migration, or failure to record events, proportionately during the entire period), so that at any one time one obtains a notional population which is consistent both with starting and finishing populations and producing plausible intermediate vital rates.[58] This is legitimate up to a point, but it does produce a tendency to 'put the cart before the horse', and in 'normalising' the vital events, sets up distortions by hiding the real changes which took place.

If our initial tests for the completeness of the registers and the suitability of the group have been made, it will in general be found that there is little to be gained from the elaborate attempts to apply correction factors. It is certainly dangerous to conclude from evidence of the gap in 1837–40, between baptisms and births, that the intermediate discrepancy was in proportion. This would depend on a great many local factors.

Base populations – observed and intermediate

We may now assume several base populations for each intermediate decade – one is that obtained by joining the terminal dates by a straight line, another depends on an aggregation of recorded baptisms and burials during each period. Other lines are curved based on certain theoretical models of population growth, e.g. an exponential curve of the type which often figures in models of growth during the industrialising period, or a 'growing rate of increase' curve. None of these methods is in itself preferable to any other, all may be equally far removed from the true state of affairs. But the straight line is inherently the least plausible. On the whole, therefore, it seems better to construct a hypothetical total population curve which fits in between the extreme ends, but which is based neither on a constant rate of increase, nor on any such general principle as the exponential one, but on observations consistent with at least the more reliable parts of the total picture. This involves the construction of intermediate base points by calculation. One such method is described in Appendix A to this chapter, and consists essentially in trying to find out what total population, over a short period of years around the desired base point, would bear a relationship to the observed births and deaths of that period which was both plausible within the general range of observed values for that period elsewhere, and consistent with the long-term growth rates necessary to link the initial with the final population. But we have to admit that any such devices involve a certain amount of circular reasoning, and that the more one makes assumptions of the kind required in these complex operations, the less reliable will the final birth and death rates be.

If, because of doubts about the reliability of registration in the quinquennia in which the intermediate base periods lie, it is thought undesirable to apply this method, then the next best method seems to be to adopt the exponential curve (see Appendix B).

It seems worth stressing that the construction of *rates* as opposed to the gathering of absolute figures should not be pursued too far. Rates are an easy method of making comparisons over time, and between places, but if they cannot be obtained except by a great deal of guesswork, the fluctuations in absolute numbers of events (and especially in natural increase and such measurable matters as infant mortality and marital fertility) can go a long way towards providing answers to the questions which we ask.

Averages, rates and their interpretation

When we last left our raw data, we had them collected on annual sheets, and in quinquennial, decennial and twenty-five year summaries. This applied to single parishes, as well as to groups, for which information had been collected at individual parish level. We need now to convert these raw data into indices suitable for comparative purposes.

We begin by producing some averages, which facilitate the process of comparison. It is best to collect such averages on the twenty-five year summary sheets (see specimen at p. 70 for baptisms; the same form can be used with appropriate headings for burials and marriages). Spaces should be left on these forms for totals as well as averages, at intervals. In practice, there is no point in producing averages for very short periods where absolute quantities are small (e.g. where only two illegitimate baptisms occurred in a quinquennium, an average of 0·4 per annum is not very meaningful).

From these averages, we proceed to the construction of rates in the manner described – that is, producing a notional base population for each period of account and relating the vital events to this. There is usually little to be said for the labour of constructing annual baptism, burial or marriage rates for single parishes. Instead, the quinquennial average should be applied to the notional population of the middle of the five-year period. Alternatively, series may be produced giving annual rates for a group of parishes. Anything more detailed is likely to lead to spurious precision.

The crude birth, death and marriage rates should produce at any rate a general outline of movements for the group of parishes under investigation. As has already been pointed out, such measures cannot go very far in explaining the network of interaction between population and economy. They mainly serve to pin-point with greater precision the years and places of change – the crises of subsistence, the epidemics and other sudden catastrophes; and in arriving at them we shall probably have discovered the period of immigration and emigration, the impact of Nonconformity, and other long-term basic structural changes in the local community.

At this stage we have to see whether any of the other measures described will fill in the picture. General mortality may be further explained by reference to infant and child mortality. Nuptiality may be illuminated by statistics relating to the proportion of women dying (demonstrably) ever-married, i.e. those specifically referred to as widows or 'wife of' (this is no guarantee that others mentioned only by name were not also wives or widows, but the indications given may serve as an index). Fertility may possibly be inferred by the method outlined, of dividing marriages into baptisms. According to the merits of individual registers, the researcher may devise his own further measures – where ages at marriage or death, occupations, or causes of death are given, there is clearly scope for further refinement.

Thus a typical list of measures to be tabulated from a parish yielding material along the lines of our forms might be as follows:

1. Total growth (or decline) by natural increase (or decrease) from beginning of period under investigation to the end year chosen (usually a census year):

   (*a*) crude figures
   (*b*) corrected for under-registration (where applicable).

2. Using initial and final populations and any intermediate points, as well as the natural increase figures taken from (1) above, construct population curve.

3. Refer annual or five-year average figures to base population to produce:

   (*a*) crude baptism rates (corrected to produce birth rate) by sex
   (*b*) crude burial rate (corrected to produce death rate), by sex
   (*c*) marriage rates.

4. Using total of marriages and baptisms, produce marital fertility rates.

5. Using baptisms and infant burials, produce infant mortality rates (including sex differentials).

6. Mobility of population:

   (*a*) Proportion of marriages in each period between persons of same parish, and in other categories such as adjoining parish, county and so on.
   (*b*) Listing names from one decennial period, count how many of these still occur 10, 20, 30, 40 years later.

7. Nuptiality: proportion of women buried with and without indication that they were or had been married. Age at marriage by sample attempts to trace baptisms of partners.

8. Illegitimacy.

9. Miscellaneous statistics: remarriage of widows and widowers, proportion of burials referring to paupers, burial in woollen, tax paid on burials or baptisms, ascertainable mortality from epidemics, and any other features regularly listed in the registers.

We have now arrived at an intermediate stage of exploitation. The process outlined in this chapter will take considerably longer than the simple head-count which is measured in a few hours in Dr Wrigley's chapter. On the other hand, even if all the work described here is performed, the total amount of time will still be much less than the 1,500 hours required for the full reconstitution of a single fairly small parish. No general time scale can be laid down, but experience suggests that the full aggregative exploitation of a group of ten parishes of a combined terminal population of about 10,000 people over a period of 150 years might be about six months' full-time work, assuming that some attempt is made to produce also the subsidiary economic and social information for the locality which needs to be considered in conjunction with the demographic data. But this will vary depending on whether registers are already transcribed or printed, and whether checks against the originals in this case reveal inaccuracies of a serious kind; on the size of individual registers (for searching backwards for the baptisms of infants buried); on the feasibility of some of the more elaborate procedures outlined by way of partial reconstitution (e.g. to discover the age at marriage); on the gaps encountered; on the diversity of local names; on the experience of the research worker; and so on. A project which might take a year for someone new to the work can probably be done in half the time by someone who has already become familiar with some of the complications listed.

In general, teamwork is preferable to single-handed exploitation. For instance, one person dictating categories of events from a register to another entering strokes on the form can work more than twice as fast as one undertaking both reading and entering. A calculating machine greatly speeds up processing – preferably an electric desk calculator, with a rapid dividing mechanism. For adding up series of annual events, a 'comptometer' type of machine is preferable to an ordinary adding machine.

The final stage of the work consists in comparing all the series with each other and in checking them against the available background information. As soon as peaks (and troughs) of mortality emerge, we look for either documentary evidence of famine, epidemics and natural diseases, or for periods of exceptionally good harvests, high wages, or labour shortage. We compare nuptiality with the price of corn, with wage rates, with what is known about the growth of urban or industrial areas in the vicinity.

We observe the mechanism of recovery after high mortality: the marriages, the births, the lower levels of mortality in years immediately following. We follow the 'bulge' generations through to the point where they reach marriageable age. We enter on our charts events like enclosure, civil war or the raising of militia, and relate breaks in the continuity of vital rates to these points of time. We check marital fertility against female mortality rates, infant mortality and opportunities for women to find work. There is no limit to such operations. In each case, the data need examining, and if, as is almost invariably the case, they exhibit sharp fluctuations, our task is to see whether we can relate these to events. If the figures are sufficiently reliable, there may be an opportunity of carrying out correlation and regression tests – the course of grain prices with nuptiality, industrial production with fertility, and so on. These matters are within the normal scope of the work of the modern economic historian, and need no elaboration here. The reader is referred to the authorities already cited in this chapter for examples of the uses to which the material may be put.

D. E. C. Eversley

NOTE. See Appendix A for a method of estimating base populations; Appendix B for a discussion of population growth curves; and Appendix C for sampling problems.

NOTES

1 J. C. Cox, *The Parish Registers of England* (London 1910). J. S. Burn, *The History of Parish Registers in England*, first published in 1829, is much less systematic. See also R. E. Chester Waters, *Parish Registers* (London 1870), and A. M. Burke, *A Key to the Ancient Parish Registers of England and Wales* (London 1908), W. Bradbrook, *The Parish Register* (London 1910).

2 See Census 1831, III, *Parish Register Abstracts*. Also Cox, *The Parish Registers*, 234.

3 37 Harrington Gardens, London S.W.7. An entirely new *National Index of Parish Register Copies* is in the course of preparation and will be obtainable from the Society.

4 See below, 263.

5 This is partly due to the fact that the transcriptions were often prepared for purely genealogical purposes, and the possibility of exploitation for social or demographic history was not envisaged. But the great majority of those edited by the principal societies are of a high standard of accuracy.

6 Cox, *The Parish Registers*, 240 ff. They have been used very effectively, for instance, by Professor Chambers.

7 See Cox, *The Parish Registers*, App. I, 241 ff., for list of known cases where the Bishops' Transcript is of earlier date than the first extant register.

8 Cox, *The Parish Registers*, 8.

9 There is some evidence that the marriage rate is the most stable of all indicators, and that at any rate in the eighteenth century it was generally round about 8 per thousand. For details see P. Razzell, 'Population Change in Eighteenth Century England: a Reinterpretation', *Econ. Hist. Rev.*, xviii (1965), 312–32.

10 M. Dickens, *A Thousand Years in Tardebigge* (Birmingham 1931), 113.

11 There are a number of good general histories of British dissent, e.g., J. T. Wilkinson, *1662 and After, Three Centuries of English Nonconformity* (London 1962); E. A. Payne, *The English Free Churches* (London 1952). Many details will be found in local histories, and histories of particular denominations.

12 There are exceptions to this generalisation. See K. M. Drake, 'An Elementary Exercise in Parish Register Demography', *Econ. Hist. Rev.*, xiv (1962), 427–45. This study very carefully takes into account the effects of both chapels of the Anglican church, and of Nonconformity. Dr Drake's notes on 427–8 may be taken as an example of how to assess the extent of dissent.

13 Examples: *V.C.H. York*, I, 404–19; *Warwick*, VII (Birmingham), 411–85; *Stafford*, VIII, 276–307, etc.

14 Cf. Cox, *The Parish Registers*, 258. Since his time many Nonconformist registers have been published. In some counties there are now guides to these. See, e.g., N. Caplan, 'Sussex non-parochial Registers', *Sussex Notes and Queries* xv (1962), 334–8; and 'Original Records of Nonconformity in Sussex', *ibid.*, 217–21. See also by the same author, *Annals of Lingfield Congregational Church 1810–1959* (Bedford 1959). For an assessment of Nonconformity in this context, and other references to quantitative estimates, see J. T. Krause, 'The Changing Adequacy of English Registration, 1690–1837', in *Population in History* (ed. Glass and Eversley), 383 ff.

15 The Quaker registers are in the Library of the Society of Friends at Friends House, Euston Road, London N.W.1. Copies are also available at the offices of local Quarterly Meetings. Listings of the Quaker Registers are in the Reports referred to in footnote 16 below, especially the 1859 Report, pages 110–32. Additional lists in the 1858 Report. The Commissioners for 1838 praised the accuracy of the Quaker Registers highly (page 12).

16 There is a printed list of registers based on the original hand-over of Non-Parochial records to the General Register Office under the Act of 1836: *Lists of Non-Parochial Registers and Records in the Custody of the Registrar-General*, London 1859 (P.R.O. Press Mark R 3 A 128 M: since this volume is apparently one of those which does not fit into the normal sequences of parliamentary papers, the exact location is given here). There is a copy in the British Library of Economic and Political Science at the London School of Economics (Ref.: R (O.S.) Y 327). The copy in the P.R.O. has been amended from time to time by hand. See also *Report of the Comimssioners*. Most Registers are in the Public Record Office in classes RG 4–8 but there are others in

public depositories which are listed in the Appendix to the General Register Offices' *Abstract of Arrangements respecting Registration of Births, Marriages and Deaths* (H.M.S.O. 1952). Useful additional information of registration will also be found in B. Dale, 'Non-Parochial Registers in Yorkshire', *Trans. of the Congreg. Hist. Soc.* vol. I (1901–24). And: *The Story of the General Register Office* (H.M.S.O. 1937).

17 For evidence of the extent of Nonconformist use of Anglican facilities cf. Drake, *Econ. Hist. Rev.*, xiv, 427–45. Amongst striking instances known to the author are a whole family of Presbyterian ministers and missionaries in the churchyard at Ambleston (Pembrokeshire), and, by way of contrast, Church of Ireland clergy in the Quaker burial ground at Rosenallis (near Mountmellick, Laois).

18 Cf. Caplan, *Lingfield*, where the chapel served a large tract of the county. With Nonconformists who were not organised in parishes, a much larger part is played by famous chapels and, even more, famous preachers, so that people would come from many hours' walk or ride away to hear sermons – or to baptise and bury.

19 *Fifth Annual Report of the Registrar-General*, Abstract for 1841 (London 1843), 76.

20 *Thirteenth Annual Report of the Registrar-General*, Abstract for 1850 (London 1852), iii. There is a very useful local breakdown, 2–27. This can be taken as an index of incidence of Nonconformity.

21 *Report on the State of Registers other than Parochial Registers* (London 1838), 10–11.

22 *Thirteenth Annual Report*, x.

23 J. T. Krause, 'Changes in English Fertility and Mortality, 1781–1850', *Econ. Hist. Rev.*, xi (1958), 52–70, and 'The Changing Adequacy . . . ', in *Population in History*.

24 By contrast, it is believed that the returns of communicants and noncommunicants made by incumbents in reply to diocesan inquiries, often overestimated the proportion of the faithful, perhaps in order to demonstrate the zeal of the clergy or to ward off too detailed inquiries into the state of the parish.

25 See above, note 9.

26 See below for methods of calculating marital fertility 74–5.

27 For a discussion of methods of constructing base populations, see below, 76–82 and 85–6, and App. A. There are now elaborate statistical devices for inferring total populations from partial registration data, or vice versa, of age structures from mortality statistics. These are in use, for instance, in Latin America. It has

yet to be demonstrated that they could be used in 17th or 18th century Europe, where the range of possibilities of combinations seems much larger.

28 For exceptions, see E. J. Buckatzsch, 'Occupations in the Parish Registers of Sheffield, 1655–1719', *Econ. Hist. Rev.*, i (1949), 145–50.

29 But see Drake, *Econ. Hist. Rev.*, xiv, for short periods when ages were available.

30 More frequently at times of epidemics. Many of the English Quaker burial notes give the cause of death – they had a great interest in medical matters. It is worth noting that such details exist only in the original notes, and not in the transcripts at Friends House Library, another instance where it is necessary to consult the original (e.g. Soc. of Friends Register no. 857 at the P.R.O.). An interesting possibility of analysing the causes of deaths of an important category is provided by the records of the British Lying-in Hospital, Endell Street (P.R.O. R 68, 52–66) covering the years 1749–1868, and including over 42,000 cases.

31 But it is not usually worthwhile making the recording forms unwieldy by including columns for classes of entry which are very rarely encountered. It is best to make a separate note of these as required, and tabulate at a later stage.

32 But Baptist registers often record the actual date of birth.

33 Cox, *The Parish Registers*, 254, and Krause, 'The Changing Adequacy . . .', in *Population in History*, 383 ff.

34 D. V. Glass, 'A note on the under-registration of births in Britain in the nineteenth century', *Pop. Stud.*, v (1951), 70–88.

35 Cox, *The Parish Registers*, 76 ff.

36 But, as we have noted, this regulation may actually have resulted in failure to state the place of origin with the apparent increase in the number of 'local' marriages that this entailed. See below, 64.

37 Skipp, *Bickenhill*, 39–40.

38 Styles, *Univ. of Birm. Hist. Journ.*, ix (1963), 37, 39, 43, 63.

39 For details of the history of the change-over, cf. H. Watkins, *Time Counts. The Story of the Calendar* (London 1954), or A. Philip, *The Calendar: Its History, Structure and Improvement* (Cambridge 1921). The experience of the author's study of Irish Quaker registers suggests that with a little practice the conversion of old style into new style dates becomes a very rapid operation.

40 The examples given here are for the annual accounts of baptisms, marriages and burials, and quinquennial and twenty-five year summaries of baptisms. Similar summary sheets should be prepared for marriages and burials. If material is assembled for

longer periods, it is advisable to group into decades, fifty and hundred year periods, but no special forms are necessary for this.

41 In practice, where large numbers are involved, it may be found advisable to use punched card systems at this stage, rather than a multiplicity of forms (see Mr Armstrong's chapter below).

42 There is little in English sociological literature about the pattern of marriages in the geographical or sociological sense. A good deal has been done in Germany, mainly by Prof. I. Schwidetzky of Mainz, and her staff. Some of it may not have been noted abroad because it appeared first in journals like the *Archiv fur Rassen- und Gesellschaftsbiologie* which were suspect after 1933. But the work continues under unexceptionable auspices. See specially: H. Walter, *Bevölkerungsgeschichte der Stadt Einbeck* (Hildesheim 1960); Schade and Rietz 'Untersuchungen zur Auflösung eines kleinen sozialen grossbauerlichen Isolates', *Akad. f. Wissensch. u. Literatur*, Mainz, Abt. Math.-Naturwissensch. Klasse, 1959 (Wiesbaden 1960).

43 Cf. Lewis, *Topographical Dictionary*. The volumes of the English Place Name Society are also indispensable.

44 The county as such probably meant little. But the assize town and the petty sessional divisions were realities in most people's lives. Moreover, in many counties the network of communications centred on the county town. On the other hand, there were many enclaves of one county within another, and in some cases the road pattern, the eccentric position of the county town, or the accident of a coalfield, may lead to much more centrifugal movement. Herefordshire and Leicestershire are examples of counties with a strong orientation towards their centre, Oxfordshire of the opposite. Counties like Cheshire and Staffordshire, close to rapidly developing industrial areas, tended to produce concentrations of population on their borders, and therefore much movement into other counties.

45 E.g. as found in Griffith, *Population Movements of the Age of Malthus*, 40.

46 For the history and significance for registration of these taxes, see D. V. Glass, 'Two Papers on Gregory King', in *Population in History* (ed. Glass and Eversley), 170 ff., and Cox, *The Parish Registers*, 8 ff.

47 For an English demonstration of the possibilities of counting backwards from 1801 and 1811, see the paper by W. A. Armstrong 'The Population of England and Wales, 1789–1815', to be published in French in *Etudes et Chronique de Démographie Historique*, 1965.

48 See P. H. Styles, 'Introduction to the Warwickshire Hearth Tax Returns' in *Warwickshire County Records: Hearth Tax Returns* (ed. M. Walker), I, Hemlingford Hundred: Tamworth and Atherstone Divisions (Warwick 1957); and C. A. F. Meekings, 'Surrey Hearth Tax, 1664', *Surrey Record Society*, xvii (London 1940); *Dorset Hearth Tax Assessments*, 1662–4, pub. by Dorset Nat. Hist. and Arch. Soc. (Dorchester 1951).

49 See D. V. Glass, 'Two Papers on Gregory King', both on the tax and the conversion factors. See also P. E. Jones and A. V. Judges, 'London population in the late seventeenth century', *Econ. Hist. Rev.*, vi (1935).

50 Ed. C. W. Chalklin, 'The Compton Census of 1676: the Dioceses of Canterbury and Rochester', *Kent Records*, xvii (Kent. Arch. Soc.: Ashford 1960), 153–74. Sir William Dugdale, *Antiquities of Warwickshire*, revised by Wm. Thomas (1730).

51 The land tax has been extensively exploited to gauge the changes in tenancy and settlement, and more recently, with a view to throwing light on population changes as well. Cf. J. M. Martin, *Warwickshire and the Parliamentary Enclosure Movement*, unpublished Ph.D. thesis (Birmingham 1965).

52 See Mr Armstrong's chapter, below.

53 Talbot Griffith, *Population Movements of the Age of Malthus*, 28.

54 J. Brownlee 'The History of Birth and Death Rates in England and Wales, taken as a whole, from 1570 to the present time', *Public Health*, xxix (1916), 211–22 and 228–38. See also a discussion of Brownlee in D. E. C. Eversley, 'A Survey of Population in an Area of Worcestershire from 1660–1850', in *Population in History* (ed. Glass and Eversley). Also D. V. Glass, 'Population and Population Movements in England and Wales, 1700 to 1830', in the same volume.

55 See J. T. Krause's two articles listed in fn. 14 and 23 above, and the article of D. V. Glass in the last footnote.

56 J. D. Chambers, 'Population Change in a Provincial Town: Nottingham 1700–1800', in *Studies in the Industrial Revolution* (ed. L. Pressnell, London 1960); Sogner, *Pop. Stud.*, xvii, Eversley, 'Worcestershire' in *Population in History*.

57 Cf. Cox, *The Parish Registers*, 94, for Dale Abbey and Chapel of the Peak.

58 Cf. Sogner, *Pop. Stud.*, xvii, 140.

4

FAMILY RECONSTITUTION

FAMILY reconstitution is the bringing together of scattered information about the members of a family to enable its chief demographic characteristics to be described as fully as possible. The family reconstitution method is not new. Genealogists have √ for generations searched out the dates of birth and death of the partners to marriages of the rich, the well-born and the famous, and have listed the dates of birth of their offspring and the dates of their marriages and deaths to establish lineages and relationships. The tracing of family histories and the recording of details of this sort is actively prosecuted to this day. But it is only very recently that attempts have been made to apply this method to a sample of the families of a whole community by making use of parish registers as a source of information. Where this is possible the community's demographic history can be examined in greater detail and with greater precision than by any other method.[1] It is, of course, not possible to reconstitute fully all the families in a parish by making use of the register of that parish alone, if only because no parish was ever a closed community. Individuals and families moved in and out, so that only in a small percentage of cases can families be fully reconstituted. A much larger proportion can be partially reconstituted and used in the calculation of some demographic indices. If the total number of reconstituted families is large enough to reduce the risk of random error to an acceptably low level and if the families reconstituted can reasonably be held to be a representative sample of the population of the whole community, a detailed reconstruction of its population history and demographic mechanisms is possible.

Family reconstitution is complementary in its nature to other methods of investigating population history. It might be characterised as the study of demographic characteristics in depth where other methods deal chiefly with their study in breadth. Aggregative methods are comparatively economical in labour and large populations over long periods of time can be covered quickly in this way. For example, an experienced worker can count the entries in the registers of a large parish of about a thousand inhabitants over a period of three centuries and record the monthly totals of baptisms, burials and marriages on standard forms[2] in ten to fifteen hours. A further three or four hours with a calculating machine totalling columns and lines will show the number of events by calendar year, by harvest year if required, and seasonal fluctuations. Family reconstitution of the same parish for the same period might take, say fifteen hundred hours, though any estimate must be very rough both because individuals work at very different speeds and because the time taken varies so much according to the material in the register and the length to which the analysis is pushed. In the time necessary to undertake family reconstitution on a parish register, therefore, a hundred times as many analyses of registers by simple counting methods can be carried out. More refined aggregative methods require much more time, of course (e.g. when calculating the proportion of babies dying very early in life[3]), but the difference between reconstitution and aggregative methods remains great in both time and expense.

The great strength of the family reconstitution method lies in its ability to penetrate more effectively into the demography of a parish than aggregative methods. For example, it is possible to gain a clear idea of trends in total population by aggregative methods but often difficult to discover what changes in fertility and mortality produced the trends in question. Figure 4.1 may serve to illustrate this point. It shows the nine-year moving averages[4] of baptisms, burials and marriages in the parish of Colyton in Devon, and suggests that population was rising steadily between the middle of the sixteenth and the middle of the seventeenth centuries, but that during the next hundred years there was a tendency for the population to fall. The graph, of course, is a product of aggregative methods and much of interest can be learnt directly from it. The notable negative correlation between baptisms and burials, for example, suggests that in this parish periods of hardship not only caused a rise in

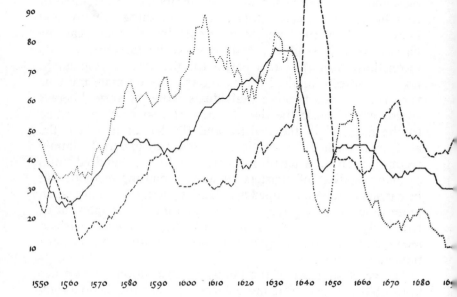

Baptisms ———
Burials ------
Marriages (×5) ··········

Figu

burials but also discouraged marriages and the formation of new families.[5] The tremendous surge of mortality in the mid-1640s stands out clearly and the peak can be located exactly if the standard forms are consulted for monthly and annual totals (there was an upward trend in burials during the early 1640s culminating in a period of twelve months from the beginning of November 1645 to the end of October 1646 during which 392 people were buried, perhaps a fifth of the population). The connections between this peak and the campaigns of the Civil War, the presence of epidemic disease, the price of grain, the condition of the woollen industry, and so on, can all be investigated. Or again, aggregative methods can be used to

98

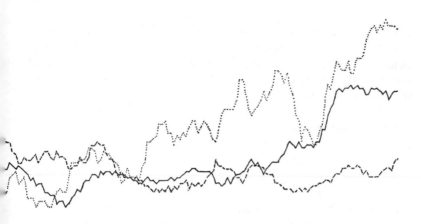

measure the size of the natural increase or decrease of population. But even refined aggregative methods cannot penetrate very far into other questions; for example, the mystery of the century of slow fall and stagnation between two periods of growth. Family reconstitution, on the other hand, is helpful here. It will show whether the change was due to a rise in the average age of first marriage for women, or a rise in the average interval between births, or a rise in infant mortality, or other changes in nuptiality, mortality and fertility which singly or in combination can account for the altered balance between baptisms and burials.[6] Thus, while aggregative methods may enable gross population trends to be established and some features of demographic change to be studied, a fuller analysis is difficult in the days before state censuses unless family reconstitution can be carried out.

The precision and detail of the results obtained by family reconstitution are, of course, limited by the accuracy and fullness of the record, but within these limits family reconstitution comes close to exhausting the possibilities for population history contained within parish registers. In particular family reconstitution overcomes one of the most inhibiting features of aggregative methods, the problem of deriving rates.[7] In western countries today, and elsewhere if the bureaucratic machinery is equal to the task, the state both collects vital statistics and periodically conducts censuses. By relating information from the first source to information from the second a rate can be calculated for any type of demographic event. Thus the crude death rate relates the total number of deaths per annum to the total population; an age-specific death rate relates, say, the total number of deaths of boys 10–14 to the total number of boys in that age-group; and so on. In each case the data for the divisors are provided by the census while the data for the dividends come from the vital statistics. To have one type of information but not the other severely restricts demographic analysis. The registers provide the vital statistics of parishes but no equivalent of the modern census. Both estimates of total populations based on annual totals of baptisms, burials and marriages in parish registers and those based on such sources as the Hearth Tax or Protestation returns are subject to large margins of error (especially for single parishes), and in the case of the former cannot be used as a basis for the calculation of crude birth or death rates since this would involve a circular argument.[8] This problem does not arise where family reconstitution is possible since the size of the population at risk is discovered in the process of reconstitution just as the number of events in a particular category is known. Thus, for example, it may be possible to follow the reproductive histories of, say, 200 women married between 1650 and 1699 through to the end of their reproductive period, and calculate age-specific fertility rates since both the number of births to women in each five-year age-group and the number of years lived by them in each age-group is known.[9]

The results produced by family reconstitution work have a considerable, strictly demographic interest[10] and their own intrinsic fascination. The work can give rise to chains of reasoning which have a great charm because of their elegance and ingenuity.[11] But the most pressing reason for prosecuting research into population history, whether by family reconstitution or other methods, lies in the importance of population history to the understanding of a wide segment of social and economic history. This has been underlined by a number of recent books which should help to encourage further work in population history.[12] There has also been a renewal of interest in the general theory of the inter-relationship between demographic characteristics and social function and change.[13] The demographic structure and behaviour of populations change in sympathy with social, economic and environmental changes, and, since they develop at times, as it were, a momentum of their own, themselves provoke changes in their economic, social and physical environments. If sufficiently full information is available population can be one of the main focuses in the study of social and economic history. It is a nexus, the centre of a web of related events some of which, when taken out of this context may attract the attention only of the antiquarian, the topographer or the genealogist, but which by acquiring a common focus in the demography of the community, also achieve a wider significance. To use Koestler's term, Goubert and others recently have succeeded in bisociating areas of knowledge which were previously less well integrated and they have greatly benefited both individually and collectively. Whether one studies the balance between numbers and the supply of cultivable land; the importance of harvest and weather to the community; the frequency of turnover of holdings; the views of contemporaries on the idle poor; the upbringing of children and their relationship to their siblings; the structure of authority in the family; the place of the unmarried and widowed; sexual mores; the relationship of master and man in pre-industrial society; the changes in real wages; in later times the flow of people from country to town; or more specifically demographic issues like the average size of families; the proportion of the 'tail' of the population beneath working age; the impact of the great killing diseases; or expectation of life at various ages, a knowledge of the society's demographic character is a part of the proper context of the discussion.

All this is feasible, however, only if the sources are good enough to allow an elaborate study of population history. To make family reconstitution possible it is essential to have a running record of baptisms, burials and marriages in a parish with enough detail at each entry to enable the person concerned to be identified with confidence. This means that family reconstitution methods cannot be used in England (except possibly for aristocratic families) before the injunction which required parish registers to be kept.[14] From 1538 for a period of three hundred years parish registers are the prime source of knowledge about population changes in this country. The state took over responsibility for the collection of vital statistics in 1837 after having already taken the first four national censuses (1801, 1811, 1821, 1831). After the state began to collect vital statistics the parish registers are less useful for family reconstitution because their cover becomes less complete. The end of the fourth decade of the nineteenth century is also a convenient point at which to conclude a family reconstitution study based on parish registers because the enumerators' notebooks of the 1841 census record the names of all the inhabitants of each registration district. This provides a firm anchor to one end of the study and can serve as a check upon the accuracy of reconstitution of families over the previous half century.[15] Earlier censuses do not afford this facility.

It is obvious that family reconstitution requires a comparatively long period of well-kept records since the dates of baptism of parties to marriages for some years after the register begins will lie in the period before the register was kept, and similarly the dates of burial of individuals born towards the end of the register period will also be unattainable. Therefore the minimum period for which it is worthwhile to undertake family reconstitution is quite long, perhaps as much as a century, and the proportion of families which it is possible to reconstitute fully will rise with the length of time for which the record is complete, other things being equal. Work on a register which is complete for two hundred years will yield considerably more than twice as many reconstituted families as work on the same register over only the first or second half of the period.

102

Furthermore, it is not enough that the record should be full in the sense that each baptism, burial and marriage in a parish is recorded in its register. It is also necessary that the entries should be sufficiently full to identify the men, women and children who are listed. For example, a baptism register which contained only the Christian names of the babies baptised would be unusable since the family to which each baby belonged could not be known. To learn that John was baptised on 8 April 1693 tells one nothing of value in family reconstitution (though it is quite enough to know only this in simple aggregative work). To learn that John Wilson was baptised on that date is no more useful unless it is also known that only one family of that surname existed in the parish. To learn that John Wilson, son of Henry, was baptised, on the other hand, is normally enough to enable him to be allotted to a particular family. If the mother's Christian name is given there can seldom be any ambiguity; and if her maiden name is also given (as happens sometimes in very full registers) then the odds against a wrong identification become astronomically high.

Most baptism registers do fairly consistently give at least the name of the father as well as that of the baby, and therefore do not normally present severe problems. Nor is the marriage register a source of difficulty since a simple convention produces satisfactory results in identifying the bride and groom at each wedding even when only their names are known.[16] With the burial register, however, it is otherwise, and special attention should be paid to the quality of the burial register in considering the possibility of family reconstitution. It is unfortunately the case that whereas most baptism registers provide more than the bare name of the baby baptised, many burial registers record only the name of the dead person. To know that Jonathan Abbot was buried on 8 December 1612 is seldom enough to identify the man with confidence. Sons often bore their fathers' and daughters their mothers' names so that where the burial register is of this type very few attributions can be made confidently. With more detail ambiguities are rapidly reduced to manageable proportions. Many registers, for example, include detail of the relationship between the person buried and the head of the family (as, for example, Peter, son of Jonathan Abbot; or Tamsyn, wife of Jonathan Abbot). In such registers a

103

widow is usually described as such after her death, and where a name appears without any further information it is usually a male name, and the man in question is usually the head of a family or a bachelor who has survived the break-up of the family into which he was born without having formed another himself.[17] Registers in which this degree of detail is given are also common, and they are normally usable. In many of the better registers this fuller form is usual, but there are also periods of relapse, as it were, into the short form of entry. If such periods are not frequent or prolonged they need not prohibit family reconstitution work since the surrounding periods of good registration will help to reduce the number of ambiguities in the periods of relapse. It is unusual for registers to record age at death until after 1812,[18] but where this is done even the short form of entry is usable since knowing age at death reduces ambiguities as effectively as giving a relationship with the entry.

There is one other consideration which should be borne in mind in selecting a register for family reconstitution work. This is the size of the parish, both in population and in area. There were thousands of parishes in England in the parish register period with populations of only a few hundreds where there were at most two or three score families in existence at any one time. Since only a small fraction of these families can be reconstituted, serious random errors are likely to appear in any rate derived to measure population characteristics unless a very long period is treated as a whole to increase the number of families in the sample to an acceptable level. But this is a self-defeating procedure since it makes it impossible to measure changes within the period. If these changes were important the result of lumping together families over a long period of time is to produce average figures which may not have been true for any of the sub-periods.[19] If parishes which were small in population were also small in area the difficulties are aggravated. The chief reason why only a small proportion of the families in a parish can be reconstituted is the prevalence of migration across parish boundaries. The chances of this occurring tend to rise as the area of the parish decreases, since a move which would mean crossing a parish boundary in a small parish would leave one still within a large parish. Many large parishes included several

104

villages and hamlets rather than a single inhabited place. For example, the parish of Colyton contained two substantial settlements in Colyton itself and Colyford as well as a number of small hamlets. If the two main settlements had been in separate parishes, as might easily have been the case, family reconstitution work in either of the two halves must have been much less easy. Similar considerations tell against parishes whose main settlement is close to the parish boundary. To take the limiting case, if the main street of the village is also the parish boundary[20] there is sure to be a very high level of inter-parish movement. The more eccentrically placed the settlement in a parish, the greater the probability of a high 'wastage' through migration. Again a number of parishes were split up into two or more separate pieces which also entails, of course, special difficulties. The great bulk of migratory movement was over small distances of less than seven or even five miles.[21]

It is pointless to attempt to set rigid limits of size of population, still more of area, beneath which family reconstitution work will not yield worthwhile results. An ideal parish for reconstitution might perhaps be one whose population lay between 1,000 and 2,500, whose area was, say, 10,000 acres, whose main settlement lay towards the centre of the parish, and whose registers were complete and full for the whole period from 1538 to the inception of civil registration. Parishes where the number of marriages was below *c.* 3–6 per annum, and of baptisms below *c.* 12–20 per annum are most unlikely to yield sufficient reconstituted families to afford useful results, and even those where marriages were at a rate of *c.* 5–8 and baptisms at a rate of *c.* 18–30 per annum may prove rather small unless the quality of the register or the low level of migratory movement enables a comparatively high proportion of the families to be reconstituted.

It is always possible that by combining the information from the registers of a number of small contiguous parishes the same results can be achieved as may be had from a single large parish. Good registers are, however, not common and the chance of finding a group of small parishes all possessing good registers is small. In some important areas of the country, nevertheless, this possibility deserves careful attention since some of the most densely settled and richest farming areas contained few or no large parishes. Where parishes were very large in area, as in Lancashire, for example, many of them had chapelries as well as a parish church. These parishes need very thorough examination before family reconstitution is attempted since many baptisms were recorded in the chapel registers even though all marriages are to be found in the church registers. Some chapels also possessed graveyards and kept a burial register. In general, the proportion of parishes which offer good prospects for family reconstitution rises, of course, as the period for which results are required grows shorter. There are many more registers which can be used for, say, a century and a half than for the full three hundred year period.

The parish registers of big towns will probably prove much more difficult to use than those of country parishes. The fundamental problem is once more the high level of movement across parish boundaries. But in addition urban parishes are often large in population so that much more time than usual is necessary to transfer the information from the registers and carry out reconstitution.[22] Moreover, big cities have many parishes. The chances of all the parishes having good runs of registers is slight but work on any one parish is likely to yield results that are difficult to interpret. Successful family reconstitution work may eventually be done for towns as well as for the country but rural parishes are more promising. It is significant that even in France where reconstitution work on country parishes has shown excellent results no attempt has yet been made to extend the work to large towns.

No parish register combines all the characteristics making for swift, full and simple family reconstitution. Before turning to the details of method it is perhaps useful to rehearse some of the typical drawbacks of parish registers as sources of information for reconstitution work. There are very few registers with entries for every year from 1538 onwards. Nearly all have odd years missing. Very many have much longer gaps due to the loss of whole books from carelessness, theft, fire or decay. In many registers no entry was made for months or years at a time because of the death or neglectfulness of the incumbent or the parish clerk. Since they, like other men, were in greater danger of death at times of plague and famine than in more tranquil periods, the register is often irritatingly blank when it is most

106

important that it should be complete.[23] Very often there are
blank years in the Civil War period after the ejection of an
incumbent. Sometimes it may be impossible to decipher entries
because of staining or because the ink has largely disappeared.
Even registers which are complete in the sense that no book or
page once existing has been lost or become illegible may still be
very defective. In many registers, for example, there are years
in which entries are clearly incomplete even though not disappearing entirely. At Ottery St Mary the baptism register
shows an average of 60 baptisms per annum in the period 1719–
28 (max. 78, min. 49); from 1727–39 the average fell to only 13
(max. 25, min. 4), before rising once more to about its earlier
level in the 1740s. Occasionally gaps in the parish register can
be filled by consulting the Bishops' Transcripts,[24] but often the
omissions cannot be made good. For family reconstitution a gap
in the marriage register is less important than gaps elsewhere.
In all parishes in any case the marriages of many resident
couples were contracted outside the parish and a gap in the
marriage register just produces an effect similar to that produced by a rise in the proportion of marriages celebrated in
neighbouring parish churches. Deficiencies in the other two
registers are more serious since they increase the margin of
error in calculations involving any families which existed at the
time of the gaps. A missing year or two in a century is tolerable
since margins of error must in any case be allowed but any
substantial period of deficiency or serious defectiveness in a
register[25] constitutes a barrier. Family reconstitution work can
be carried out on either side of the barrier but not across it.

Another problem in using parish registers for family reconstitution is that the event which the register records is
usually not the event whose date of occurrence the demographic
historian would like to obtain. The registers normally contain
details of baptism and burial rather than of birth and death.
Only the marriage register is free from this type of difficulty.
The problem is trivial in the case of the burial register since
burial usually took place within three days of death and almost
invariably within a week. But it is serious in the case of the
baptism register since, at least by the eighteenth century when
customs had become laxer, it was fairly common to wait for
months and even years after birth before having a child baptised.

107

Parents sometimes brought two or more children to be baptised together even though they had been born years apart.[26] Sometimes the same child appears twice in the baptism register (private baptism followed by a public ceremony in church). This can also lead to confusion if the date of birth of the child is not entered with his baptism. Many children died before being baptised. Some of these appear in the burial register without a corresponding baptismal entry.[27] Family reconstitution work is subject to much greater uncertainties when social and clerical custom permitted late baptism than when baptism followed as quickly after birth as burial did after death.[28]

The fact that baptisms and burials of those who were not Anglicans were often not recorded in parish registers is not necessarily a serious problem for family reconstitution work. It means only that Nonconformist families are not included in the sample of families reconstituted. Nonconformists were usually married in the parish church and sometimes buried there too, but most of their children were baptised in the chapel. Nonconformist chapels in short behaved much like Anglican chapels in this respect. A family which became Nonconformist did not necessarily disappear from an Anglican register completely but entries about the family become too few to be useful for family reconstitution unless indeed the Nonconformist register survives to fill in the gaps.

It is probable that even in the best kept registers there are inaccuracies and omissions on a finer level of detail to add to the grosser deficiencies already discussed. Registers were often not made up from day to day but periodically from rough notes or even from memory. From time to time no doubt notes were lost, or mistranscribed, or memory failed. The registers were kept on paper until 1597. From that date they were required to be kept on parchment. The old registers were to be transcribed on to parchment for their better preservation.[29] Few originals now survive and while the transcribing was sometimes beautifully done and provides fine examples of Elizabethan penmanship errors must have crept in. Parish clerks were subject to lapses in concentration and would sometimes record a married woman in her maiden name or would transpose the Christian names of mother and daughter. The process of reconstitution however carefully carried out will tend to produce further errors, mis-

108

transcriptions and omissions. If the work is done from a printed register or other transcription a further generation of errors creeps in. A large number of judgments about, for example, the correct reading of a faded name or the entries in a register where the clerk's concentration failed him must be made in the course of reconstitution and some of these will be wrong. Furthermore, the very possibility of reconstitution, especially on data as sparse in detail as parish register material, turns on the acceptance of certain conventions. Each convention establishes a criterion which makes it possible to distinguish between entries which are sufficiently specific to be used and those which are not; to establish a threshold in the continuum of probability, as it were, above which an attribution of an event to a known individual is regarded as certain. Here too there must be some inaccuracy, though if the conventions are well judged the inaccuracy may be slight.[30] Something must be left to individual judgment in using register material even though a full set of conventions has been formulated. For example, there may be a period of transition in a burial register between the fuller type of entry with details of relationship given for all except the heads of families and the short form of entry where only the name of the dead man or woman is given. Different conventions govern these two variants.[31] In the period of transition when the register no longer reflects a uniform practice, discretion is needed in judging when to change from one convention to another. In attempting family reconstitution on English parish registers it must be recognised that a margin of error will exist on either side of any demographic indices which emerge from the exercise.

All this is not to say that family reconstitution work is subject to such large margins of error that its utility is in doubt. Indeed it is perhaps a virtue of this method that the sources of error are necessarily in the forefront of one's consciousness in carrying through the work. Other demographic measurements including modern censuses give an impression of accuracy which is spurious. One ought perhaps to replace the last four or five digits of any totals of British population with noughts to underline the wide margins of error of any census figures.[32] For many historical purposes, in any case, it is less important to know the absolute level of fertility and mortality rates than to know the direction of their shifts over time. It is probable, for example, that material drawn from English parish registers will tend to understate the true level of infant mortality by an amount which is difficult to determine exactly.[33] Yet to discover a period during which the rate rose or fell by, say, a third would nevertheless be of great interest and importance. Many errors in reconstitution work tend to be self-cancelling in the sense that they do not introduce a bias into the result but represent rather a peppering of scores round the true mark.[34] The published work on parish registers in France has shown how very accurate and detailed the results of reconstitution work can be when the records are good. English registers give less information at each entry than the French but this is counterbalanced by the fact that in France reconstitution work is very seldom possible before the last quarter of the seventeenth century whereas in England it is sometimes possible to begin in the middle of the sixteenth century and thus to examine fully the remarkable changes of the mid-seventeenth century.

It may be asked what proportion of families in a parish can be reconstituted in favourable circumstances. No simple answer to this question is possible. Information about a family may be so complete that it enters into the calculation of all the major demographic indices, but this is rare. It is much more common to be able to use what is known of a family for some purposes but not for others. Sufficient may be known about a family to make it usable in the study of infant mortality even though the age of the wife at marriage may not be known; another family may yield information of value in the study of the frequency of pre-nuptial pregnancy but not in the calculation of age-specific fertility; and so on. The greater the completeness of information required the smaller the proportion of families which can be used. Thus, working on the Crulai registers Gautier and Henry were able to establish age at marriage of women in the period 1710–42 in 45 per cent of the marriages, but in only 27 per cent of the marriages was the age of both parties known, while in only 19 per cent of the marriages in this period was the date both of birth and death of the parties to a marriage known.[35] For some purposes a high, for others a low proportion of the families will yield useful results. Because of the sparser information in English registers and also perhaps because of the greater mobility of the English population, the proportion of English families providing useful information for any given purpose will probably prove to be lower than in France as a rule though it is much too soon to be dogmatic on the point. As an example, however, in Crulai over the period 1674–1742 the age of the bride could be established in about 38 per cent of all marriages.[36] In Colyton over the period 1538–1837 age at marriage for women is known in only about 30 per cent of the cases.

Very little is known even of the crude totals of population in this country before 1801. Many of the figures still widely quoted are derived from the work done largely by Rickman and published in the 1841 census. Still less is known of the demographic mechanisms which produced changes in population totals – the interplay of nuptiality, fertility and mortality. Yet the materials are to hand in parish registers to remedy this ignorance in large measure. A judicious mixture of aggregative work and family reconstitution studies should add immensely to what is known at present about the history of population in England.

FAMILY RECONSTITUTION: THE SEQUENCE OF OPERATIONS

What follows is a description of the main stages of family reconstitution. Parts of the operation are rather intricate (especially the fourth stage, D) and the text may prove difficult to follow when read 'straight'. It may be compared to a chess manual in which the significance of the later moves is apparent only when the earlier moves have been played out on a chess board. In the same way some of the operations described in D become much easier to follow when the earlier operations on the slips and forms have already been carried out and the work has reached that stage. The work divides into six stages.

A. Preliminary analysis of the register.
B. Transfer of raw data from the register to the standards slips.
C. Sorting of the slips into sets.
D. Reconstitution of families on Family Reconstitution Forms (FRFs).
E. Calculations done on the FRFs.
F. Derivation of measures of fertility, mortality, etc.

A. Preliminary analysis of the register

Before embarking upon the first stage of family reconstitution proper it is useful to know the trends in gross numbers of baptisms, burials and marriages. This is useful both positively and negatively: positively in that the information derived from the count will be complementary to that from reconstitution, and negatively because an analysis of this sort will reveal the presence of any gaps in the register or periods when it was seriously deficient.[37] Indeed it is often only after comparing the results of several preliminary analyses that one can assess the merits of a number of possible parish registers and select the most promising. On the Preliminary Extraction Forms (PEF I, pink, for baptisms; PEF II, green, for burials; PEF III, white, for marriages), the monthly totals of events are recorded. Annual totals can then be calculated, either by calendar or harvest year, by summing the lines, while summing the columns permits an analysis of seasonal variations in baptisms, burials and marriages. Provision is made for the calculation of totals by harvest year as well as by calendar year because it sometimes happened in pre-industrial agricultural communities that the whole pattern of life and social activity was drastically upset by a bad harvest. One bad harvest meant much suffering. Two or more in succession might bring disease, starvation and death on a large scale. In some local cases in continental Europe as late as the eighteenth century a quarter of the population died during a food crisis of this sort. The harvest year in England seems rarely to have been a significant unit of time in English population history during the parish register period in marked contrast with parts of contemporary France or Norway.[38] But a negative result is important. If this contrast can be fully established[39] it suggests a significant difference in economic conditions between England and the continent. The harvest year on the forms runs from the beginning of August to the end of July so that the number of burials, for example, in the harvest year 1684 equals the number of burials August-December 1684 plus those of January-July 1685.[40] The matter is a little more complicated in the case of baptisms since any effect of bad harvests on fertility would show itself primarily not in the number of current baptisms but rather in current conceptions

112

BURIALS

PARISH: COLYTON

County: Devon

YEARS: 1661–80

YEAR	Jan.	Feb.	Mar.	Apr.	May	June	July	Aug.	Sept.	Oct.	Nov.	Dec.	Civil Year (totals)	Jan–July	Aug–Dec.	Harvest Year (totals)	Chrisom Children	Wanderers	Comments
1661	0	0	4	3	1	5	8	3	3	2	3	4	36	21	15	33			
1662	2	2	7	3	3	3	8	3	1	6	2	3	33	18	15	34			In these two
1663	2	1	3	2	1	2	4	2	0	6	1	2	30	19	11	29			decades the
1664	3	1	3	2	2	6	1	3	2	2	3	1	29	18	11	27			registers
1665	2	1	2	3	4	3	1	2	1	4	1	2	26	16	10	34			consistently
1666	5	4	2	4	4	8	3	1	4	5	1	7	39	24	15	45			used to
1667	4	1	5	6	5	8	1	1	6	5	3	10	55	30	25	53			'full' form
1668	2	1	8	8	4	1	4	5	3	9	1	8	46	28	18	53			of entry,
1669	5	6	9	3	5	2	5	7	6	9	7	6	70	35	35	74			and is
1670	7	13	8	3	1	3	7	14	20	6	7	9	95	39	56	93			usable for
1671	8	4	8	2	7	2	3	7	6	4	2	7	63	37	26	57			reconstitut.
1672	8	3	6	2	2	2	3	6	3	3	4	2	49	31	18	29			Details of
1673	3	3	0	3	2	0	0	1	1	2	2	7	24	11	13	48			residence are
1674	4	4	9	5	5	3	3	0	3	1	2	4	45	35	10	35			often given,
1675	5	3	0	4	5	7	5	4	2	3	2	6	42	25	17	60			but
1676	6	8	2	3	5	10	5	4	7	7	6	6	73	43	30	62			
1677	5	6	3	3	3	5	7	7	4	0	6	6	55	32	23	61			occupations
1678	2	6	7	6	7	5	5	3	4	7	4	7	65	38	17	56			very seldom
1679	5	1	7	7	6	1	2	2	2	4	0	6	47	29	18	43			
1680	5	2	2	2	2	4	4	2	4	6	4	4	41	25	16	37			
TOTAL	83	70	93	82	81	75	70	77	82	80	63	107	963	554	409	963			

viii 64

Figure 4.2

This burial form is pale green in the original. The colour coding of all printed slips is a great assistance to quick, accurate work. Note the large fluctuations in the annual totals of burials. After a period of high mortality 1669–72, there were very few burials in 1673 because of the 'weeding-out' of the previous four years.

It is, of course, only a coincidence that the totals in the harvest year and civil year columns are the same. Usually they are slightly different because the last harvest year overlaps into 1681 (just as the first half of 1661 is taken back to the 1660 harvest year).

113

with perhaps an increase also in miscarriages and abortions. Since the register records baptisms attention must be projected forwards nine months, as it were. As far as fertility is concerned the harvest year 1602 does not consist of the baptisms August 1602-July 1603, but the baptisms May 1603-April 1604. The accompanying diagrams may help to make this clear.

Other information can be recorded on the PEFs (bastards on the baptism form; chrisoms – those buried within a month of baptism – on the burials form, for example). There is also space for comments. This should be used for notes which are relevant in judging family reconstitution possibilities (for example, 'here the register begins to name mother as well as father on the baptism entry'; or 'between these dates occupations are regularly given'; and so on).

Points to remember:

1 Each PEF should start with the first year of an even number decade (for example, 1601, 1621, 1641; not 1611, 1631). This may mean that much of the first form is unused but results from different parishes are then much easier to compare. Similarly if there is a gap in the register leave the corresponding period on the form blank.

2 The modern calendar year begins on 1 January. This is the year used on the forms. Until 1752, however, the year began on 25 March. This means that until 1752 dates in the early part of the year must be converted to conform with modern practice. The period 1 January to 24 March is moved forward by one year (for example, February 1679 becomes February 1680).

3 Any prolonged period of under-registration is as serious a drawback for family reconstitution as a complete break in the register. It is important, therefore, to watch carefully for this. It is often helpful to plot annual totals of baptisms, burials and marriages on a graph to make it easier to appreciate fluctuations. Periods of exceptional mortality, of unusually few marriages, and so on, are also then immediately evident. Nine-year moving averages of baptisms, burials and marriages may also be plotted at this stage.[41] They sometimes reveal clearly longer term trends which are difficult to pick out from annual totals.

4 In general the number of baptisms should over long periods be between three and five times the number of marriages. Where

PARISH: COLYTON County: Devon

YEARS: 1601-20

YEAR	Jan.	Feb.	Mar.	Apr.	May	June	July	Aug.	Sept.	Oct.	Nov.	Dec.	Civil Year (totals)	Jan-July	Aug.-Dec.	Harvest Year (totals)	Comments
1601	3	3	0	1	0	1	1	2	0	0	2	0	13	9	4	10	
1602	0	1	1	1	1	2	0	0	0	4	3	0	13	6	7	16	
1603	3	2	1	0	1	2	0	0	0	2	4	1	16	9	7	23	
1604	4	5	1	4	0	2	0	3	0	3	2	1	25	16	9	25	
1605	3	1	0	5	5	1	1	0	2	1	3	0	22	16	6	13	
1606	1	1	1	0	6	2	2	1	4	1	1	3	17	7	10	24	
1607	3	6	1	0	3	1	0	0	0	1	2	1	18	14	4	9	

P.E.F. I

PARISH: COLYTON County: Devon

YEARS: 1601-20

YEAR	MONTH OF CONCEPTION												Baptisms by Civil Year (totals)	Jan.-Apr.	May-Dec.	Conceptions by Harvest Year (totals)	Bastards	Comments
	Apr.	May	June	July	Aug.	Sept.	Oct.	Nov.	Dec.	Jan.	Feb.	Mar.						
	MONTH OF BAPTISM.																	
	Jan.	Feb.	Mar.	Apr.	May	June	July	Aug.	Sept.	Oct.	Nov.	Dec.						
1601	3	5	4	4	3	3	5	3	4	4	7	4	49	16	33	48	1	
1602	7	7	4	2	3	5	6	5	5	2	4	5	51	20	31	49		
1603	5	5	4	3	3	5	2	4	1	6	4	1	43	17	26	47		
1604	8	5	5	5	6	4	3	4	3	0	2	7	52	23	29	57		
1605	5	8	2	3	3	1	3	9	1	4	1	6	49	18	31	49		
1606	2	8	7	9	3	2	0	0	8	6	3	3	53	26	27	57		
1607	3	5	8	5	3	2	3	4	4	2	6	4	57	22	35	55		

Figure 4.3

115

the ratio is much lower than this the parish church in question may either be surrounded by chapelries at which many baptisms were recorded, or have been a popular church for marriages with couples from other parishes, or there may simply have been serious under-registration of births (sometimes due to strong Nonconformity). Where the ratio is much higher than this it may mean that the local church was unpopular for weddings. In either case further investigation is called for before beginning reconstitution.

5 It is vital to make full notes on the content of entries in the register in the Comments column on the PEFs or separately if necessary. At any time the burial register may adopt the stark form in which only the name of the dead person is recorded without indication of residence, occupation, relationship or age. Unless the period is short this will prevent family reconstitution. Sometimes in the sixteenth century marriage registers give only the name of the groom (thus, 'John Hargreaves was married, 9 Aug. 1571'). This is fatal to full reconstitution. In the sixteenth and seventeeth centuries many registers in Wales and the West Country did not normally record surnames except for the gentry (so that a typical entry might be 'John, son of Hugh of Burndean, baptised, 8 Feb. 1594'). This may not absolutely preclude reconstitution but it becomes much more difficult – a further degree of indeterminacy is present. Without notes of this sort to consult beforehand reconstitution is a lottery, though the counting of entries is, of course, in itself a very valuable exercise. The register may be, as it were, quantitatively very full and accurate, while being qualitatively too thin to permit reconstitution.

Other points to consider before beginning reconstitution:

1 It is always prudent to examine the Bishops' Transcripts. Entries in them should be collated carefully with those in the register. They may fill gaps, provide additional entries, or give alternative readings of some register entries, all of which are important.

2 If there are chapelries in the parish which also kept registers, their registers should be examined. A very large number of parishes in the north of England possessed chapelries (some Lancashire parishes ultimately contained a dozen or more

chapelries with registers). Some of these parishes were very large areas and the chapelries remote from the main settlement. A knowledge of local history and geography is of great value here. In general, however, if the chapel registers are complete they should be used. If they are defective it should be recognised that it will prove difficult to find reconstitution information for a high proportion of the marriage entries in the church register.[42]

3 The distribution of settlement within the parish should be studied. If the main settlement is very close to the edge of the parish more difficulty may be experienced from inter-parish movement (see 104–5 above).

B. Transfer of raw data from the register to the standard slips

In principle this should be done from the register itself, rather than from a transcript so that the proportion of errors due to mistranscription can be kept as low as possible. In practice the best printed transcripts contain very few errors of transcription and can be used with confidence. Some handwritten or typed transcripts are also good. It is possible indeed that working from the best transcripts may even be better than working directly from a register since some transcriptions were done by men with great skill in deciphering sixteenth and seventeenth century hands and a long experience of the work. Sometimes, too, the transcript incorporates collated material from the Bishops' Transcripts. Working from a transcript, of course, normally takes less time than working from the original. Nevertheless the original or a good photocopy should always be kept at hand and consulted frequently. This is necessary both as a check upon the accuracy of the transcription and because almost all transcriptions either suppress some types of information present in the original altogether or adopt a convention in recording it which may give rise to misunderstanding. The Colyton register, for example, has been transcribed with great care and contains only a few score of mistranscriptions in many thousands of entries.[43] The transcriber did, however, adopt one convention which makes the transcription less valuable than the original for reconstitution work. He transcribed the parish of residence from the register only when the entry named a parish other than Colyton. No mention of the parish of residence in the printed transcript may, therefore, mean either that

there was nothing in the register about the parish of residence
or that the parish named was Colyton. This is a comparatively
trivial matter, but in other transcriptions more important
details may be omitted. This is particularly true of marginal
notes which are often most illuminating (for example, there
may be information of the greatest value about local weather
conditions, or the agricultural fortunes of the parish, or even
about the manner in which the register was kept).[44]

Three standard slips are used in the transfer of data from the
register; for baptisms (pink), for burials (green) and for
marriages (white). In addition there is a fourth slip (white), the
marriage recall slip, which is filled in at a later stage of the
work.[45]

Points to note:

1 A separate slip must be made out for each event in the
register. Occasionally the same register entry may record both
the baptism and burial of a young baby. If so fill in two slips.
Fill in two slips also for an entry recording the baptism of
twins.
2 Unless there is good reason to act otherwise[46] slips should be
filled in for the whole period from the beginning of the register
until 1841. The nominal lists in the enumerators' notebooks of
the 1841 census provide a good anchor for one end of the
period. It is immaterial, however, in the actual making out of
the slips whether one moves forward in time from the first
entry in the register or backwards from the last.
3 Ink should be used for all entries on the slips unless a pencil
entry is specified.
4 Surnames should always be printed rather than written in a
cursive hand. They, and they alone, are written to the right of
the heavy vertical line in the top half of each slip. All names
should be written out in full and the spelling of the register
always retained.
5 The dating system used is that of the modern calendar.
Before the introduction of the modern calendar in 1752 the
year ended on 24 March (or in sixteenth-century registers sometimes at other dates early in the present calendar year). Any
entries in the register after 31 December in any year should
therefore be recorded on the slip as occurring in the following

118

Married	23-4-1609	Banns/licence

Husband

name	*Theodor*	surname	MARWOOD

age	residence	*Mynchenholme* t.p.
	occupation	*carpenter*
	bachelor / widower / __unknown__

father	
residence	t.p.
occupation	maiden name
mother	

Wife

name	*Katheryn*	surname	HOOKE

age	residence	t.p.
	__spinster__ / widow / unknown

father	
residence	t.p.
occupation	maiden name
mother	*Winefride**	"
late husband's name	

Remarks	✗ *widow*

Signatures		Mark	Signed
husband			
wife			

Parish *Colyton*

No. 732

E.S. III (a)   viii 64

Figure 4.4. The baptism slip (E.S.I. – Extraction Slip I) is pink in the original; the burial slip (E.S.II) is green; and the marriage slip (E.S.IIIa) is white. The slip reproduced here is a 'real life' example from the Colyton register.

year (for example, 6 Feb. 1678 becomes 6 Feb. 1679). Dates should be written thus: 21–2–1678, with a dash between the day and month and between the month and year. Dots between the numbers invite errors (for example, 21.2.1678 might be read as 2.12.1678).

6 When a range of alternatives is presented on the slip (for example, male/female/unknown) the appropriate word should be underlined.

7 On the lines on the slips devoted to residence the letters t.p. stand for this parish and should be underlined where appropriate. When a man lived in the parish many registers record the tything, hamlet, farmstead or even occasionally the street in which he lived and this information should, of course, be entered as well as underlining t.p.

8 Where an indication of status is given (gent., Esq., Mr, etc.) put this in under 'occupation'.

9 If an entry makes reference to someone already dead (for example, 'Thomas, son of Henry Marwood, deceased') place the sign (†) before the name of the dead person.

10 Where a name is difficult to decipher and a doubt remains about its spelling place a question mark in square brackets [?] immediately after the doubtful word. After an unusual entry, such as a girl christened in a name usually reserved for boys it is useful to put [sic] after the word.

11 Any standard slip inevitably fails to cover all possibilities. The space for Remarks is for information which cannot be placed in any other part of the slip but which is potentially of use (for example, the burial entry in the register may carry information about the cause of death; a baptism entry may note that this child is the tenth of the union; and so on). If more space is needed than is available in the Remarks section, put it on the back of the slip, being careful to put P.T.O. on the front.

12 Incumbents sometimes made interesting notes in the register about the weather, harvest conditions and prices, interspersed with ordinary entries. These may be of great importance and they should be transcribed in full into a notebook kept for the purpose.

13 Great care should be taken to record any aliases which may be found in the register. Besides recording them on the appro-

priate slips it is convenient to keep a separate running list of all aliases.

14 It is very easy to miss an entry in the register from time to time or even to make out two identical slips for the same entry, especially if the work is done in long spells or is broken off abruptly for any reason. To make sure that any mistakes of this sort are discovered it is wise after finishing the copying on to slips of, say, all the baptisms of the year 1690 to count up the number of entries in the register for that year and the number of slips made out to ensure that the number is in each case the same. This should be done with special care when entries for several years are jumbled together, or when there is only one single register in which baptisms, burials and marriages alike are recorded (in this latter case the whole register must be gone through three times, once each for each type of entry).

15 Sometimes information in a later hand is added in a register or the transcriber in a printed register may supplement entries (for example, the date of birth of a marriage partner from another parish). Where this is so it should be transferred to the slip with a note indicating its provenance.

16 If the measurement of the spread of literacy through the population is one of the aims of the study, the signature section of the marriage slip should be filled in. Place an X in the relevant box for each party to the marriage. If a finer degree of differentiation is wanted a more sophisticated system of marking may be used (for example, XE in a box for those who sign their name with ease). Work on literacy should only be attempted from the register itself or a photocopy, and is not possible until the second half of the eighteenth century after the passage of Hardwicke's Marriage Act (1753).[47]

C. Sorting of the slips into sets

When a slip has been made out for each event in the register the next operation is to create surname sets in chronological order for each of the three types of event, baptisms, burials and marriages.

1 It is convenient to begin the work of subdivision by sorting the original pile of slips into smaller letter piles (all surnames beginning with A, B, C, etc.).

2 Each letter pile can then be taken in turn and further sub-

divided by surname (Abbot, Abrahams, Adams, Alford, etc.). Variants of the same family name should be kept together. If in doubt keep them together. Make sure that variants of a surname that have been kept together in, say, the baptism surname sets are also kept together in the burial and marriage surname sets.

3 Consult the list of aliases made when filling in the slips. The surname sets connected by an alias should then be amalgamated (for example, Baker alias Tucker: all Tucker slips should be added to the Baker set). Always add the surname which is later in the alphabet to the earlier one, even though it is commoner to find, say, Tucker alias Baker than Baker alias Tucker. Amalgamate all the slips in the two surname sets even if the alias appears for the first time only after each surname has been current for some time.

4 If the work has been done systematically the slips will be in approximate chronological order but each surname set should be checked to make sure that strict chronological order has been obtained.

5 As each surname set is arranged in chronological order it is tied as a separate bundle with a slip knot. This holds the set firmly but the knot slides easily along the string so that the whole set or any individual slip can be removed and replaced without making it necessary to undo the knot. A separate bundle is tied whenever there are three or more slips of the same surname in the set. The remainder within any one letter pile are sorted alphabetically and tied in a single miscellaneous set.

6 Each slip is numbered when all the letter piles have been sorted into sets, beginning with the first surname set in the A letter pile and proceeding through the alphabet. Within each set the numbering is, of course, chronological. Thus all the Newton baptism slips may run from 6724 to 6851. The slip 6724 is the earliest baptism and 6851 the latest. Each of the three types of slip (baptism, burial and marriage) begins at 1 and runs upward as far as necessary. A mechanical numbering device which trips forward after each application is useful. The slips in the miscellaneous set in each letter pile are also, of course, numbered. This can conveniently be done last after numbering the surname sets in the letter pile in question.

7 When the marriage slips have been numbered in this way a parallel series of marriage recall slips should be copied out. On the marriage recall slips detailed information is filled in for the wife alone: only the name of the husband is recorded. *It is best to use red ink* in making out the recall slips to prevent any confusion with the marriage slips. Give to each recall slip the number of its 'twin' marriage slip. Sort the recall slips into surname sets by maiden name as in 1–5 above. Recall slips recording the remarriage of widows should be sorted by the surname of the earlier husband and placed in the surname set of those with that name as a maiden name (for example, a widow named Gaiche who marries again is sorted into the same surname set as women whose maiden name was Gaiche).

8 It is convenient when all the sets from a letter pile have been finished to re-form the letter pile from the constituent sets and to make out a card on which all the surnames which have been separately bundled are listed. The card can then be placed at the top of the pile to make it easy to find any set which may be wanted.

D. Reconstitution of families on Family Reconstitution Forms (FRFs)

D1 Transfer of information from the slips to the FRFs – In D1 the first steps in the transfer of information from the slips to the FRFs are described. Complete the operations of D1 for any one surname set before passing on to the next, and proceed in alphabetical order (i.e. take the marriage, baptism and burial surname sets of Abbot, if that is the first surname, and carry out D1a, D1b and D1c on Abbot before going on to repeat the sequence with Abraham).

D1a Marriage slips. Take the first set of marriage slips and make out an FRF for each slip transferring all information from the former to the latter. If one of the partners to the marriage is from another parish put the name of the parish in pencil in the box for place of birth. If he or she is described as a sojourner put soj. in pencil in the box. If the parish of residence is given as the home parish put t.p. (this parish) in the box in ink. If no parish is given put an X in pencil in the box. If the rank of marriage is in doubt (1st, 2nd, 3rd marriage, etc.) put

Married	27-11-1574	rank	1

Wife

name _Ellyn_   surname TREDEW

age

residence .... t.p.

<u>spinster</u> / widow / unknown

father .... _Thomas_

residence .... _Colyford_ ...... t.p.

occupation ....   maiden name

mother ....

late husband's name ....

baptised ....

buried ....

wife / widow / unknown

Husband

name _John_   surname TORNER

Remarks ....

....

....

....

....

....

....

Parish _Colyton_

....

No. 280

E.S. III (b)   iii 65

A marriage recall slip

Figure 4.5

124

Family Reconstitution

in the likeliest solution in pencil and in brackets (for example, if a marriage partner is described as a widow put 2+ in pencil). The FRF should be given the same number as its twin marriage slip. When the transfer has been effected the marriage slip *must be marked U in ink* to show that it has been used. When the surname set is exhausted check to ensure that all slips have been used, and replace the set in its string loop after making sure that it is in chronological order once more.

D1b Baptism slips. Next take the set of baptism slips of the same surname as the marriage slips and transfer the information from each slip to the appropriate FRF. Where no FRF exists to which the baptism information can be transferred (i.e. when the marriage in question took place outside the parish or before the beginning of the register), take a new FRF putting the name of the father (and mother, of course, where possible) in the upper half of the FRF as well as recording baptism details in the lower half as usual. In the box for date of marriage pencil in, for example, 'before 9–9–1685' if this is the date of the first known baptism. These FRFs can be numbered from any arbitrary figure upwards (say, 10,000), provided, of course, this is higher than the number of marriages in the parish over the period of reconstitution. It is useful to have a pile of FRFs available already numbered since it may be difficult to locate the last numbered FRF of the same type in the pile of FRFs if the numbering is done one at a time. *Each baptism slip when used must be marked U in ink.* As the set of baptism slips is gone through in this way the children born to the marriage recorded in the upper half of each FRF are listed one by one in the lower half of the form until the family is complete. The fact that the slips are in chronological order ensures that the children of each marriage appear in their proper sequence. Where the date of birth as well as that of baptism is given it should also be entered as the upper of two dates on the appropriate line (see fig. 4.9). If only the date of birth is known make this clear by an asterisk and a note in the remarks section. Beware of the possibility that the same child may be recorded twice in the baptism register. This can usually only be established with certainty if dates of birth are also given.

A separate list must be kept of illegitimate children in which

HUSBAND	*surname* alias BAKER *name(s)* TOCKER	Robert			Son						Occupation husband			
WIFE	NEWTON	Susan			Daughter	John, Agnes					husband's father / wife's father			

MARRIAGE *solemnized at*		Marriage			Dates				Age at end of union	Remarriage				
m. 269	Colyton	rank of	age at	marriage 21-2-1574	end of union 5-6-1615	length 41				Widowhood (months)				
HUSBAND	*born at* Getsayne *t.p.*	*residing at* (1) *t.p.*	X	*baptism* X	*burial* 5-6-1615	*age* X								
WIFE	Hambrayne	I	23	16-9-1550	26-6-1623	72	64							

Age groups	Years married	No. of births	Age of mother	Interval (months)	sex	rank	Baptisms date	Burials date	status / age	Marriages date	age	Name(s)	Surname of spouse
15–19			24	9	F	1	26-11-1574	10-1-1579	s. 4			Jertrude	
20–24	1.5	1	25	14	M	2	2-2-1576	20-6-1583	s. 7			Robart	
25–29	5	3	27	24	M	3	22-2-1578	25-3-1643	m. 65	28-8-1624	46	Wyllyam	BUSHELL (244)
30–34	5	2	29	24	M	4	2-3-1580	20-9-1658	X 78			John	
35–39	5	2	31	27	F	5	22-6-1581			30-4-1623	40	Garthrud	LONGE (930)
40–44	5	2	34	33	M	6	27-3-1585					Symon	
45–49	5	0	36	28	F	7	13-8-1587			7-7-1623	35	Cattren	HAYDON (934)
TOTAL 10	39	29			M	8	14-1-1590			4-2-1626	36	Robart	PARRETT (959)
boys 5	40	13			F	9	14-2-1591	22-2-1591	s. 8d			Susan	
girls 5	41	15			F	10	15-5-1592	3-2-1615	s. 22			Mary	
Remarks in 3rd baptism slip						11							

FRF ii 65

This is a copy of an FRF filled in during the reconstitution work on Colyton. The children of this marriage appear to have waited until the death of the mother before marrying. Even in Garthrud's case it may have been clear that her mother's end was near.

Figure 4.6

the date of baptism and the name of the mother, etc., is recorded. Slips recording the baptism of an illegitimate child should be marked L (listed) in ink when used.

Some entries may be ambiguous. For example, at a period in the register in which only the name of the father is given with a baptism entry, there may be two families each headed by a John Smith. Sometimes the clerk showed himself conscious of the danger of ambiguity and named either the place of residence or the occupation of each John Smith to enable them to be distinguished. Sometimes only a few of the entries concerning the two families are ambiguous and then the spacing of the

126

List of illegitimate children (cont.)

name	surname		mother	bapt.	bur.	remarks
James	BOLE	s.	Elizabeth	23-4-1809	6-4-1812 12-4-1812	not called base
Joane	BONDFEILD	base d.	Alyse	11-12-1594		
Edward	"	base s.	Doratye	25-4-1610		A Coliton
James	"	base s.	Dorothie	25-2-1617	21-8-1617	
Margerie	"	base d.	Johane	19-4-1635		
Johan	BOWDON	base d.	Jayes	16-12-1589		A Colyforde
Amy	"	base d.	Amy		11-12-1634	

Figure 4.7

other births when they have been transferred to the FRFs may make it clear to which family each of the doubtful entries should be allocated. If there is still ambiguity, the allocation which seems most likely should be made but the entry done in pencil on the FRF. The slip is marked U in ink as usual. Later some of the ambiguities may be cleared up (for example, when the burial entry of a child gives more information than its baptism entry).

Some entries may seem obviously wrong in the register. For example, there may be an entry recording the baptism of Peter, son of John and Mary Brown, which proves to be the only entry referring to such a family. Suppose further that it occurs at a date at which a baptism in the family of John and Margaret Brown is likely because it is in the middle of a lengthy gap between two other baptisms. The clerk may well have made a mistake but once again it is advisable to wait to see whether any further information can be gleaned later in the reconstitution before making a decision to include the child in John and Margaret's family. A note on the FRF of John and Mary may be made to prevent the matter being overlooked. It is also convenient to keep a separate running list of points of this sort to be checked through at the end of stage D.

Occasionally a baptism slip carries only the name of the mother but with no indication that the child is illegitimate. When this happens add the child to the list of illegitimate children with the comment that it is not called base in the register, but always make sure before doing so that it is not the legitimate child of a marriage in which the father has recently died. Usually the clerk makes reference to a recently dead father but occasionally he may only name the widowed mother.

It may happen that a baptism or burial slip contains details of the father's occupation not given at his marriage, or other details not previously known. When this is so record the information at the appropriate place on the FRF, putting the date, type and number of the slip after the entry (thus, 'husband-man [1681, bap. 3852]'). Do the same if information on a baptism or burial slip shows a change of occupation, etc., on the father's part since his marriage.

When this operation has been completed for any one surname set of baptism slips all slips in the set should have been marked either with a U or an L in ink and the set should be checked to make sure that this has been done. The set can then be re-placed in its string loop in its original chronological order.

D1c Burial slips. The third operation in this stage of reconstitution is the transfer of information from the burial slips. Take the set of burial slips of the same surname as the marriage and baptism slips and work through the set in chronological order, transferring information to the appropriate FRF whenever a firm attribution from slip to FRF can be made. *The slip should be marked with a U in ink* when this has been done. Where the date of death as well as the date of burial is known it should be entered above the date of burial (see figure 4.9). If only the date of death is given make this clear with an asterisk and a note in the remarks section.

In a good register most of the entries are unambiguous – John, son of Peter and Joan Hewes; Alse, wife of Peter Abraham, etc. Where the register consistently gives full detail of relationship even a name without a relationship is often unambiguous, since it refers to the head of a family or the un-married survivor of a family which has broken up as a household. A full register often shows that the clerk was alive to the problems of identification. If Peter Hewes is the head of one household himself and has a married son of the same name, he will always be recorded in such a register as Peter Hewes, senior or the elder, after his son's marriage, while his son will then be called Peter Hewes, junior or the younger until his father's death. A man or woman may often be entered in the register as son or daughter of, say, John Abbott, even though he or she was fully adult at death, provided that he or she was not married and that the parental household still existed.[48] Occasionally the age of the deceased is given (commonly after 1812) which is a great help where other information is sparse, though the age of older people was often not accurately known and more often than not exaggerated. If such a slip is used put the year of birth in the baptism box of the individual concerned in ink but also in brackets (thus [1730]). Later in the process of reconstitution an exact date of baptism may, of course, be established.

Sometimes the burial of a child is recorded for whom there is no baptismal entry. Put this entry beneath the baptism entries on the FRF in question (for example, on the fifth line if there are four baptisms on the FRF: see figure 4.9 below).

Frequently a burial slip which is ambiguous when the set is first gone through can be used if the slips which have not yet been marked U in ink are examined a second time. For example, the later burial of Hugh Newton, cordwainer, may remove the uncertainty about a Hugh Newton who was buried at an earlier date. Therefore it is important to go through the unused slips a second time (and occasionally even a third time). It is helpful when going through the slips for the first time to note on the FRFs a date of burial in pencil when an attribution seems very probable but an element of doubt remains. When this is done the slip should be marked with a U in pencil. It may be, for example, that the register records the burial of Thomasine Percy without other detail and that a mother and daughter of that name were alive at that time. If, after the burial of Thomasine Percy no further children were born to this marriage when several had been born in rapid succession previously, it is probable that it was the mother rather than the daughter who had died, and an entry might be made in pencil on the FRF. Suppose further that a later FRF in the same set shows

129

that John Percy, the husband of Thomasine, remarried. If between the dates of burial of Thomasine and the date of remarriage of John no other Thomasine Percy was buried then there is no longer any ambiguity and the date of burial of Thomasine can be entered in ink when the slips are gone through a second time. The slips can also then be marked with a U in ink.

There are, of course, many ways apart from details of relationship in which ambiguities can be narrowed to the point where a confident attribution can be made. Details of occupation or place of residence are frequently given in the registers and can be of great value. The cumulative effect of the transfer of information to the FRFs is often apparent at this stage of reconstitution, since, for example, the Hugh Newton described as a cordwainer in the burial register may only once elsewhere have been referred to by occupation as well as name in the register, say at the baptism of his fifth child, but this may be enough to distinguish between him and another Hugh Newton who was a husbandman.

Where the burial register is without detail apart from the bare name of the dead person, ambiguities multiply and the proportion of attributions of burial entries to FRFs which can be made with confidence falls to a low level. In these circumstances an entry can be considered unambiguous only if there is only one individual of the name known to be alive (in the sense of not being known to be dead) at that time and under the age of ninety.[49] A particularly difficult problem in working with a register which gives only the name of the dead person is the danger that burial slips may be attributed to an individual on an FRF but then, lower down in the surname set, there may appear another slip bearing the same name. For this reason it is sometimes helpful during the period of poor entries in the register to group all the slips bearing the same Christian name together. It will be clear from the above that in a register where the fullness of entry at burial varies the register itself (or a photocopy or reliable transcript) must be kept at hand because the degree to which an entry is unambiguous may depend as much upon its context within the register as upon the entry itself. In a period of full entry if William Purse is buried and there were two William Purses in the parish at the time, father

130

and son, aged five and forty-five respectively, then the dead man is the father. But in a period when the register gives no detail beyond the bare name of the dead person the uncertainty cannot be resolved unless there is other evidence in addition to the register entry (for example, the subsequent birth of other children to William Purse the father).

Do not overlook the possibility that a burial entry may refer to an illegitimate child whose baptism is recorded on the list of illegitimate children. There is a space on this list for the entry of burial information. The slip should be marked with an L (listed) in ink after the transfer of information.

Note that two children of the same Christian name sometimes appear on the same FRF. This is often an indication that the first of the two died young and the same name was used again, but not necessarily so. The christening of a child in the same name as an older child of the same family is not *ipso facto* proof that the older child had died.

It is wise to recognise that in general a greater element of uncertainty attends the transfer of information from burial slips to FRFs than is the case with marriage or baptism slips. Some groups, however, are seriously affected while others afford few problems. Uncertainty is least about the deaths of children under fifteen (those still living in their parents' households) and married couples. In section F it will be shown that for other reasons mortality studies must be concentrated on these two groups in the population. In periods when the register gives a full form of entry very few ambiguities about children are found, and comparatively few about married couples, widows and widowers. Where the register gives only names without other information the two groups are affected as much as others in the population. Such periods are necessarily short since otherwise no reconstitution study would have been attempted (see above 103–4). In calculating mortality rates periods of the short form of entry should be treated separately (for example, for infant mortality) or if this is impracticable mention should always be made of their possible effect. Entries on the FRFs which remain in pencil after the slips have been gone through a second time should be ignored in the calculation of mortality rates, or else two rates should be quoted, one including and the other excluding them.[50]

131

It is rare to find that all the slips in a set can be used. Usually some refer to people who were neither baptised nor married in the parish and who therefore do not appear on any FRF unless their children were baptised in the parish. Such slips cannot be used. After the operations described above unused slips and those bearing a U in pencil only should be placed on top of the used slips (each subset being in chronological order) before the set is again tied up. If reconstitution is later undertaken in neighbouring parishes the information on some of these slips will find its place on the FRFs of these parishes.

Note that the box for the date of end of marriage should be filled in at this stage. If the date of burial of both parties or of neither party is known there is, of course, no difficulty. If the date of burial of only one is known there are three possibilities. When the entry takes the form, 'Jane Hall, wife of John', the marriage ends on the date of the wife's burial. When the entry takes the form 'Jane Hall, widow, buried 6–2–1678', put 'before 1678' in pencil for the date of burial of the late husband and X in ink for the date of end of marriage (proceed similarly if the entry is of the form 'John Hall, widower'). When the entry simply gives the date of burial of one party with no other detail, put X in ink for date of end of marriage and for burial date of spouse.

D1d General. When D1a–c has been completed for any one surname set (all marriage and baptism slips should carry a U in ink), take the next surname set and repeat the sequence of operations. When all the marriage surname sets in any given letter pile have been done, work through the miscellaneous marriage set. When this is finished go through the baptism letter pile abstracting any surname sets not yet done (where all the marriages, as it happened, took place in other parishes) and using, of course, the parallel burial sets. Finally, check that all the marriage and baptism surname sets and miscellaneous sets are done before turning to the next letter pile.

D2 The coupling of baptism and marriage slips – This is a vital stage in reconstitution work since it yields information about age at marriage which can reasonably be held to be the most important single statistic about pre-industrial populations.

132

D2a Marriage slips. Take a set of marriage slips and a set of baptism slips of the same surname and work through them attempting to couple baptisms to subsequent marriages. This is a simple matter if the Christian name of the groom's father is given on the marriage slip. Otherwise work to the convention that any baptism entry of the same name as the groom occurring in a period not less than sixteen or more than forty-nine years preceding the marriage may be the record of his baptism. There are five possibilities: that there is no earlier baptism of the same name in the specified period $m(0/1)$ – i.e. no baptism associated with this male marriage partner; that there is only one baptism of the same name $m(1/1)$; that there are two or more baptisms of the same name $m(2+/1)$; that there is only one baptism but more than one groom to whom it might refer $m(1/2+)$; that there are two or more baptisms which might refer to two or more grooms $m(2+/2+)$. Where $m(0/1)$ is found nothing can be done. Where $m(1/1)$ is found mark both the baptism and marriage slips with a P (marriage partner) in pencil. In an $m(2+/1)$ situation mark each baptism slip and the marriage slip P2/1 in pencil if there are two baptism slips, P3/1 if there are three, and so on. The ambiguity may resolve itself if comparison with the relevant FRFs reveals that all except one of the children died before the date of the marriage. Where $m(1/2+)$ is found mark the baptism slip and each marriage slip P1/2, etc., in pencil. This situation may be clarified if the marriages all prove to concern one man only, being in fact remarriages except in the first instance. It was common for registers to fail to distinguish between bachelors and widowers in the marriage entry, though widows were much more commonly described as such on their remarriage. If $m(2+/2+)$ is found mark the baptism and marriage slips P2/2, P3/4, etc., in pencil. A combination of the circumstances mentioned under $m(2+/1)$ and $m(1/2+)$ above may remove the uncertainties in the situation. Ambiguities of the $m(2+/1)$ and $m(2+/2+)$ types may also be resolved if an age at death is given on the FRFs when they are consulted.

If the groom's parish of residence is not the parish in which the marriage took place, or if he is described as a sojourner, he should be assumed to have been born elsewhere and should not be further considered in this connection.

There is a further possible source of confusion. It may be

that a man, say Peter Newton, was born in the parish, married a girl from another parish in the church of that parish, and returned to live in his home parish. An FRF for him is built up by the information given at the baptism of his children. Suppose that another Peter Newton was married in the parish at much the same time as the first Peter Newton was married elsewhere, and that there was a baptism entry in the same name some thirty years earlier in the register. The method described here will associate the baptism slip with the second Peter Newton when it might just as well be the first. No account should, however, be taken of this possibility. Occasional mistakes will occur for this reason but they will be rare and will not upset the results seriously.[51]

D2b Marriage recall slips. Repeat this for the marriage recall slips of the same surname set (by maiden name). The rules to be followed are the same except that any baptism slip of the same name as the bride in a period not less than fourteen or more than forty-nine years before the marriage should be considered. Clearly $f(1/2+)$ cannot be resolved in the same way as $m(1/2+)$, unless indeed the woman's first marriage was to a man of the same surname as her own. Categories $f(1/2+)$ and $f(2+/2+)$ are retained nevertheless and the slips should be marked accordingly because details gleaned later may remove ambiguities (for example, if the age at death of the wife is given this may make it clear which is the correct baptism slip). Marriages of widows in the surname sets are dealt with later.

D2c The FRFs (I). All marriage, marriage recall and related baptism slips marked with a P in pencil and of the same surname set are now collated with the parallel FRFs. Begin with the grooms (marriage slips and related baptism slips). In the case of $m(1/1)$ make sure that the boy to whom the baptism slip refers did not die in childhood or youth (which will, of course, appear from the FRF). If he did not, add the date of his baptism, the names of his parents and any details of their occupation or residence to the top half of the FRF of his marriage. The rank of marriage, if it was not already known, can be entered in ink. Transfer back to the appropriate part of his FRF of baptism the date of his marriage, the surname of his bride, the FRF number of his marriage, and the date of burial where this is known (see figure 4.6). When this has been done change the pencil Ps on both slips to ink and cross through. If the boy did die in infancy or youth cross through the two Ps in pencil. In the case of type m(2+/1) discover whether death has eliminated all but one of the possible 'starters' and made the position unambiguous. If so, proceed as above, converting the P on the marriage slip and the surviving baptism slip to ink before crossing through. Cross through the pencil Ps on the other baptism slip or slips. If the position is still ambiguous because two or more of the boys survived cross out all the Ps on both the baptism and marriage slips.

In the case of type m(1/2+) a knowledge of the burial dates of the wives of the marriages in question (or strictly speaking of the marriages other than the latest in time), will make it clear whether the later marriages are remarriages. If all the marriages concern the same man the procedure for interchange of information between the FRFs is the same as above though, of course, the number of FRFs involved is larger and there is more shuttling to and fro of information between them. The Ps on all the slips can now be made in ink and crossed through, and note can be made of the appropriate FRFs of the fact that the groom was a widower while entering in ink the rank of the marriage in the box for rank of marriage. If the marriages prove to relate to more than one man the Ps on the slips should remain in pencil and be crossed through. The position cannot be made unambiguous. In the case of type m(2+/2+) if all the ambiguities are cleared up by a combination of the two last sets of possibilities the transfer of information and the marking of slips is done as above. If not the pencil Ps are crossed through (see also *D3a* below).

Uncertainty about which baptism slips should be coupled to a later marriage may also be resolved if the age at death of the husband is known from the burial slip. Ages at death are often inaccurate in registers especially if death took place at an advanced age, but if the possible baptism dates are widely spaced and the date of birth calculated from the burial slip is very close to one alternative this evidence may be used.

Make sure that all the Ps have been crossed through before returning the baptism and marriage slips to their respective surname sets.

D2d The FRFs (II). Next take the marriage recall and related baptism slips of the same surname in order to do for brides what has just been done for grooms. The procedure is in general the same as for grooms, but the following points should be noted.

Only the FRF of baptism of brides is to hand (the FRF of marriage is, of course, in a different surname set of FRFs except when the groom has the same surname as his bride). On it are entered the date of the marriage, the name of the groom, and the number of the marriage FRF (which is, of course, the number of the marriage recall slip). *The date of baptism of the wife, her parents' names, and any details of residence and occupation are entered in the appropriate place on the marriage recall slip* (see figure 4.8).

Cases of the type $f(1/2+)$ and $f(2+/2+)$ may be resolved when the FRFs of marriage are examined. For example, where one baptism might be linked to more than one marriage uncertainty may be resolved on consulting the FRF of marriage because it may appear (to take the simplest case) that to associate the baptism with one of the two marriages would be impossible since it would mean the woman having children in her fifties. This must mean that the baptism slip should be linked to the other marriage. Or knowledge of the age at death may help as in the case of men. Abstract therefore the relevant FRFs of marriage for each $f(1/2+)$ and $f(2+/2+)$ case from their sets to see if further progress can be made. This is laborious but cases of this type arise relatively infrequently. Note that the wife's parentage may be apparent when the FRF of marriage is consulted because it is recorded at the baptism or burial of one of her children, though it was not given at her marriage.[52] *If this is so the date of baptism should be marked with an X in pencil on the FRF of marriage, the date of baptism being recorded only in the remarks section.* The reason for this is that only the fact of her having borne children makes it clear what the date of baptism of the woman was. In the later calculation of age-specific fertility rates to include wives whose age is known in this way would introduce an element of bias since the date of baptism of childless women cannot be recovered thus.[53]

When this operation is complete for any surname set of marriage recall slips check that all Ps are crossed through and return all baptism slips to their surname sets. Do the same with all marriage recall slips with pencil Ps, *but set aside all marriage recall slips with Ps in ink* (i.e. those now carrying details from the FRF of baptism).

Repeat *D2c* and *D2d* through the surname sets and letter piles till all piles have been dealt with.

D2e The FRFs (III). At this juncture none of the FRFs will carry the dates of baptism of brides on the upper half of the form.[54] This information is on the marriage recall slips but has not been transferred to the FRFs of marriage. Equally, although the FRFs of baptism carry the dates of marriage obtained by coupling baptism and marriage recall slips, they do not carry any burial dates or dates of remarriage because these acts occurred under a different surname. Therefore an exchange of information must be effected between the FRFs of baptism and marriage for each woman whose age at marriage is now known. It would be very laborious to do this by bringing together the pairs of FRFs but the same result can be achieved more simply by using the marriage recall slips set aside in *D2d* above. These are re-sorted into sets by the groom's surname. Each set is then related to the corresponding set of FRFs. The date of baptism of the wife can now be transferred to the FRF of marriage together with any other information abstracted from the FRF of baptism and noted on the marriage recall slip (parents' names, occupation of father, etc.). The date of burial where known is transferred from the FRF of marriage to the marriage recall slip. The recall slips which now carry a date of burial are sorted by maiden name once more so that the date of burial and the status of the woman at her burial can be noted on the FRF of baptism. The other recall slips are kept aside for the time being.

This stage *D2e* may reveal a small percentage of mistaken couplings of baptism and marriage recall slips. This will occur if when the marriage recall slips and FRFs of marriage are collated the wife apparently has children above the age of fifty. There is always a possibility of a wrong attribution being made because migration may bring a woman to the parish having the same name as a woman already living there. If the marriage entry does not record the fact that the woman was of another parish, it will be assumed as a result of the method

137

employed that the woman married was the woman born in the parish. Some wrong attributions will reveal themselves in the way outlined above. Physiological absurdities must, of course, be rejected but careful note should be made of each instance as the frequency of occurrences of this sort affords some check on the accuracy of the method employed.[55]

D3 Widowers and widows – The last main operation in filling in FRFs concerns the marriages of widowers and widows. The former present difficulties because parish clerks were not scrupulous in distinguishing between bachelors and widowers when making a marriage entry; the latter because their names change.

D3a Widowers. The FRFs in each set are examined to try to detect those grooms who were widowers (this will already have been done in a small number of cases in *D2c*). The convention to be observed is that if the marriage of, say, John Gaiche occurs within ten years of the burial of the wife of an earlier marriage in which a John Gaiche was the husband, and if there is no baptism slip which could be associated with the second marriage, then the John Gaiche of the second marriage is assumed to be the same man whose wife died earlier. A very high proportion of remarriages took place within two years, often indeed within a few months of the death of the first wife and the attribution, though arbitrary, is correct in a very high percentage of cases. When these conditions are satisfied any information on the earlier FRF about baptism, etc., or on the later about burial, which is not already on the other FRF is exchanged to make each as complete as possible. There is in short a full exchange of information between the upper halves of the FRFs. Whenever the groom's status as a widower is established in this way the box on the FRF for date of remarriage should, of course, be filled in and the name of the new bride added together with the FRF number of the later marriage. If several remarriages of the same man are involved the operation is more complicated but the principle remains the same. There may also, of course, be men explicitly called widowers at marriage. Procedure here is simpler but conforms to the rules already described. *It is important that the box for the date of remarriage should be filled in when it is known.*

Note that this operation will involve modification of some of the date of end of marriage entries made in *D1c*. Under *D1c* the box for date of end of marriage was marked with an X in ink when the date of burial of one partner was known without other detail (see 132 above). If a later remarriage of the other partner is now established the date of end of marriage is now known and the box should be altered accordingly.

The FRFs built up entirely from baptism and burial entries (because the marriage was performed elsewhere) will enter into consideration at this stage, since the date of end of marriage is often known for them and the survivor may remarry. Such an FRF may therefore show a dated marriage to be of the second or higher rank or may intervene between two dated marriages and change the rank of the last marriage accordingly. FRFs which have no marriage date may in this way acquire a date of baptism for the husband.

D3b Widows (I). It was rarer for a clerk to fail to note that a woman on marriage was a widow than that a man was a widower, but this does happen. Therefore it is necessary to test whether there are among the marriage recall slips any where the bride could have been a widow. Proceed as above for men except that the information about name of first husband, parentage, date of baptism, etc., is noted on the marriage recall slips to be transferred later to the FRF of the second husband. Marriage recall slips bearing a P in ink can be ignored since they necessarily relate to spinster marriages. On some recall slips the bride is described as a widow. Information from the FRF of first marriage should be noted on them also. *Do not forget to make an entry in the box for the date of remarriage where appropriate*. The name of the new husband should be added next to the box for date of remarriage together with the FRF number of the later marriage. If the remarriage is that of a woman already widowed note the fact on the marriage recall slip by numbering the rank of marriage 3+ in pencil. All recall slips of widows are set aside.

As with widowers, remarriage within a few years of widowhood was normal if any remarriage occurred, though it was much less common for a widow to marry within, say, three months of the end of her previous marriage than for a widower to remarry within the same period.

D3c Widows (II). The object of this sequence of operations is to ensure that information about a woman who married more than once is fully collated so that all that is relevant appears on each FRF on which she figures, her FRF of baptism, of first marriage, and of all subsequent marriages.

First examine the marriage recall slips of widows. Any which bear a date of baptism taken from the FRF of first marriage can be coupled to one of the marriage recall slips set aside in *D2e* (since the date of baptism on the FRF of first marriage was itself obtained via one of the slips set aside in *D2e*). The latter can easily be found since they are also in sets by name of first husband. When any two are coupled in this way, clip them together with a paper clip with the recall slip of the later marriage uppermost. Set to one side any marriage recall slips known to relate to a marriage of the third or higher rank.

The marriage recall slips are now re-sorted by the surname of the new (second) husband and collated with the corresponding FRFs. The details of baptism, parentage, rank of marriage and so on, carried on the recall slip can now be transferred to the corresponding FRF of the second husband, while the date of burial of the wife, if it is recorded on the FRF, is noted on the marriage recall slip of the widow.

The slips are now sorted once more into sets by the surname of the first husband. The date of burial can be transferred to the parallel FRFs from those slips which now contain a burial date. Where a recall slip of a first marriage has been clipped underneath a recall slip of a widow's marriage, details of the later marriage and of burial are transferred from the upper slip to the lower. The recall slip of the first marriage is then detached, re-sorted by maiden name and collated with the FRF of baptism on which fuller information can now be recorded.

Note, however, that when the marriage recall slips are collated with the FRFs of second marriage it may appear that some married a third time (i.e. that there was a remarriage recorded on the FRF of second marriage). When this happens find the marriage recall slip of the third marriage (which will, of course, be among the marriage recall slips of widows) and clip it on top of the marriage recall slip of the second marriage. At the same time take any recall slip of third marriage previously set aside and do the same. In some instances this will mean, of

Married	14-2-1735	rank	2		

Wife				surname	
name	Deborah			TILMAN	

age

residence ....t.p...

spinster / _widow_ / unknown

father	George			BUCKNOLLE	

residence ....t.p..

occupation... *maiden name*

mother .... Amy .... SWEETLAND

late husband's name Humphrey (1701)

baptised .... 14-4-1699 ....

buried 30-11-1735

wife / widow / unknown

Husband		surname	
name	Samuel	BANKS	

Remarks..

....

....

....

....

Parish Colyton

E.S. III (b)   iii 65 | No. 1733

Figure 4.8. This is the marriage recall slip of the second marriage of a woman who was to die quite soon after her second marriage. Underneath it, of course, at this point would be the recall slip of her first marriage to Humphrey Tilman (recall slip 1701).

course, clipping three recall slips together, one for each of the three marriages. Exchange the information between the slips now linked together because they concern the same woman. Then re-sort the slips by the name of the third husband in the chain of slips, compare each chain to its parallel FRF of third marriage, transferring to the FRF information on the chain of slips about baptism, parentage, earlier marriages, etc., and add to the chains of slips dates of burial where known. Each slip in a chain will now contain all the information to be transferred to the earlier of the two marriages FRFs with which it is concerned (except, of course, in the case of a recall slip of a first marriage where the transfer is to the FRF of baptism). This means unclipping each chain and re-sorting the slips once more by the name of the earlier marriage (for example, the slip of the third marriage is re-sorted by the name of the second husband, the name which the woman bore at her third marriage). Information lacking on the parallel FRF (notably, date of burial) is then transferred to it. The recall slips have then fulfilled their purpose and can be returned to their original surname sets.

If it appears when the recall slips are compared with the FRFs of third marriage that the woman in question married for a fourth time (because the FRF of the third marriage carries mention of remarriage) proceed as above. The number of recall slips and the rank of marriage involved are different but the principle of operation is the same. Deal similarly with any marriages of a still higher order which may appear. Marriages of the third or higher rank are, of course, only a small percentage of the total of widow marriages.

It is important always to complete the sequence of operations for a higher rank of marriage before proceeding to a lower (this is because recall slips may be wanted for a chain of slips of a higher rank marriage which would have been re-sorted and returned to their original surname sets if a lower rank of marriage were dealt with first). Therefore, although it is convenient to explain the whole sequence of operations for each rank of marriage as a continuous process, the last stage (when the recall slips are re-sorted by the name of the earlier husband) should be delayed until the marriages of the highest rank have been identified and all the chains of slips built up. The re-sorting by name of earlier husband can then be done first for the slip chains of women who married, say, four times before passing on to marriages of lower rank. Ultimately all marriage recall slips are returned to their original surname sets.

D4 Final check – The transfer of information from the slips to the FRFs is now complete but some 'clearing-up' remains to be done.

It is useful to look through the upper half of each FRF to make sure that the following boxes have been filled:

date and place of baptism
date and place of burial
date and place of marriage
date of end of marriage
rank of marriage.

Where date and place are unknown check that the box has been marked X in pencil. The rank of marriage should appear either as 1, 2, 3, etc., in ink, where the rank is known, or 1, 2+ and occasionally 3+, in pencil, where the rank is not known certainly and the most probable rank is recorded.

In checking the box for the date of end of marriage note that, *although it may be possible to establish the fact that the date of burial of, say, the husband is also the date at which the marriage ended, because the widow is mentioned at the later marriage or death of one of her children, the box for the date of end of marriage should be marked with an X in pencil.* A note of the date can be made in the remarks section. This is done because marriages whose date of ending are known are used in the calculation of marital fertility, and if the date is known only because there were offsprings to the marriage this will bias the results (see below 147–8).

If a running list of doubtful cases has been kept (see 127 above) this is a convenient time to work through it in order to settle questions set aside earlier in the hope that more information would come to light.

E Calculations done on the FRFs

Before the whole body of information on the FRFs can be used for the calculation of general measures of fertility or mortality work upon each FRF must first be carried out. This provides the individual figures of age at marriage, interval between births, etc., which taken together describe the population as a whole.

The main calculations to be made are:

In the top half of the FRF
 1 Age at marriage
 2 Age at burial (death)
 3 Age at end of marriage
 4 Length of marriage
 5 Interval between end of marriage and remarriage
In the bottom half of the FRF
 6 Age at marriage for children of the marriage
 7 Age at burial (death) for children of the marriage
 8 Duration of marriage in age periods
 9 Age of mother at baptisms (births) of children
 10 Intervals between baptisms (births)
 11 Number of children (total, and by sex).

The calculation of 5 and 10 is done in months. The calculation of 7 is done in days if burial occurs within one month of baptism, in months if age at burial exceeds one month but is less than one year, and in years at greater ages (7d., 3m., 2y., etc.).[56] The calculation of all other intervals (1, 2, 3, 4, 6, 8, 9) is done in years.

All calculations done in years or in months are made in completed units. For example:

baptised 17–4–1577
 buried 25–9–1611   age at death 34 years
 buried 20–2–1611   age at death 33 years

or (interval between end of marriage and remarriage)

burial of spouse 15–6–1753
 remarriage 19–10–1758 $5 \times 12 + 4 = 64$ completed months
 remarriage 13–10–1758 $5 \times 12 + 3 = 63$ completed months
 remarriage 13– 3–1758 $5 \times 12 - 3 - 1 = 56$ completed
                                                  months

Calculations done in days are made by simple subtraction.
 baptised   15–4–1630
 buried   2–5–1630   age at death 17 days

144

In the calculation of 8 above (duration of marriage in five-year age-groups) the number of years lived in any age-group is 5 if the marriage began before and ended later than the period in question. If this is not so the figure is equal to the number of completed years lived in the period plus 0·5. Thus:

length of married life in age-group 20–4
woman married at 18, buried at 41=5   years
woman married at 18, buried at 21=1·5 years
woman married at 21, buried at 41=3·5 years.

It is important to note that in the case of marriages being broken by the death of the husband, the widow may have a legitimate child at any time during the first nine months after her husband's death. *In such case the marriage should be treated as continuing for nine months after the death of the husband.* Thus:

woman married at 18, widowed at 21=either 1·5 or 2·5 years
if woman born 5–6–1701, widowed 12–6–1722=1·5 (21 at 12–3–1723)
if woman born 5–6–1701, widowed 16–10–1722=2·5 (22 at 16–7–1723).

In the case of the marriage beginning and ending within the same age-group its duration is equal to the number of completed years of marriage plus 0·5 (if widowed add 9 months to the duration of the marriage as above). Thus:

woman married at 21, buried at 24=either 2·5 or 3·5 years
if woman born 5–6–1701, married 12–10–1722, buried 13–9–1725=2·5 years
if woman born 5–6–1701, married 12–10–1722, buried 15–12–1725=3·5 years.

It is convenient when performing these calculations to deal also with FRFs which record the burial of children for whom there was no corresponding baptism slip (see 129 above). A large proportion of these have no baptism slip because they died within a few days of their birth. Allot to each of them an approximate date of birth even when some measure of guess-work is inevitable. Indicate with an arrow the placing of the child in the birth order. Give to each an age at burial in brackets.

HUSBAND _SKINNER_ | Richard   Son | Richard / Rose PHILLIPS   Occupation husband _glazier_

WIFE _BRADDICK_ | Joan   Daughter | Joseph   husband's father _glazier_   wife's father _husbandman_

MARRIAGE	solemnized at		Marriage		Dates		length	Age at end of union	Remarriage	
2088	Colyton	rank vii	age at	marriage 3-7-1784	end of union 2-6-1799	14		24-8-1800	SEARLE (2241)
	born at i.p.	residing at i.p.		baptism	burial	age		Widowhood (months)	buried at i.p.
HUSBAND	2	29	21-8-1754	14-11-1819	65	44		14	i.p.
WIFE X i.p.	Shute i.p.	1	(24)	(1760)	2-6-1799	(39)			i.p.

Age groups	Years married	No. of births	Age of mother	Interval (months)	sex	rank	Baptisms date	Burials date	status	age	Marriages date	age	Name(s)	Surname of spouse
15-19		25	11		F	1	24-6-1785 / 25-7-1785	6-10-1835	wid	50	24-9-1821	36	Rosamund	COLE (2509)
20-24	0.5	0	27	22	F	2	16-5-1787 / 1-6-1787				19-10-1807	20	Sarah	SELLER (2322)
25-29	5	3	29	22	M	3	6-4-1789 / 2-5-1789	2-9-1808	s.	19			Richard	
30-34	5	3	31	23	M	6x	3-12-1792 / 25-12-1792	16-7-1793	s.	7m.			Robert	
35-39	4.5	1	31	0	F	7x	4-7-1796 / 1-9-1796				5-8-1820 / 7-11-1835	24 / 39	Jenny	SMITH (2484) / PORSE (2763)
40-44		32	20		M	4x	30-3-1791 / 3-4-1791		s.	(0)			Robert	
45-49		36	43		F	5x	30-3-1791 / 3-4-1791		s	(0)			Rebecca	
TOTAL	7					8								
boys	3					9								
girls	4					10								

Remarks: * Twins (?)

FRF ii 65

This FRF is based on one which was filled in during the reconstitution of Colyton. The original has been slightly amended to enable more points to be illustrated.

Figure 4.9

Since many will be assumed to have died at or shortly after birth a nought in brackets will be a common entry (0). Include these children in the calculation of birth intervals and the number born in each five-year age-group. FRFs with entries of this sort should be included in the subsequent calculation of infant mortality, age-specific fertility, and so on, but it is wise always to calculate two rates, one including and the other excluding families of this sort. The inclusive rates will be found to be higher than the other in most cases, as might be expected.

F Derivation of measures of fertility, mortality, etc.

This is a very large topic. The rates derived and to some extent the methods used will vary according to the aims of each piece of research. An exhaustive treatment is therefore not possible, but some problems of material and method are always present.

F1 The problem of movement into and out of the parish – It is evident that both the completion of FRFs and the subsequent calculation of measures of fertility and mortality would be greatly simplified if parish populations had been closed populations. But migration affected all parishes to some extent, and some, notably those in cities or on main highways, to so great an extent that family reconstitution may prove very difficult or impossible at least when attempted for single parishes. All demographic rates are calculated by relating the number of occurrences in a class of events to the total population at risk. If the total population at risk is not accurately known no dependable rates can be derived. For example, it may be known that a baby was born in the parish because of an entry in the register, but if he is to be included in the group for which an infant mortality rate is calculated it is essential, whether or not his burial is recorded in the register, to have an independent method of establishing his presence in the parish. For the calculation of some demographic characteristics of a population, in short, *it is essential to have a criterion by which the presence or absence of a family in the parish can be judged*. Such a set of conventions will be arbitrary but can also be reasonable.

It is essential that the criterion should be independent of the phenomenon studied. For example, suppose that there is an FRF which contains the date of baptism of the mother; the date of the marriage, but not the date of the end of the marriage; the dates of baptism of several of the children of the marriage, and the dates of burial of some of them who died in infancy (i.e. while they still lived in the family unit). The information on this FRF may properly be used for some calculations but not others. Suppose that the second child of the marriage died when four years old and that there were baptisms in the family at a later date. Then information about the second child can be used in the calculation of the mortality of children who lived through their first, second, third, fourth and fifth years (in the last case in the numerator, in the other cases in the denominator), because there is later evidence independent of the child's life and death of the presence of the family in the parish. If the entry of the child's burial in the register were the only evidence of his presence in the parish during his four years of life, the knowledge of his life and death could not enter into the study of child mortality. To do so would tend to exaggerate the level of child mortality. If in these circumstances he had not died his presence could not have been established. Nor is it enough to show evidence of the later burial (as opposed to baptism) of other children since this would tend to overweight the sample with families in which child mortality was high. If, to take another possible situation, the child had not died and if the last child of the family had been born when he was nine, then he would be included in the population of children at risk for each year of life up to and including the eighth.

Following the same principle it is clear that evidence from this FRF could not be used in the study of marital fertility. The continued residence of the family in the parish is known only because of the baptism and burial of children. The burial of the parents is not recorded in the register. If they had been childless nothing would have been known of them after their marriage and they would not have been included in any study of marital fertility. If families whose residence in the parish is known only from entries about their children in the baptism and burial registers are included in the calculation of marital fertility rates, the rates which result will be higher than the true rates.[57]

If the date of the end of a marriage which is recorded in the register is known, it should be assumed that the couple were continuously resident in the parish between the two dates unless there is direct evidence to the contrary.[58]

It is unwise to assume that children continued to live with their parents above the age of ten, or at the latest fifteen. Therefore age-specific mortality rates for the whole population can only be calculated with confidence up to this age since above it it is so difficult to apply a satisfactory independent criterion of presence in the parish. Amongst adults it is probable that only the married population will offer any scope for mortality studies.

The discussion of criteria of presence in the parish underlines the 'stay-at-home' nature of the group of reconstituted families. The more fully reconstituted they are, the less migratory they

148

must have been. It may be asked whether this does not seriously undermine the usefulness of any results obtained from family reconstitution. Is it fair to consider the 'stay-at-homes' representative of the population as a whole? No decisive evidence has yet been produced to settle this question. Since most migration was over very short distances it may be possible to solve the problem when a group of parishes are reconstituted together so that individuals and families who move can be followed as easily as those who do not. It may well prove to be the case that only those who moved long distances – to London, or Bristol, or Exeter, for example – fell into a different pattern of life. Those who moved only to neighbouring parishes remained in the same social and economic framework of life. Parishes varied greatly in size. Big parishes which included several villages contained within their bounds movements which would be inter-parochial elsewhere. Many men held land in more than one parish or had other economic ties with several places. Men and women appear to have chosen marriage partners indifferently over a radius of six or seven miles from their home village. The parish boundary was probably not a demographic boundary of much consequence in most parts of England,[59] and for this reason results obtained from the family reconstitution of a single parish are unlikely to be seriously misleading because of the 'stay-at-home' bias in them.

F2 Calculation – A very large number of calculations can be made using the data on the FRFs – age at marriage, average length of marriage, interval between end of marriage and re-marriage, average family size, frequency of families of different sizes, age-specific fertility, intergenesic interval, percentage of illegitimate births, percentage of pre-nuptial conceptions, infant mortality, child mortality, mortality of married couples and so on. Each main branch of investigation can be sub-divided (for example, the mortality of first or last children in the family can be contrasted with that of the others). Treatment in detail of all possible calculations is beyond the scope of this chapter,[60] but it seems well to mention a few general issues and to include a few worked examples.

All figures calculated on the FRFs in years and months will on average understate the true figures by one half of the unit interval. Thus in calculating the average interval which elapses between marriage and first birth it must be remembered that as many of the children baptised 10 months after marriage will have been over $10\frac{1}{2}$ months as under. An adjustment must be made to allow for this. Example:

622 marriages

total of time elapsed in completed months
between marriage and first baptism   9,952
add 622×0.5 311

Total   10,263

average interval between marriage and first baptism

$$\frac{10,263}{622} = 16.5 \text{ months.}$$

In the study of the age of men and women at first marriage, perhaps the most important single demographic variable in the study of pre-industrial societies, it is important to remember that the distribution of ages of marriages is skewed and that the mean age is often significantly higher than the median. It is therefore of value to know both.
Example:

1. Mean.
No. of women 373   total of their ages at first
marriage in completed years   9,904
add 373×0.5 186

Total   10,090

mean age at first marriage $\frac{10,090}{373} = 27.1$ years

2. Median (age at marriage of middle woman of population such that as many women were older as younger than her)
there were 153 women under 25 at first marriage
there were 37 women 25 years of age at first marriage
the median is the 187th in order

therefore the median age is $25 + \dfrac{187 - 153}{37} = 25.9$ years.

150

Many other demographic frequency distributions are strongly skewed (the interval between marriage and first baptism, for example) so that the difference between the mean and the median may be worth calculating in other instances also.

Infant mortality is one of the key variables which can be calculated after the FRFs have been completed. In principle if there were in, say, the period 1558–75 522 children born in the parish whose parents were still present in the parish a year after the births in question, and if 89 of the children died before reaching their first birthday, then the level of infant mortality is $\frac{89}{522} \times 1,000 = 170$ per thousand. In practice difficulties arise when using English registers to calculate infant mortality because many infants died before public baptism which, by the eighteenth century was often delayed weeks and even months after birth. This is a great contrast with French practice where baptism on the day of the birth or the day next following was the rule. In Crulai a third of all deaths under the age of one took place on the day of baptism when the child was only a few hours old, though this very high percentage may include some still-born children.[61] It is not clear how many of the English children who died before public baptism appear in the burial registers. It may well be that practice varied in different parts of the country. The rather low figures of infant mortality which are often obtained in England should therefore be treated with reserve.[62] Where the size of the population permits it is useful to calculate rates for the first week and first month of life and compare the results with specimen tables of the distribution of infant deaths within the first year of life to gain some indication of the reliability of the figures.

All the calculations done on the FRF data can be carried out manually, and indeed the time necessary to derive the main rates, though large, is less than is needed in the earlier stages of family reconstitution. But it is also possible, of course, to transfer the FRF data to punched cards after the end of section E. This has not yet been done in England[63] but it seems likely that if an exhaustive analysis of a good register in a large parish is undertaken, involving many calculations on sub-groups in the population over short period of time, the use of punched cards will preserve greater accuracy and save time.

The importance of the 'by-products' of family reconstitution should not be overlooked. For example, the marriage registers often noted the parish of origin of any partner to a marriage who came from another parish. This makes it a simple matter to assess the degree of 'endogamy' which existed in the past and the distances customarily travelled to find a partner if one was not found within the parish. Movement over short distances of up to seven miles in order to marry was very common from the earliest times covered by parish registers. Or again, the marriage registers after Hardwicke's Marriage Act (1753) usually carry the signature or mark of the bride and groom. This makes it possible to study the growth of literacy during the Industrial Revolution period, and the difference in this respect between the sexes, between town and country, and between different regions of the country. All three registers may give the occupation of men mentioned in entries. If this is done for all entries over a period an occupational census of a sort may be taken. It may not be easy to know the absolute numbers engaged in any one occupation at a single point in time, but the percentages of the population employed in different trades and industries over a period of years may be calculated accurately.

Just as FRFs can be used for purposes other than demographic history, so documentary sources other than parish registers can be used to supplement the information recorded on the FRFs. Overseers' accounts, churchwardens' accounts, constables' accounts, and so on, if used in conjunction with parish registers will enable more detail to be entered on the FRFs and may resolve some ambiguities (for example, about date of death) which cannot be resolved when using the register alone. Experience of the use of other records in conjunction with parish registers for family reconstitution is slight as yet. It may introduce difficulties of principle which are hard to overcome (for example, if the effect of the use of one class of record were to increase the proportion of full reconstitutions of a single social type, it would bias the sample of families used in calculating demographic rates). Equally some classes of record may prove to be very helpful without introducing a bias. Nominal lists of inhabitants are the best type of record for use in conjunction with the registers, both as a source of information and as a check upon the accuracy of results, but they survive for a comparatively small number of parishes only and these often have poor registers.[64]

Experience of the use of Catholic, Nonconformist and Quaker records, whether used separately or to supplement parish registers, is also limited, and may again prove important in the future. Already family reconstitution methods have been applied to the British nobility and to the Irish Quakers with very interesting results.

Family reconstitution has so far only been attempted in three English parishes and in only one is the work complete. Much remains to be done in extending and improving the technique of reconstitution. Indeed a chief reason for writing this chapter is the wish to hasten the day when it becomes obsolete or at least needs supplementation. The quality of English registers as a whole is still a subject for argument. Some of the conventions on which the operations described in this chapter are based may prove to need modification to produce the best results. Yet these uncertainties should be a spur to further work rather than a curb, for the prize is very rich. Family reconstitution work in France has already shown its great significance to many branches of history, as well as its strictly demographic interest and it is vital that its possibilities should be fully explored in England. Used in combination with other methods of measuring population changes in the past, it can serve as a warp for a broad range of historical analysis. The weft may be weather fluctuations and harvest yield; or the impact of a major epidemic and its associated social and economic consequences; or the size of the family and the structure of family life; or the play of secular economic change in pre-industrial and industrialising areas; or the interplay of them all. In each case a knowledge of population history, if it is sufficiently detailed to enable changes in fertility, mortality and nuptiality to be measured accurately, is invaluable. The fruit of work of this sort is mastery gained over a sector of life which both affected and reflected much else, and in a precision of detail rare in the study of the past.

E. A. Wrigley

NOTES

1 The development of this method stands largely to the credit of Louis Henry, and can be traced through three of his publications.

In his study of the Genevan bourgeoisie he put genealogical material to new uses; in the *Manuel* of the same year he defined his method; and the study of Crulai which followed shortly after showed what a wealth of detail could be had from a good parish register.

L. Henry, *Anciennes familles genevoises*, I.N.E.D., Cahier 26 (1956). M. Fleury and L. Henry, *Des registres paroissiaux* à *l'histoire de la population*, I.N.E.D. (1956). E. Gautier and L. Henry, *La population de Crulai*, I.N.E.D., Cahier 33 (1958).

This chapter was written in the hope of making English readers familiar with the techniques pioneered at the *Institut National d'Etudes Démographiques*. A direct translation of Henry's *Manuel* would not have been useful since English parish registers are very different from the French, but this chapter draws heavily upon his work. I should like to acknowledge the extent of my debt.

2 See section A below.

3 See above 71–2 and 76.

4 See below fn. 41 for details of their calculation.

5 A marked positive correlation is also common, especially perhaps in areas where a period of high mortality caused many holdings to fall vacant, making it possible for new marriages to take place and new families to be formed.

6 In fact in Colyton in the second half of the seventeenth century there was a sharp rise in the average age of first marriage for women, a pronounced fall in age-specific marital fertility, and a rise in the death rate among young children. The changes all point in the same direction, as it were, and may well account for the population failing to maintain its numbers. It is interesting to note that the ratio of baptisms/marriages actually rose in Colyton in this period which shows how dangerous this ratio can be as an indicator of marital fertility. I hope in the future to publish a monograph on Colyton's population history in which the remarkable changes in the parish in the three centuries, 1538–1837, will be examined fully.

7 See above 76–83 where Eversley discusses this point more fully.

8 Accurate counts of the inhabitants of individual parishes do exist (see chapter 5 below), but only for a small number of parishes at scattered points in time.

9 In other words reconstitution is essentially a cohort rather than a current method of measuring demographic variables, in contrast to the types of measurement discussed by Eversley in chapter 3. One of the chief difficulties of reconstitution is the problem of keeping the time span of each cohort as small as possible so that

changes in fertility and mortality can be pin-pointed in time. Successive decennial cohorts are perhaps the ideal, but in practice the number of reconstitutable marriages in each decade is too small in most parishes to make this feasible unless a group of neighbouring parishes are reconstituted together.

10 It is interesting to note that one of Henry's motives in developing reconstitution studies on French registers was the desire to study the levels of fertility reached in populations in which little or no artificial control of conception is thought to have been practised.

11 See, for example, Henry, *Anciennes familles genevoises*, 93–110, in which the timing of the onset of family limitation is examined, and its nature discussed.

12 The work of Goubert is outstanding in this connection. P. Goubert, *Beauvais et le Beauvaisis de 1600 à 1730*, S.E.V.P.E.N. (1960).

13 See especially A. Sauvy, *Théorie générale de la population*, 2 vols (Paris, 1952 and 1954).

14 For details see J. C. Cox, *The Parish Registers of England* (London 1910).

15 But see above 53 and 60 where Eversley discusses the deterioration in many registers after 1780. This may prevent the study going so far forward in time in some parishes.

16 See below *D2*. The problems are discussed in greater detail in my paper, *Some Problems of Family Reconstitution using English Parish Register Material*, mimeographed paper for Section VII, Third International Economic History Conference, Münich 1965.

17 See below *DIc*.

18 One of the provisions of Rose's Act of that year was that the age of the deceased should be recorded in the burial registers. The legislation took effect from 1 January 1813.

19 See above 29–32 for a further discussion of this problem.

20 This does sometimes occur. The village of Elstree provides an extreme example of this phenomenon. It was divided into four quadrants by the cross roads, each quadrant being in a different parish, the two northern ones in Hertfordshire, the two southern in Middlesex. My attention was drawn to this example by Mr W. Newman Brown.

21 See also above 20–7.

22 Some methods of reducing the time taken may prove worthwhile. For example, only families whose surnames began with certain letters might be reconstituted, say A–D. Unfortunately since A–D families were not endogamous this does not cut down slip filling as much as might be supposed at first sight.

23 Some incumbents and clerks may even have found it prudent to leave their parishes in time of plague.

24 See Cox, *Parish Registers,* for further details of the Bishops' Transcripts.

25 The terms deficient and defective are taken from the survey of parish registers in the 1831 Census where they were used to distinguish between registers in which for a period no entries survived and those in which there were some entries but clearly too few. The 1831 Census is still the only general inventory of parish registers, though lists of transcripts have been prepared by the Society of Genealogists.

26 This happened, of course, in the Colyton register as in others. But it is easy to exaggerate the time-lag between birth and baptism even in the later eighteenth century. In the decade 1771–80 at Colyton, for example, 50 per cent of all children were baptised within a month of birth, 68 per cent within two months, and 75 per cent within three months.

27 At Linton in Cambridgeshire in 1780 the vicar made the following note in the register 'N.B. It has not been usual for many years past to register the sickly children who are named at home, till they are brought to Church to be incorporated. Consequently all that die and are never incorporated come into the List of Burials but not of Baptisms. This circumstance should be known to the curious who may be inclined to form their ideas of population from these lists.' Mr R. L. Stevens of Linton was kind enough to draw my attention to this entry.

28 In France it was rare for more than a day to elapse between birth and baptism. This clearly makes for far fewer uncertainties.

29 By a constitution of the Convocation of Canterbury of 25 October 1597.

30 See Wrigley, *Some Problems of Family Reconstitution using English Parish Register Material,* mimeographed paper for Section VII, Third International Economic History Conference, Münich 1965.

31 See below section *DIc.*

32 After the United States census of 1950 a sample check revealed a net omission rate of 1·4 per cent, or about two million people in all. See M. H. Hansen, W. N. Hurwitz and L. Pritzker, 'The Accuracy of Census Results', *Am. Sociol. Rev.,* xviii (1953), 420.

33 At Colyton the rate calculated without any adjustment for possible under-registration never rises much above 100 per 1,000 in the three centuries 1538–1837. But it would be unwise to assume that all English parishes had very low infant mortality

rates calculated without adjustment (it is premature even to assert that the true rate at Colyton must have been much higher than the apparent rate). At Wrangle in Lincolnshire, for example, a rate of about 240 per 1,000 for the period 1597–1642 has been found by Mr F. West who is working on the demographic and social history of the parish and to whom I am indebted for this information.

34 This is true, for example, of the occasional mistakes made about age at first marriage.

35 See Gautier and Henry, *La population de Crulai*. The first two percentage figures are taken from a table on 77, the third is calculated from data in this table and that on the following page.

36 The figure for Crulai is calculated from Table 1, 242–4 and from a table on 77 of Gautier and Henry, *La population de Crulai*.

37 See above 54–6 and 107.

38 See Goubert, *Beauvais et le Beauvaisis* and K. M. Drake, *Marriage and population growth in Norway 1735–1865*, unpub. Ph.D. thesis (Cambridge 1964).

39 Work at present in train at the Cambridge Group for the History of Population and Social Structure should throw much more light on this issue shortly.

40 But see Eversley 31 above for a critical examination of the value of the harvest year as a unit.

41 A nine-year moving average is obtained by adding together, say, the baptisms of the year 1580–8 inclusive. The sum is divided by 9 and related to the middle year of the sequence, 1584. The figure for 1585 is obtained by adding the baptisms of 1589 to the total for 1580–8 and subtracting those of 1580 to produce a new total for the years 1581–9 to be divided by 9 as before; and so on. Moving averages damp down violent annual swings.

42 For similar reasons, and especially in small parishes, it is always wise to become acquainted with the registers of neighbouring parishes. If they are also good the possibility of joint reconstitution should be considered. See J. Ganiage, *Trois villages de l'Ile de France*, I.N.E.D. Cahier 40 (1963).

43 The transcription was done by A. J. P. Skinner and published by the Devon and Cornwall Record Society, 2 vols (1928).

44 Printed forms had been in common use for marriage, of course, from the time of Hardwicke's Marriage Act (1753).

45 See below 123.

46 For example, it may be known from aggregative work that an important change in the demography of the parish took place in, say, the period 1720–40. If time did not permit the reconstitution

of the whole register one might study simply the families formed by marriages over the period 1700–60 to make it possible to pinpoint the timing and nature of the changes in the 1720–40 period.

47 I should like to acknowledge my debt to Mrs Susan Stewart who made a number of valuable suggestions about this section of the chapter. She also made illuminating comments on the sequence of operations in section D.

48 In the Colyton register there are many examples of this: Elizabeth Seward was given as daughter of Ralph on her burial at the age of 33 in July 1654; William Follett was entered in the register as the son of Charles on his death at the age of 29 in December 1645. Many other instances could be quoted with some ages as high as the forties.

49 It was very rare indeed for men and women to exceed this age.

50 It is interesting to note that Hollingsworth in his study of the British peerage always attributes an age at death to each individual where the exact age is not known. This he does even though it may not be possible to state it more accurately than that it falls within a span of 64 years (the longest of the twelve classes of order of accuracy of data which he uses). The method leads to a bunching of deaths at certain ages and some circularity of argument because of the way the ages at death are allotted in cases where little is known of the individual. But the method also possesses countervailing merits. Further work may show that it could be adapted with profit for reconstitution work on parish registers. See T. H. Hollingsworth, 'The Demography of the British Peerage', supplement to *Population Studies*, xviii (1964).

51 See Wrigley, *Some Problems of Family Reconstitution using English Parish Register Material*, mimeographed paper for Section VII, Third International Economic History Conference, Münich 1965.

52 This is a rare form of entry.

53 See 147–8 below for a fuller discussion of this point.

54 Except for a few obtained as a result of the work done on f(1/2+) and f(2+/2+) in *D2d* above.

55 In Colyton only 5 in a total of 886 marriages produced an absurdity of this sort. It is interesting to note that it is possible to make an entirely independent check of the accuracy of the attribution of baptism date to bride for 84 women in Colyton in the eighteenth century. In each case the check could be carried out only *after* the coupling of the baptism and marriage recall slips had been done. In only 3 cases had a false attribution been made when following the principles of *D2d*.

56 If the date of birth is known it, rather than the date of baptism, should be used in making these calculations.

57 Marital fertility data from this marriage could legitimately be used, however, in studying the fertility of women in any one age-group who had further children in a later age-group, since then it would be on a par with other families and would not bias the results.

58 The assumption behind this convention is not beyond challenge. In some parishes, for example, it was quite common to bring back bodies for burial from neighbouring parishes. This clearly affects the validity of the assumption where it occurs.

59 Except perhaps where 'estate' and 'peasant' villages alternated with each other (essentially those which were dominated by a single landowner and those which were not), or where enclosure acts had affected one parish without touching its neighbour.

60 Gautier and Henry, *La population de Crulai*, specify many operations which may serve as a guide here.

61 Gautier and Henry, *La population de Crulai*, 170.

62 See fn. 33 above.

63 Hollingsworth has used them extensively in his studies of the British peerage.

64 See chapter 5 below.

5

THE STUDY OF SOCIAL STRUCTURE
FROM LISTINGS OF INHABITANTS

WILLIAM SAMPSON, Rector of Clayworth in Nottinghamshire, took up residence in the village on 27 November in the year 1675. Five months later, on 9 April 1676, he read a *brief* from his pulpit, requesting his parishioners to subscribe for the relief of the town of Northampton, where there had been a serious fire. 'Whilst they were collecting this brief' he goes on to say in his *Register*,[1] 'I took occasion to enquire, at the same time, the names of all my parishioners; which were these that follow *nominatim et (ad evitandam invidiam) alphabetice*.' There follows a list of 401 names, in alphabetical order certainly, but in households, the surname of the head of the household determining the place in the order and so 'avoiding envy'.

Now it is clear that the 'collection' which was going on whilst Sampson wrote out his list must have been from house to house, because it is scarcely likely that even in this village, regular as it was in church attendance, every head of household can have been in the congregation on that April Sunday morning. It is also probable that the list was composed fairly quickly, perhaps within a few hours of his address from the pulpit, or within a couple of days; certainly within a week. Sampson's listing then may fairly safely be supposed to have had one of the distinguishing marks of what the demographer would allow to be a *census*, that it should be a house to house enquiry carried out by qualified and knowledgeable people. It may also have possessed the second such mark, that it should be made at a point in time, recording all the persons actually present in that place on a particular day. This is by no means certain, however. The enquiry could have spread over several days and does in fact contain a subsequent addition; the Rector had forgotten

160

his own family and one other. Moreover, there is nothing to show that the respondents confined their replies to the names of persons actually resident in the household at a particular time. It is indeed more likely that they told Sampson, or his churchwardens, not only who was, in fact, present, but also who should have been present as well. Therefore, the servant who happened to be at the local market selling butter at the relevant time, or the son who was away fetching cattle, may well have been recorded, though absent. There may have been omissions of the same kind as well: the journeyman tailor who was at a house making clothes for a day or two might have been left out because he would not ordinarily have been there.

Sampson's list of the inhabitants of Clayworth in 1676, in fact, probably ought to be classed as *ideal* rather than *actual*. Nevertheless, its quality must be regarded as high, very high indeed, when compared with other such lists which have survived to us from before 1841, that is from before the time when, by Government decree, every household in the country had officially to be described in full every ten years as part of the Census. The circumstances of its composition are quite exceptionally clear. The slight weakness we have noticed cannot have affected the list in more than a very minor way, and might actually be a help to the historian of population engaged in trying to reconstitute families in this parish in the way described in the last chapter.[2] Before we go on to further details about those listings of inhabitants which concern us in this chapter, we must make it clear what it is that they all have in common.

Only those documents can enter into the analysis of the social structure of communities which bear immediate and convincing signs that the whole population is covered. Partial listings have their value; those which name heads of households only, for example, or those which are concerned only with adults. But the whole point of our argument will be that principles of recreating past social structure must be based on the complete community. Specifically they must be worked out from as many local samples of the complete community of the country as can possibly be found, local samples which are themselves communities. It will be asked at once how we shall finally decide that the evidence we have chosen does refer to such complete communities. Our full answer must be to some extent a circular one; we accept only those listings as complete which, when submitted to the full analysis contained in the tables which we shall describe, yield answers which we know from experience to be probable answers. We can also examine our evidence for internal consistency and check it at some points against the parish registers when they are available. But our initial concern is with the claim which any document makes, at first sight, to belong to the class which alone interests us. The list of Clayworth in 1676 has already been shown to be one of them. It contained everybody, it was compiled by a fully competent person, probably going from house to house, and so on. Still, as we have hinted, there are other headings under which it has to be judged, and these reveal its limitations.

Its major defect is that no ages are given. It might perhaps be urged that to expect a clergyman in the year 1676 to recognise the importance of ages in a matter like this is to expect too much, even though, like William Sampson, he had been a university teacher until he had taken up his benefice, and though he was related by marriage to the tiny group of scientists then already active. It is true that recordings of the ages of inhabitants have so far been recovered for only four or five English communities for any date earlier than 1706, but one such record survives from as early as 1599 (Ealing in Middlesex) and another for the mining community dominated by the family of Newdigate at Chilvers Coton in Warwickshire as it was in the year 1684. The list for Clayworth in 1676 also falls short of those for Chilvers Coton and Ealing in another important respect. It does not give an occupation for more than about a third of the heads of households, whereas in these other communities, and elsewhere, also, it is possible to gain an almost complete picture of how every family made its living.

But in one crucial feature this particular list is as good as any we have. The marital status of every head of household is given, so that we can tell at a glance whether a man listed first in his household, but without a wife, is, in reality, a widower, and so on. We can also tell, because Sampson tells us so, whether a woman coming at the end of a succession of sons and daughters is in fact a widow, and even if she is the mother-in-law. Indeed, not simply the status of each head of household, but the relationship of every member of each household to its head, is

162

made amply clear, and this is a crucial requirement for a list of inhabitants which is capable of being analysed for demographic and social structural purposes. In one particular, curiously enough, the 1676 listing for Clayworth is below the standard of many others, in such a way as might make it useless for the purpose of any analysis at all if it had not been written out alphabetically. Sampson does not indicate in any other way where one household ends and another begins.

That each family should be unmistakeably differentiated from every other is perhaps the first of all features which must be looked for in a listing of inhabitants to be used for historical purposes. We have begun this consideration of the study of social structure from listings of inhabitants with the example of Clayworth in 1676 not only because it serves to bring out very clearly some of the qualities which have to be sought for in such documents, but also because it makes evident the kind of knowledge which studying them can yield. It is obvious that the size of the household, the structure of the household, the precise number of inhabitants, their division into sexes, into children and adults, into married, unmarried and widowed, can all be very easily recovered from what Parson Sampson wrote down in that year. A village of 400 inhabitants is too small to be free of quite random variation in any of the features we have mentioned. But the preparation of similar results from ten or a dozen such communities would give a rather more revealing set of conclusions for the whole country, or at least of its rural areas, provided that they all fell within the same decade and were not confined to a particular region. Even at the present time the preparation of such conclusions for the decades 1691–1700 and 1701–10 is well within our reach. Some forty lists of inhabitants of English communities are already available for the first decade of the eighteenth century, mostly from a particular area of Kent it is true, but including some townships in the cluster known as Stoke-on-Trent in Staffordshire in 1701. A dozen lists date from the last decade of the seventeenth century, and they are well scattered over the whole country; there is, moreover, a very large collection for the parishes comprising the city of London and its suburbs.

The other lists of inhabitants so far registered by the Cambridge Group for the History of Population and Social Structure

163

are about twenty-five in number and are spread over the remaining decades of the years between 1599 and 1800. The existence of most of them seems to have been unknown to historians and demographers until very recently, and some of them are quite new discoveries, made in the chests of parish churches, in the muniment rooms of County Record Offices and libraries, even in the printed pages of local histories. Since little concerted effort has yet been made to collect records of this type, and since so many have, nevertheless, come to light within a few years, it seems reasonable to suppose that many more will be found in the near future.[3] It is of considerable consequence that they should be found. For the fact is that those questions about population and social structure which can only be answered from complete lists of persons comprising communities, cannot be answered at all for England before the year 1841 except from sources of this kind. Let us return forthwith to the example we have chosen to see what further items of social structural information it contains, and to see what bearing they may have on historical and social study. Parson Sampson's motives in the year 1676 can also tell us something of the various reasons why such documents must once have existed in considerable numbers, and so may reappear at any time.

The most straightforward and important advantage which an accurate list of inhabitants gives to the historian of population has still to be mentioned. As Dr Eversley has shown, it provides a base line for any calculations he may wish to undertake about the course of growth or diminution of the numbers of the settlement which it covers. Together with the parish registers it also gives an opportunity of discovering that which is so very important to demographic study and which is so exasperatingly rare for societies without a census – accurate vital statistics. Sampson numbered his parishioners not once, but twice; in his *Register* for the year 1688 appears a further complete list of inhabitants as they were 'about May-day'. At that point in time, twelve years and three weeks after the 1676 enumeration, 412[4] men, women and children were present in Clayworth. At first sight it would seem that the population was fairly constant. A figure of 400–10 can fairly be assumed to cover its total over the twelve years; perhaps, indeed, for many years since a net loss of seven by the excess of burials over baptisms was more than made up by the movement of eighteen persons into the village which kept the community at about the constant level. If the total of inhabitants was steady in this way, then it would seem safe enough to take the yearly baptisms, marriages and burials and work out a series of vital statistics based on a population of this order. Between 1 May 1676 and 30 April 1688, there was a total of 190 baptisms, 33 marriages and 197 burials entered into the registers by the meticulous Rector. At a population of 405 this represents a baptismal rate of 39·1, a marriage rate of 6·8 and a burial rate of 40·5 per thousand of the population. It is always possible that an odd birth escaped him, or that some dead baby went unburied in the churchyard. But these vital statistics are as reliable as will ever be worked out from an era so remote from modern methods of registration.

These facts should serve to underline the enormous value of finding two, not one, accurate listings of the inhabitants of a community. It will be noticed that the unexpected evidence from Clayworth, evidence which, as we shall see, appears already to be available for several other communities, including London parishes in the 1690s, shows the difficulty of calculating the totals of population at varying dates by the addition and sub-traction of differences between totals of baptisms and burials. If we had not known that the population of Clayworth in 1688 was 412 we should have reckoned it at 394, and going down rather than up, since there was a surplus of burials until 1695. If, moreover, we had been content to suppose that a fairly constant *total* of inhabitants was accompanied by a static *composition*, by a small turnover in persons, during the twelve years, we should have made an error of considerable propor-tions. No less than 244 of the 401 persons at Clayworth in 1676 had disappeared by 1688, that is 61 per cent and 254 of the 412 who were there in 1688 were newcomers since 1676, that is 62 per cent. Of the 244 who disappeared, less than 100 were buried in Clayworth. The survival of these two full and accurate listings of a completely rural parish at a time before modern industry or transportation began to have an effect in England shows that the turnover of persons could be almost as high as two-thirds within twelve years.

This may be thought a very striking extension of historical knowledge of the demographic kind, providing information which could not be obtained in any other way. Enough has been said, or hinted at, to show the ways in which listings of inhabitants, when systematically analysed, can serve as a supplement to other forms of demographic study and as a standard, even as a corrective, both as to methods and results. The great difficulty of evidence of this kind, its abiding and incurable disadvantage, is that its occurrence is fortuitous, a matter of good fortune.

So far, no other opportunity quite like that at Clayworth has presented itself and the figure we have quoted for turnover of persons there itself suffers severely as information, because we have no adequate means of appreciating it by comparison, no proper frame of reference for it. Still, similarly complete and apparently reliable evidence is already known to exist for other places, and more successive listings of inhabitants may well come to light. At the present time, early in 1965, we can compare turnover at Clayworth with turnover at only one other community, a community even smaller in size and removed by fifty years in time, since all the information comes from the years 1618–28. In this village, that of Cogenhoe, near Northampton, the turnover was 54 per cent in the ten years.[5] What is more, the total number of inhabitants fluctuated considerably from year to year. There were 185 in the village in 1618, 150 in 1620, 154 in 1621, 176 in 1622, and 180 in 1628. Even the number of households varied, between 30 and 34.

Parson Sampson's second list of the inhabitants of Clayworth made in 1688 has claims to be the most revealing of all those so far analysed for any community in our country before the year 1841. If he had only included ages it could, with justification, be called a 'census' in the twentieth century sense. In fact, no official census for the whole of our country and not confined to a particular sample for special statistical purposes has ever covered all the questions which can be answered from it. It tells us the facts which show how many orphans there were amongst the villagers in that year (orphans reckoned as children who had lost either one of their biological parents), and even how many times each husband and wife had been previously married. Not even the almost unbelievably detailed listing of the inhabitants of the town of Corfe Castle, Dorset, at some time in the 1790s gives this final item of marital status, though it does include ages and, which is unique, a statement of the income of each individual.[6]

Nevertheless, the reason why Sampson decided to make this second listing is uncertain and it is possible that in one other respect it is slightly below the quality of its predecessor of 1676. The differences are worth mentioning, because the same issues are raised by almost every other listing of this type. Here is what he writes in his *Register* about the action he took in 1688.

'About May-day I took the names of the inhabitants of this my parish of Clayworth, and placing them according to the order of houses and families, down the north side of the town, and up the south side, and lastly those of Wiseton, and were as follows.'

The word 'town' at that time meant any settlement, including what we should call a village. Wiseton was a separate hamlet within the parish. This statement suggests that though Sampson wrote out his list in the house-to-house fashion he did not necessarily call at every dwelling and interview a member of the household. He could have simply sat at his desk in the Rectory and thought up each house and household one by one, as they succeeded each other along the village street. In this case he might well have reminded himself by looking up notes made for different purposes, or by making some calls at cottages, or by summoning some people for interview. The method used now, that is asking each householder to fill up a form, was of course not open to Sampson and not open to anyone desirous of making lists of persons, at least not until well after 1800, perhaps even after 1841. This was because there were so many illiterates: perhaps as few as a third, certainly not as much as a half, of the heads of Clayworth households could have been expected to fill up a form in 1688.

It is of great importance to remember these facts about literacy in appreciating the quality of all these returns, and also in forming an opinion about what might be expected to survive from earlier generations of use to the demographer. Many of the listings so far known seem likely to have been the result of the thinking-up process, prompted to a greater or lesser extent by consulting other documents and by interview. This is clear because so many of them are arranged in order of importance of inhabitants, their social rank order. Sampson was able to start

167

his list of 1688 with the name of the squire, 'Mr Thomas Wawen, Lord of the Soil', because the great house was in fact the northern end of the series which made up the village. But when in April, 1676, Francis Nicholson, curate-in-charge, began his 'account of the present inhabitants of Goodnestone-next-Wingham, according to their families, quality and religion' with the name of Edward Hales, Esq., he was starting at the natural point for the men of that day, with the most exalted individual and family in the village. Since social rank and economic consequence went with size of household, the general rule is simple. Where a list begins with the large households first, it can be assumed to be in social rank order, even if there is absolutely no evidence as to why it was drawn up, by whom, or on what occasion.

Francis Nicholson divided the inhabitants of Goodnestone in Kent in 1676 into four classes according to their 'quality', gentlemen, yeomen, tradesmen, labourers and poor men. No other list so far discovered provides quite such overt evidence for the student of the overall social structure of our country during the period before official statistics. But it must be evident that very valuable and even reasonably systematic information of this character can be extracted from many such documents. As we have said, the larger the number of lists we can discover, the wider they are spread in time and in area and the more detail they contain, the completer will become the body of fact available to the student of social change. There seems to be no reason why the more advanced and intricate sociological questions should not be capable of being given an answer: those concerning the formation of classes or even of political elites, for example, as well as those concerning industrialisation may possibly be tackled always supposing we can find sufficient good lists. Changes in the familial system, even the kinship system, could certainly be exactly followed, as we shall try to show.

The present chronological limit for evidence of this sort is at the year 1599, when the aging Elizabeth was still on the throne and when Richard Phillips and William Gurnall, constable and headborough of the rural village of Ealing in the county of Middlesex, drew up a list of names of 'everyone living within the parish'.[7] There is nothing to show why they decided to include the ages of all inhabitants and the exact constitution of

168

each family, which makes their record so valuable. But there is no reason why this should have been the first time that questions from superior authorities, lay or spiritual, elicited such replies. The occasion of the return from Ealing seems to have been somewhat local and even rather trivial, connected with the prevalence of paupers at that particular time and in that particular area. Within the next few years it may become possible to trace social development in our country from evidence of this kind from the reign of Victoria to dates even earlier than the last years of Elizabeth, perhaps even into the reigns of the previous Tudors or into medieval times.

It is quite justifiable, in spite of the rarity of such documents, to begin by hoping that a listing was carried out at some time for any given community, and no particular reason for such an enterprise having been undertaken need be borne in mind. There are certain general types of list known to us, nevertheless, and we have come to recognize certain occasions on which such lists may, or even must, have been made out, though not necessarily in a form which we should accept for our purposes.

In the years before 1841 lists of persons were drawn up either for the convenience of administrators, as they have been systematically since that time, or for spiritual and ecclesiastical purposes. When the position of the Christian Church in the life of every single individual in England as it was before the nineteenth century is remembered, it is not surprising that a good proportion of the complete listings should have been drawn up for spiritual and ecclesiastical purposes, and that a number of the particular occasions on which such census-type activities are known to take place were ecclesiastical and religious too.

The year and month of both the Goodnestone and the first Clayworth listing was April 1676: Francis Nicholson dated his on Friday the 7th of that month, and William Sampson, as we have seen, on Sunday 9th.[8] This was, in fact, the month of the so-called Compton census, for which every parish priest in England was required to make a return to his Archbishop, that is, either to Canterbury or to York, containing the following facts:

1 'What number of persons are by common estimation and account in your parish inhabiting.'

169

2 'What number of Popish Recusants, or persons suspected for such recusants, are inhabiting.'

3 'What other Dissenters are in the parish.'

These are the exact words used by Nicholson in his return to the Archbishop of Canterbury, and for him Roman Catholics were Popish Recusants, Nonconformists were Dissenters. The record of the number of such people in each parish may turn out to have an important bearing on the reliability of all the evidence contained in the parish registers. By the 1670s these records begin to be suspect as sources for total vital statistics because Nonconformity had become so widespread.

Neither Sampson nor Nicholson was actually required to write out the names of inhabitants on that occasion, or even to count them very exactly. The fact that both of them went far beyond what the Archbishop had requested and took such care to record every individual soul under their spiritual guidance shows that each was an exceptionally conscientious clergyman. But it also points to the existence of a particular tradition of the Western Church, a tradition which was probably much stronger on the Continent than in England and which may turn out to be of the very first importance to the historian of social structure. This was the pastoral precept that each parish priest, besides keeping separate registers for baptisms, marriages and burials, should keep a special book with the title *Liber Status Animarum*. In this volume – the rather odd Latin title means something like 'register of the number and condition of souls' – he was to record every family, with everyone living in it, noting down those fit to take Holy Communion, those fit for instruction and those fit for confirmation.[9] If, as has been commented elsewhere, 'If all the beneficed priests of the English Church had, in fact, kept all these four registers, above all, if some of them, a very small proportion would suffice, had kept a *Liber Status Animarum* to hand down to us, then the task of the historian of social structure would be transformed.'

But it would seem that very few clergy of the Church of England were stimulated by the enquiry of April 1676, to draw up a listing of this character for their parishes as Sampson and Nicholson appear to have done. Most of the returns so far examined contain nothing more than the bare answers to the four

170

questions listed in Nicholson's document, giving very rough and sometimes incredible figures. Some divide up parishioners by households, however, and some list by name every person capable of communion. If it was not social scientific curiosity which led Sampson to make his second listing of 1688, then it may well have been a residual feeling for the tradition of the *Liber Status Animarum*; more probably a combination of both, with ordinary inquisitiveness thrown in.

We have dwelt on the details of the Compton Census and of the pastoral duty of listing souls in order to draw the attention of all keepers and users of parish registers and of parish records generally to the possibility that documents of this character once existed and may, perhaps, still exist. It is true that no document bearing the title *Liber Status Animarum* has ever been found in an English parish chest, nor is their conceivable presence mentioned in the standard works on local archives.[10]

Nevertheless, the listings made by the Rector at Cogenhoe in the decade 1618–28, just after the registration of souls became part of the ritual of the Roman Church, look very like a rough record of this kind. And one document is known which approximates quite closely to a *Liber Status Animarum*. This bears the date 2 June 1701, and it presents, with admirable clarity and completeness,

A collection of the names of every particular and individual person in the parish of Stoke-upon-Trent, in the County of Stafford, as they are now residing within their respective Liberties and Families within the said parish; together with the age of every such person, as near as can conveniently be known, as also the number of families and souls qualified (as to their ages) for communicating, in each family.

Unfortunately, this recording is imperfect from our point of view, in a way which is much more typical of documents drawn up for fiscal than for ecclesiastical purposes; it covers not the whole substantial parish of Stoke-on-Trent, but only some of its constituent *Liberties*. This is not necessarily because the priest got tired of his task, but much more probably because the transcriber who made the only surviving copy in the year 1705 failed to finish it. For the general rule as to listings carried out for and by the Church is this. Since they always refer to the parish there can be no doubt of the unit of population concerned.

171

Since their object was pastoral, they tended to include Non-conformists, and back sliders. The parish was a very ancient and well demarcated area, whose boundaries were 'beaten' every year by the inhabitants: they actually went in procession round them on a particular date, headed by their parson. No such difficulties as those which Mr Armstrong describes for the Enumerators' Books of the early Census ordinarily arise with parish records.

Listings of communities made for ecclesiastical purposes then ordinarily cover the whole of a population, though not necessarily by naming every individual. They may mention families only, adding the numbers within each, or they may list only those capable of communion, that is those over sixteen years of age. But they are likely to include persons of every occupation and standing, rather than be confined to landholders or property owners generally. There is some tendency, as we have tried to show, for them to approximate to the form of a *Liber Status Animarum*, and this is just what the demographer would like them all to do. An enquiry of this kind in 1676 seems to have prompted some priests to make a return in such a form, and there were other such occasions in the history of the English Church. A very similar survey of the condition of souls in every parish in the kingdom took place in 1603, and returns for individual dioceses have been printed.[11] Bishops sometimes requested similar information from all the priests under their jurisdiction,[12] and even a zealous archdeacon may have acted at some time in such a way as to lay down in the records a whole series of documents which might extend our present information. A great deal depends for the future of social structural history on the skill of archivists and historians in tracing documents belonging to such surveys which have the necessary characteristics, and upon the vigilance and goodwill of clergymen, churchwardens and everyone interested in local records.

The story of the Clayworth registrations demonstrates by itself how much depends on the arousing of interest in studies of this kind if the required evidence is to be forthcoming. When Sampson's *Register* was published in 1911 as *The Rector's Book*, ecclesiastical historians were not slow to recognise its importance as a record of the everyday life of a parish at an interesting period, and it soon found its way into the footnotes.

172

Economic historians used it too, since it contains interesting information about the use of land, and even a yearly list of prices of produce grown upon the parson's glebe. But apart from a casual reference made in the course of a study of population in another county,[13] no one seems to have realised that it might have demographic value.

When we turn from the Church to the State, from listings of inhabitants made for ecclesiastical purposes to those made for administrative purposes, we find ourselves in an even more miscellaneous world. Secular records are much more scattered than spiritual ones and, though very many more listings were made for lay purposes than for clerical, an even smaller proportion seem likely to have been exhaustive and detailed enough to satisfy the requirements we have laid down. Still we have already commented upon the very remarkable listing for Ealing in 1599, and, we might add, another for the town of Stafford in 1623. It belongs to a fairly common class of municipal documents, but is complete enough to qualify, even if it contains nothing like the detail recorded at Ealing, Chilvers Coton and elsewhere.[14] It might seem more probable that exhaustive listings will turn up amongst the great series which are now in the Public Record Office commemorating such fiscal measures as the Hearth Taxes, the Poll Taxes, the Window Taxes and so on. But these collections, useful as they are for the purposes which Dr Eversley has mentioned and as ancillaries to those which we are here considering, have, so far, yielded no listings which could at all properly be called censuses. The one fiscal measure, moreover, which seems the most likely to provide such listings, which was perhaps even intended to provide them when it was enacted in 1694 and which has in fact already yielded the greater part of the material on which we can get to work, is far, far worse documented than the Hearth Tax and the others. Indeed its central files, those kept at Whitehall, seem to have disappeared completely.

This measure is so important to our purpose that we must dwell upon it for a little. Professor Glass, after quoting a Victorian scholar to the effect that 'every historian ought to have learned from the statute book that a thorough and complete enumeration of the inhabitants of all the parishes in England, with a full and precise statement of their several names,

173

occupations and qualities was made in 1695', has made the following statement on the subject.

This was clearly a remarkable Act. It provided for the first complete census (and no other was taken until 1801), registration of births within five days (as compared with 42 days under our present system) and the creation of a special register of statistics on differential fertility'.

In 1694 England was in the midst of William III's struggle with Louis XIV and the object of the statute was to raise money 'For carrying on the War with France with vigour'. This is the title sometimes found on documents relating to it. It imposed duties on births, marriages and deaths, which is why it is usually called 'The Marriage Duty Act'. These duties were graduated according to status and to property; they were to be in force for five years from 1 May 1695 and, in fact, stayed in force until 1705, that is eleven years. The act provided for the preparation of *certificates* for each 'Parish, Division, Constablewick, Allotment and Place' in the country to be prepared by 1 May 1695, certificates which had to be kept up to date for each successive year, so recording entries into the population concerned by birth and immigration, changes by marriage, and departures by emigration and death. So admirably were these provisions suited for determining totals of population, vital statistics and other outstanding features of the social structure, that it is hard not to agree with Professor Glass that the object of the 1694 Act may have been demographic as well as fiscal.[15]

Unfortunately the wording of the Act, verbose and repetitive as it is, does not make it clear what exactly was to be written on the *certificates*. Mention is made of a list of persons drawn up by name, by social and marital status and by property qualification. This unfortunately could be done, and obviously was done in many places, without distinguishing households. Collectors were to be locally appointed, but no particular class of individuals was named; it was not made a responsibility of the overseers of the poor, for example, or of the clergy, though the clergy were required to register baptisms, weddings and burials for the particular purposes of the Act.[16] Certificates were to be sent to the Commissioners for the Act, who were to be the same as those for the Land Tax in the first year and Justices of

174

the Peace thereafter. But no direction was given about where certificates were to be preserved, or what was to happen to the copies which must have been kept by the local collectors. Each responsible official may have been at liberty to keep his documents after they had ceased to be useful, which is, perhaps, why they turn up in so many different places; amongst private papers (as for Melbourne), in the chest in the parish church (as for Donhead, Wilts.), in the records of towns (as for New Romney) and so on. If one of the objects of the measure was indeed demographic those who drafted its provisions seem to have had only a hazy idea of demographic requirements.

Nevertheless there can be no doubt that the recovery of any considerable number of returns under this act would be of great importance, particularly if they were accurately filled in originally and contained the corrections which births, marriages, deaths and migrations made necessary for successive years. Such an event might completely alter the prospects of recreating social structure in pre-industrial England and be of considerable significance to the history of population. An adequate discussion of all the issues raised by the Statute, especially the question why it is that no vast body of returns has so far come to light in the Public Record Office, would take us far beyond our present bounds. Suffice it to say that many of the returns which have so far come to light satisfy the requirements we have laid down for a listing, even if they sometimes omit many of the details which would seem to have been necessary for the purposes of the tax in question.[17]

Collections of returns each giving an account of the population of a whole area are known to survive for two cities (London and Bristol), and for one rural area (in south east Kent). Several scholars have made use of the London returns for other purposes, but systematic work on social structure is still so much in its infancy that so far only preliminary approaches have been made in the analysis of one of these collections, that for the thirty-six contiguous places in the Wingham Petty Division of the County of Kent as they were in 1705, the last year during which the act was in force. Some 6,500 person lived in this area. At the present moment they must make up the largest known, examinable sample of persons living under the ordinary, that is to say, the rural conditions which existed all over England

175

before the time of the census, perhaps the largest in Western Europe.[18]

There are two further comments which must be made on the 1694 Act and its documents before we go on to describe how the process of analysing listings of inhabitants is actually carried out for social structural purposes. One is almost trivial. It is much more difficult to determine the boundaries of the community to which each of these returns refers than it is in the case of the ecclesiastical sources. It happens that the village of Goodnestone-next-Wingham is included in the Kent collection for 1705, but the document seems not to refer to the parish described in 1676 by Francis Nicholson (see above), but to a much smaller area. This makes it more difficult to decide than it is in the case of parish lists how far the population concerned made up a complete community. The second comment is of much greater importance and would once again soon lead us a long way from the prescribed purpose of this *Introduction*, if we were to pursue its implications for the historical demography of England. Some of the returns under this Act, including the most interesting and accurate of them, have been found amongst the personal papers of Gregory King.

Gregory King of the Herald's Office and not far distant from the Treasury when the 1694 Act was passed, may well have had a hand in the Government's decision to adopt the measure, though scarcely in drafting its schedules. As Professor Glass recognised nearly twenty years ago he seems likely to turn out to be the most important of the early pioneers of demography and of social analysis. However much the contemporary student of historical social structure sees himself as an explorer of unknown territory, he feels that King has been there before him, in the 1690s. King's *Scheme of the Income and Expense of the Several Families of England calculated for the Year 1688* has been made use of by modern historians, just as the treasury officials of the eighteenth century used it, as the only available numerical model of English society before official statistics began. It was accepted as late as the 1800s as the appropriate framework for the anatomy of the English body politic. But it has only now begun to be realised what a remarkable feat it was for him to have drawn up the one and only attempt at a complete social description ever made anywhere in pre-industrial

Europe, and to have done so 150 years before the Registrar-General began to collect the mass of complicated evidence which we now think is necessary for the purpose.

Even now the source of that *Scheme*, a finished work called *Natural and Political Observations upon the State and Condition of England, 1696*, by Gregory King, Esq., Lancaster Herald, is very little known. It was not even printed until the early nineteenth century.[19] The date 1695 on the title of the manuscript; the knowledge, which we also owe to Professor Glass, that King had access to some of the returns under the 1694 Act; the knowledge that the best of them yet recovered, that for King's own native city of Lichfield in 1695, may have been drawn up under his direction; and the presence of this return along with several others amongst King's papers: all these facts seem to point to one conclusion. The evidence produced by the 1694 Act, or at least part of it may well have been used by Gregory King to make up his *Scheme* and was the basis of the other tables in his treatise.

Not only then did a complete series of listings of the inhabitants of all the settlements in England once exist, but a very acute contemporary made out from the evidence an abstract of the total social structure. This was not the only source used by King. Indeed there are signs that he had some difficulty in getting access to what he wanted from the 1695 returns: he certainly used the central Hearth Tax records. It is not clear that all the returns made under the 1694 Act were ever assembled in London, and the search for *certificates* will have to continue all over the country, in depositories of every type; the documents can be recognised from their dates, their titles and usually from their form. Columns headed 'Titles', 'Burials', etc., are often drawn alongside the list of names. In constructing the analytic tables about to be described, we have been much influenced by the work of Gregory King and so by the framework of this particular census-type enquiry made between 1695 and 1705. This fell within the interlude when 'Political Arithmetic' was a preoccupation of English scientists, administrators and men of letters. Some of our tables are specifically designed to test particular numerical conclusions reached by King and set out in the tables of his *Observations*. It may be added that when King's figures are independently tested in this way most of

177

them look right. Some of them are so accurate, that when there is a discrepancy we are disposed to question our evidence rather than King's claims.

But there are points at which we have found it difficult up to now to confirm the numerical conclusions of this very early and very well informed demographer. One of them, rather unfortunately, is in the important matter of the size of household, where King maintains an overall figure of 4·05 for the mean number of persons whilst we are unable to confirm a general mean of less than 4·5. But such facts as these cannot concern us here. Let us turn then to the first of the forms which are used in the analysis of social structure from listings of inhabitants, listings made, that is to say, before 1841.

This form, Community Listing Form (CLF, 1st ed.) is reproduced here, made out for Sampson's listing of Clayworth, 1676. It has to be filled in twice. All analytical work on listings of inhabitants is done from photographs of the original (xerography is usually perfectly adequate) and the first purpose of the CLF is to register the photograph. The block V TABLES WHICH CAN BE FILLED is omitted at the stage of registration. But it may become necessary to fill in the whole form again and not simply block V when analysis is complete, since the answers to questions under headings other than V are often uncertain until the listing has been thoroughly explored. One of the original duplicates is attached to the photograph of the listing, and the other goes to help make up the catalogue of available documents.

The purpose of giving approximate answers to questions on the CLF when the photograph is received is to decide how much work will have to go into analysing its contents, and how reliable and complete the information yielded is likely to be. It must be evident that the full exploitation of a listing of a large community, where a great deal of social structural evidence is forthcoming, is inevitably a long and intricate business. Though not as hungry of time as the process of reconstitution of families from parish registers, it runs a similar risk, that the effort expended may not seem in the end to justify the results obtained. Still, we find that work of this kind is to some extent its own reward, since all the facts to be gone over are facts about persons, and often very interesting facts too.

COMMUNITY LISTING FORM   CLF 1st ed.
(Two to be completed)   Date _1676_

me of Community (with County) _Clayworth, Notts._

hereabouts of Original   Reference   Number of Inhabitants (approx.)
Parish Chest   _401_

TYPE OF DOCUMENT	
	a. Return under Act of 1694
✔	b. Return under Compton Census, 1676
	c. List made by Incumbent (other than b) Specify ....
	d. Fiscal Document (other than a) Specify ....
	e. Document of any other Description Specify ....

METHOD OF COMPILATION		
✔ a. House to House Survey		b. Muster
c. Recall		d. Other, Specify ....
e. Unknown		

ORDER OF LISTING		
a. By Social Standing		b. Geographical
✔ c. Alphabetical		d. Other, Specify ....
e. Unclear		

DETAILS GIVEN

	Yes	No		
	✔		a. Families Clearly Divided .	_Divisions obvious from alpha-betical order of families_
	✔		b. Names of all Inhabitants Given	
		✔	c. Only Adults (over 16) Listed	
	SOME		d. Callings of Family Heads Given	

	All	Some	None	
	✔			e. Sexes Given
			✔	f. Ages Given

g. Familial Categories Given for :-

✔ Wives	_Some_ Servants	_Some_ · Kin	
✔ Sons/Daughter	In-Laws	Lodgers	

TABLES WHICH CAN BE FILLED (COMPLETED AFTERWARD)
[If Table can be completely filled, UNDERLINE its number: if it can be partially filled, ENCIRCLE]

(1) Occupations   13 Solitaries

_2, 3_ Size of household   _14, 15, 16, 17, 18_ Resident Children

_4, 5_ Status of person   19 Orphans

_6_ In-Laws   20, 21, 22, 22a, 23 Servants

_7, 8, 9, 10, 11, 12_ Composition 25, 26, 27, 28, 29, 30 Ages
                    of households 31, 32, 33 Marriage

OTHER DOCUMENTS RELATING TO COMMUNITY

✔	a. Parish Registers	✔	c. Poor Laws Documents _Town Book (see below)_
✔	b. Other Listing(s) _1688_		d. Others Specify .... _ditto._

ANY FURTHER NOTES ON LISTING, ESPECIALLY JUDGEMENT OF RELIABILITY   _Reliability: excellent_

ayworth Town Book (in Parish) contains annual elections and accounts, including poor
s accounts; accounts of churchwardens, etc. This listing was first published in 1911. viii 64

Figure 5.1

179

The CLF is divided into blocks which are separated by double lines. The first block, the heading, should cause no difficulty. The date of the listing might have to be left approximate until some work has been done, and the rough number of inhabitants might sometimes be laborious to estimate. All the questions asked in block I–IV have been discussed in the course of the present chapter, and those in I–III can often be answered finally from a superficial survey of the document. Nevertheless II METHOD OF COMPILATION will usually have to be checked as 'Unknown' even after completing analysis. All these answers bear on the issues surveyed above, as to how long the listing took, whether it covered those and only those present in the community on a particular day, whether in fact the list is 'real' or 'ideal'. No actual opportunity is given on the CLF for expressing an opinion on this question. But unless it is possible to put a note under VII to the effect that the document appears to be 'real', a true census-type document of the modern sort, the assumption will always be that it is 'ideal'. All fiscal documents, for example, including those under the 1694 Act are almost inevitably 'ideal'.

Block IV DETAILS GIVEN demands answers to a series of specific questions, all of which must be tackled, and requires, therefore, a rather more searching examination of the document. Answers given here are the indications which make it possible to decide which analytic tables can be filled, and some of them are stoppers. We have already seen that if IV*a*, on the division between families, is checked 'no', a great proportion of the work we could otherwise do becomes impossible. The usefulness of a listing is very much reduced if any of the boxes in lines *b* to *g* have to be checked under 'No', ('Yes' for *c*), 'None' or even 'Some'.[20] The value of the Clayworth listing of 1676, as we have said, is noticeably impaired because only a 'Some' answer is possible under *d*. The status structure of the community is thereby left uncertain, though we have tried to compensate for this as will be shown below. A very great deal more is lost because 'None' has to be checked in line *f*: a whole area of the study of Clayworth in 1676 society becomes impossible because of this.

Omitting Block V at this first stage, we proceed to Block VI and reach the point where information about the settlement other than that contained in the listing becomes crucial. Almost any document mentioning the name, age, occupation, familial relationship and so on of any member of the village community at or about the time of the listing may be of value in working the series of tables listed in Block V. Rent rolls, records of the Court Leet, or (in the eighteenth and early nineteenth centuries) Poll Books can all yield useful evidence. Poor Law papers are likely to contain much valuable material and if it should happen, as it does in the case of Clayworth, that another listing exists, that is clearly of the greatest significance. Nevertheless, it is right that the parish registers should be in position *a* under this heading. If the registers survive from the period covering the lifetime of the eldest person alive at the time of the listing, and for the period during which the youngest is likely to survive (that is, say, eighty-five years either way), then a very great deal of evidence is available to supplement that in the document itself. Even an incomplete register covering only a year or two on one side or other of the census date is well worth having.

It may take a little while to determine whether the parish registers are available and what other helpful evidence exists. When these points have been decided, and the relevant information entered in Blocks V and VII, it is possible to proceed to the actual analysis, that is to the work which will go towards filling up the series of thirty-three tables whose contents are briefly indicated by the titles given in Block V of the CLF. Only after all this is done will the final block of the CLF be filled in with a judgment of reliability and, if required, any further notes. Before we go on to describe this intricate process we must pause and take breath.

First, let it be made clear that we are about to present a tentative sketch of a research programme which at the time of writing is still being designed. For that reason description will not be complete, and no claim is being made that the reader can learn from this account exactly what should be done if he is to reproduce the analysis under discussion without further information. Only a few of the series of tables we are devising are reproduced, and those, naturally, are tables which we believe may survive further discussion and criticism. But we feel at liberty to reformulate any of the tables now provisionally in use, and to add to the series as necessary. Analysis of this kind has had nothing like the history which the process of reconstitution of families from parish registers has already experienced at the hands of demographers and documentary scholars such as L. Henry and M. Fleury in France and others in our own country.

One of the objects of discussing this process in print in this preliminary way is to invite revisions and criticisms. Another is to try to ensure uniformity of category and convention, which is as important here as it is to the rest of historical-demographic study. A third is to ensure that the evidence we shall finally be publishing will be in a form most useful to everyone who finds himself in need of information about societies without statistics – sociologists, psychologists and social scientists generally, as well as demographers and historians. We are particularly anxious that the transition from the period before the census to that when the census was being taken, the period which Mr Armstrong writes about, shall be a smooth one. We want to compare, in fact, his results with ours, which means comparing pre-industrial with industrialising society in England, and we want to compare like with like.

In the second place, we shall be sketching out a method which, if it were written out in full, would, we believe, extort the greatest possible amount of relevant fact from the evidence. When it comes to submitting it to analysis by computer, a stage not yet reached at Cambridge but which we expect will be approached by the time this *Introduction* is in print, we hope that we shall be able to examine every possible useful variable along with every other. But this does not mean that nothing can be learnt from the provisional tables now in use, nor that the whole intricate and still undefined operation has to be under-taken before anything useful and reasonably accurate can be gained. Directly two numerical facts are known about a listing, the number of people and the number of households, then one figure of social structural importance is already apparent, the mean size of household. A very little further counting would reveal roughly what was the distribution between households, the number and percentage of servants and so on.

For these reasons the series under design take the form of a collection of general summary tables illustrating various aspects of the social structure, each followed by further tables illustrating the same or related points in greater detail or under different heads. Many, though not as yet all, of the main tables have sub-tables attached to them, and these may be added to at will to accord with the requirements of particular research projects. Not every table is of equal social structural importance. The filling out of main tables 1, 2, 4, 7, 14, 15, 20, 25 and, if possible, 26, would give an overall impression of the structure of society at that place at that time, adequate for most historical purposes. This would be so even if they were filled in without taking the preliminary steps we shall mention and without attempting to supplement the listing itself with other evidence (see below 189–191 for full list of tables).

These preliminary steps are as follows, and they are, of course, essential steps when the CLF indicates that the listing contains a great deal of information and looks on the face of it reliable. First the listing should be carefully copied by hand, numbering each household and each person separately, and leaving a column in which corrections and presumptions will be inserted. Presumptions are inferences about details not made clear by the words of the listing. Numeration should be by household with individuals under households; thus in household number 86, the householder is 86.1, his wife is 86.2, the first child listed 86.3, etc. Every care should be taken in copying the entries on the list that the exact spelling of each name and each description should be reproduced. After the copying is complete, every individual name should be put on to a card or slip, together with its number and all other relevant information. This, of course, is only possible to do in full where the names of all the inhabitants are given, but it should be carried out even if quite a proportion of the names are absent. These are the slips which will be used to extract information from the parish registers, and they should be kept in alphabetical order for this purpose.

If there are no parish registers, or if they have both been published and indexed, the investigator may think it un-necessary to make out slips for each inhabitant. These are so useful for other purposes, however, that he is urged not to take this short-cut, but to proceed, with his slips in his hand, to read the registers carefully for twenty or thirty years on either side of the date of the listing, transferring relevant information in full. It is possible, of course, to go much further forward or back from the listing date, but rarely worthwhile to do so. The whole of an entry should be copied on to the slip bearing the name of one of the inhabitants, because even the most casual fact, such as the village from which a bridegroom came or the calling pursued by a baby's father, may help in the analysis. For this same reason, that every detail is wanted although it may not have been included when editing the registers for print, the original registers should be used whenever possible. When this process is complete, two important decisions can be made.

One is on the precise date of the listing. If, for example, the year is 1676 and one Robert Smith is recorded on the listing as being present, but is given in the registers as being buried on November 1 of that year, we can be fairly confident that the 'census' was carried out before the last week of October. If, moreover, James Godwin is recorded on the listing and is registered as baptised between October 24 and 31 then the date must be between those two. Good fortune such as this in the relations between registers and listing cannot often be expected and dating may only be possible to within a few weeks. There can be complications too, complications which have a bearing on the time which elapsed during the taking of the list. It may record the name of an individual who died in August and the name of another who was not baptised until December, in which case we must assume that the counting went on over a period of months, or that the list has been corrected, imperfectly, at some time after its composition.

The other is a decision of a general sort about the reliability and character of the listing. Discrepancies between the ages of persons appearing on the list and their ages as calculated from registers may be slight, or they may be considerable. People may appear in the register who seem certainly to have been present when the listing occurred but who were not listed – they may have had children both before and after the indicated date, or buried a child at the approximate time. This evidence should be carefully judged, then perhaps compared with that of documents other than the registers, and a degree of reliability decided upon, which forms the basis of the judgment which will be written at the foot of the CLF. It is possible, of course, that an omission from the list, shall we say, of the family whose child was baptised so close to the census day, may not indicate incompleteness but the fact that the listing was 'real' rather than 'ideal'. The family concerned may indeed have been out of the parish on that particular day, and not included although they were normally resident.

The fresh information from the registers is now transferred from the slips to the handwritten copy of the list and inserted against the name of each affected inhabitant in the column reserved for the purpose. After this the necessary presumptions are actually made where possible for every person whose name or description was either incomplete in the original listing, or not present at all. These presumptions are of various kinds and may be considerable in number. Some are very straightforward and quite unlikely to be false. When a man of forty-five, for example, is shown as head of a household, and a woman bearing his name and the age of forty-three comes next to him, it is a safe presumption that she was his wife, although that fact is not given: it is a clear and certain presumption, of course, if their marriage has been found in the register.

But other presumptions, though necessary for analytic purposes, are far more dubious. If in the same household a woman aged seventy-five appears after some children have been listed, bearing the same name as the man of forty-five, then it is a probable presumption, no more, that she is his mother, a resident mother-in-law. But if she has a different name, though she is still of an appropriate age, it is only a possible presumption that she is the wife's mother. In either case, of course, evidence from the registers may turn the possible presumption into a near-certainty. We have found it important to assume that the person first mentioned is in fact the householder, and it is necessary to decide how each of the other members of the household is related to the head. If such decisions should prove impossible, the household in question must be looked upon as irregular.

The experience of the investigator, his knowledge of the community and its documents, the time he is willing to spend, will all enter into this process of making presumptions, and we shall go no further here in announcing rules. Good practice recommends that the degrees of probability just mentioned should be adopted, especially in the case of suspected in-laws, and kinsfolk of all sorts, as also with suspected servants. This is because the contrast between our own society and the society to which the listing refers seems likely to be particularly interesting and important in these particulars. Whereas, as might be expected, our ancestors had more servants in their households than we do and looked on them as members of the family, they seem to have had surprisingly few in-laws or kinfolk, even grandchildren, living with them. The tables illustrating these features are always better if made out twice, once with and once without presumptions. The degrees of presumption we have adopted (near-certain, probable, possible) make as many as four alternative sets of results a possibility for the specialist.

What follows is an example of one of the Clayworth households in 1676 as it appears on the master list, with the presumptions added:

List	*Presumptions, etc.*
86.	
86.1 Luke Wilson	*Householder*, buried 28–12–1676 (P.R.)
	Presumed Yeoman (R.B.)
86.2 Mary, his wife	Buried 29–11–1679 (P.R.)
86.3 Eliz. yr. daughter	
86.4 Rich. Hallyfax	Almost certainly a servant.
86.5 Tho. Morris	Ditto
86.6 Robt. Allen	Ditto

None of the Wilson household survived in Clayworth until 1688 otherwise his presence in the later list would have been recorded in a second column. The only further information on the household we have been able to find other than in the P.R. is in the *Rector's Book* (R.B.). Nevertheless the position of Richard Hallyfax, Thomas Morris and Robert Allen in the household makes it almost certain that they were servants, servants in husbandry. The very lack of further evidence about them strongly suggests that they can have been nothing else.

Luke Wilson's personal slip is now reproduced:

> Wilson, Luke.   86.1
> *Householder*
> Buried 28–12–1676 (P.R.)
> Presumed Yeoman (R.B.)

It will be clear that no information appears on the list which is omitted on the slip, whose great advantage is that it enables tables to be filled in by sorting rather than by tallying.

A further maxim is that every missing name or description should be commented upon in the presumptions column. The four males in Luke Wilson's household could not have been left without comment, and if 'Mary' had been omitted in the line devoted to his wife, it would have had to be filled in from the parish registers. Those gaps for which no safe guess can be made from any evidence, in the registers or elsewhere, should be marked 'Not recovered' (NR). Some convention may perhaps have to be adopted to distinguish information added from the Parish Registers (PR) from that from other sources. When the last inhabitant has been decided upon in this way, the presumptions should be copied on to the slips. This is the final preliminary operation, though things may come to light in the course of filling up the tables to correct or extend the original presumptions. It goes without saying that every document, the slips as well as the full copy, should be scrupulously preserved, so that anyone wishing to discover what was presumed and how information was built up will be able to do so.

He may often find that a very great deal of the analysis has, in fact, been based in presumptions in this way, or would have been impossible unless extensive presuming had taken place and much information taken from the parish registers. The six listings of the inhabitants of Cogenhoe between 1618 and 1628, for example, contain no descriptions whatsoever; everyone treated as a wife, a child, a servant, a mother-in-law is so by presumption, confirmed where possible from the extant, unprinted registers. But since there were six listings in this case, the process of inference was found particularly rewarding and reliable by Mrs Susan Stewart who carried out the experimental analysis of these listings. Names of males, who in one year were still in their parents' families, in the positions where children would be expected, would in another year be found at the head of a household, written over a feminine name traceable as now missing from the daughters of another household: the register would confirm the marriage. Males and females with surnames different from those of the family would appear at the bottom of the household one year, and be replaced by

187

different names the next; they could only have been servants. In fact, we are more confident of these Cogenhoe results than we are of some for those listings which contain more detail, but also show extensive omissions. They will form an important source for the collected list of conventions about presumption, which will have to be prepared so as finally to standardise practice.

Two further comments must be made on this preliminary process. The use of other documents to amend or extend the listing itself may introduce biases of various kinds. It may be possible to recover information on property holders only, or paupers, or those who happened to take part in a law suit affecting a single occupation. We recognise this possibility but the further information is so valuable, sometimes permitting us to fill in a table which would otherwise have to be left blank, that we find it acceptable. The other comment concerns the reading of the parish registers, especially reading forward, after the date of the listing.

This process is liable to introduce a selectiveness of a different kind because women change their names at marriage whereas men do not. The parish registers at Clayworth contain no record of the baptism of Mary Wilson or of her husband Luke. If they had been present, however, we should have picked up his age but not hers, because she was not Mary Wilson at birth. Moreover the Luke Wilson who died on 28 December 1676 could have been a different person from the Luke Wilson on the list, if it were not for the fact that in this particular case we have other evidence to confirm the identification. Those who do read through parish registers in this way will often find that a name like Wilson occurs frequently enough to leave doubt as to whether a presumption can be made. Mary Wilson, moreover, might have left the village, remarried and then have returned to Clayworth to be buried: the words of the burial entry of 29 November 1679 'Mary Wilson widow' have to be supplemented by other information to make it virtually certain that they refer to her. And when it comes to the presumed servants, it would undoubtedly be hazardous without confirmatory evidence to presume that a Thomas Morris baptised in the 1660s and buried in the 1680s was indeed the Thomas Morris in the Wilson household on the 1676 list.

The Study of Social Structure from Listings of Inhabitants

These difficulties are likewise marginal and we have no wish to exaggerate their importance. But we must not overlook the fact that some of the obscurities might be removed if the families in a listing were to be reconstituted fully in the way described in the last chapter. Deeper analysis of the social structure would be possible in this way since quite unsuspected relationships might also be discovered. Faced with one of the Clayworth documents a social anthropologist might be curious to know, for example, whether the servants were in fact related to their masters, and this type of rather remote linkage between persons could only be shown up by reconstitution. But experience with this village shows that such information is not easily obtained, and we have decided to be content with the reading of the registers in the simpler way already described. Quite apart from extending and amending his evidence, the process is important to the investigator because it gets him used to the community, its names, its occupations and so on.

The analytic tables, together with their sub-tables which we are devising for the full analysis of social structure from lists of inhabitants cover the following subjects:

STATUS AND OCCUPATION

Table 1. Households by Social and Occupational Status.
    1.1 Numbers and Classification of Occupations.

SIZE OF HOUSEHOLD

    2. Overall Size of Household.
    2.1 Size of Household by Social and Occupational Status.
    2.2 Size of Household by Age of Head.
    3. Distribution of Persons by Detailed Size of Household.

MARITAL STATUS

    4. Marital Status of Heads of Household.
    5. Status of Persons (for comparison with Gregory King).

KIN

    6. Proportion of Households with Kin.
    6.1 Number and description of Kin.
    6.2 Households with Kin by Status and Occupation.

COMPOSITION OF HOUSEHOLD

7. Composition of Households Headed by Married Couples.
8.   ,,   ,,   ,,   ,,   ,, Widowers.
9.   ,,   ,,   ,,   ,,   ,, Widows.
10. Composition of Households Headed by Unmarried Persons, by Sex of Head.
11. Proportion of Households of Irregular Composition.
12. Irregular Households by Marital Status of Head.

SOLITARY PEOPLE

13. Proportion and Status of Solitaries.

CHILDREN

14. Juveniles and Dependents by Sex and as a Proportion of the Population.
15. Proportion of Households with Resident Offspring.
15.1 Size of Sibling Group.
15.2 Size of Sibling Group by Social and Occupational Status.
15.3 Size of Sibling Group by Age of Father.
15.4 Size of Sibling Group by Age of Mother.
16. Unmarried Offspring Aged 16 and Above in Parental Household by Sex.
17. Unmarried Offspring Aged 16 and Above in Parental Household by Size of Group.
18. Unmarried Offspring Aged 16 and Above in Parental Household by Social and Occupational Status.

ORPHANS

19. Orphans by Sex and as a Proportion of All Offspring.
19.1 Orphans Living with One Parental Figure.
19.2 Orphans Living with Two Parental Figures.

SERVANTS

20. Servants by Sex and as a Proportion of the Population.
21. Servants by Description.
22. Proportion of Households with Servants.
22.1 Households with Servants, by Social and Occupational Status.
23. Servants by Groups.
23.1 Composition of Servant Groups.
23.2 Ages of Servants.

LODGERS

24.   Lodgers by Sex and as a Proportion of the Population.
24.1 Individual Lodgers and Lodging Households by Social and Occupational Status.
24.2 Households per House.
24.3 Solitary Lodgers by Sex.
24.4 Solitary Lodgers by Size of Group.
24.5 Size of Household, Landlords and Lodgers.
24.6 Servants and Children, Landlords and Lodgers.
24.7 Landlords by Social and Occupational Status.

AGE AND SEX

25.   Adults, Children and Population by Sex.
25.1 Population by Age and Sex Over and Under Age 16 (for comparison with Gregory King).
26.   Composition of Population by Age and Sex.
26.1 Population by Age, Sex, Social and Occupational Status.
27.   Means and Medians of Ages by Sex.
28.   Distribution of Persons by Age, Sex and Marital Status.
29.   Proportion of Quinquennial Age Groups 0–44 in Parental Households, in Service and Heading Households.
30.   Age at Marriage, by Sex.
31.   Maximum Notional Age of Wives at Birth of First Offspring.
32.   Proportion of Spouses Certainly Remarried.
33.   Times Remarried.

The series may seem long and somewhat formidable, but it is intended, as we have said, to wring the last possible item of social structural information from each list, and the filling in of select tables only will be satisfactory for many purposes. There are moreover very few lists so far known which can be treated at anything like full length, and none for which all the tables can be filled up. The composition of the series has been and continues to be exacting, and it will be evident that it is still by no means final. The difficulties are not simply due to the vagaries of the evidence, though the lack of uniformity in the practices of list-takers creates many of them, and makes overlapping between tables inevitable. This is particularly so in the matter of ages, for it is important to be able to compare similar things in those lists which provide ages for every individual and in those lists which merely indicate who were mature and who were not (see for instance table 14 below). Furthermore, if the results are to bring out the significant features of the social structure of each settlement, and to illustrate the important points of contrast between settlement and settlement, period and period, the tables must in effect constitute an anatomy of social structure in themselves. They must be so constructed as to represent schematically not only society as the men of the day thought of it, but as twentieth century social scientists might think of it if it existed now.

But we are not at liberty to use the Registrar-General's Social Classes and his Classification of Occupations, as Mr Armstrong does for his work. No modification of these schemes seems possible which would be appropriate to pre-industrial society, especially in the sixteenth or seventeenth centuries. Our primary object is to present the facts from every community, as registered in its listing, in such a form as will make each comparable with every other, and with later evidence about the social structure of England up to our own day. We have two secondary objects also. One is to provide a check on Gregory King's work by preparing some tables in the form which he chose, and filled in, for the whole of England in 1688; this was particularly important in framing tables 5 and 25. The other is at the moment distant and may perhaps seem too ambitious. We hope that our series may in the end make it possible to compare English society in earlier times with pre-industrial societies which can be observed in our contemporary world. It goes without saying that the tables are intended to make possible illuminating comparisons with communities in eighteenth century France, for example, or in seventeenth century Italy or Spain, or in early twentieth century Russia, even in Meiji Japan and in China before the Kuomintang. But we also hope that with appropriate additions they may conceivably be used to make comparisons of English communities before 1841 with village communities in twentieth-century societies which have fundamentally different kinship systems and social arrangements, located in, say, Ethiopia, or in Burma.

The series, therefore, is flexible, contractible and extensible. Any user is at liberty to add sub-tables as he wishes, and to leave blank those which are inappropriate, or for which he has no evidence or insufficient evidence. But in order to maintain consistency throughout the series, and comparability between results from all listings, it is essential that the same term shall always mean the same thing. Along with the final set of tables, therefore, will go a list of standard definitions, laying it down, for example, that a 'bachelor' is always a male person of mature age who shows no sign of ever having been married, or an 'orphan' an immature person for whom there is evidence that

Settlement *Clayworth* Date *1676* Pop. *401*

Table 5. Status of Persons (for comparison with Gregory King).

	Number	Percent	King (1696) Percents
Husbands and Wives	134	33·4	34%
Widowers	7	1·7	1½%
Widows	24	6·0	4½%
Children	127	31·7	45%
Servants	67	16·7	10½%
Bachelors	18	4·5	
Spinsters	16	4·0	4%
Lodgers			
Sojourners			
Not Recovered	8①	2·0	
Total	401	100·0	100%

King's percentage from <u>Natural and Political Observations</u>, 1696

Notes

① Includes the following relatives of the head of household: 1 Brother · 2 sister · 1 Nephew · 1 "Female relative". 1 "Kinsman". and 1 "Kinswoman".

Figure 5.2

193

Settlement *Ealing* Date 1599   Pop. **426**

Table 25. Population by Age and Sex, Under and Over Age 16.
(For purposes of comparison with Gregory King)

Age	Male		Female		Total		King
	Number	Percent	Number	Percent	Number	Percent	Percent
Under 1	7	3·1	5	2·5	12	2·8	3.1
Under 5	29	12·7	21	10·7	50	11·7	14.9
Under 10	52	22·7	40	20·3	92	21·6	26.7
Under 16	91	39·7	68	34·5	159	37·3	40.6
Above 16	138	60·3	129	65·5	267	62·7	59.5
Above 21	112	48·9	106	53·9	218	51·2	49.0
Above 25	103	44·9	84	42·6	187	43·9	43.4
Above 60	16	7·0	10	5·1	26	6·1	10.9
Unknown							
Total	229		197		426		

Division of Population by Sex.

	Number	Percent of Population
Male	229	53·8
Female	197	46·2
Total	426	100·0

Notes

Figure 5.2

one or both biological parents were dead at the time of the listing. Once again, it will often happen that a new listing contains a category of person for which no definition yet exists, so that the investigator will have to create a definition, carefully recording what he has done at the foot of the relevant table and in his copy of the standard definitions.

We hope that the list of tables we have presented does contain a workable beginning of a series which will in fact make possible all the comparisons which we have discussed, and illustrate the differences between the social structure at various stages of history, especially in respect of those changes brought about by progressive industrialisation. It may sometimes happen, of course, that a sub-table made up by the investigator will

be of far greater importance to his work than the main table
provided in the series. Nevertheless we would hope that he
would fill in the main table also. It seems likely, for example,
that the investigator of the social structure of an industrial
village in early Victorian Lancashire would require a different
set of categories for *Status and Occupation* from those given in
our table 1, and that he would add a table 1.2 for the purpose.
The difficulty here would be that, even after he had completed
our table 1 to make comparison possible, he would want to
use as a control for status and occupation in such tables as 2.1,
6.2, 15.2, etc., the categories provided in his own table rather
than those provided in the series. He would find himself, therefore, making a succession of additions of his own and doing a
certain amount of work twice over. On the other hand he could
use the tables dealing with *Composition of Household* without
modification.

The pattern of the series is to proceed from the general to the
particular, and from those particulars which most listings are
likely to contain, to those which only some exceptional ones
will ever mention. A few notes on the tables reproduced here
should make it clear what the investigator actually does and
what we have thought it particularly important to bring out in
composing the tables. It will be remembered that by the time
the filling up process begins both a complete copy of the list
is available, with presumptions and corrections added, and also
a complete set of slips, a slip for every name, when the list is a
nominal one. Much of the work can be done simply by sorting
the slips.

In the case of table 1, for example, all that is usually necessary
is to sort out the slips marked 'Householder', and then sort
these slips into eight piles, for 'Gentlemen', 'Clergy', 'Yeomen',
'Husbandmen', 'Craftsmen', 'Labourers' and 'Not Stated'. The
first words which are written on this table are those written on
every other made out for the listing; the name of the community,
the date of the listing and the population, at the top of the page.
It will be seen that certain of the categories used are explained
in a footnote to the table, though the full information as to
those who should be classed in the various categories will be
contained in the list of definitions which accompanies every set
of tables. The object of these shorter notes appearing on the

Settlement *Clayworth* Date *1676* Pop. *401*

Table 1. Households by Social and Occupational Status.

	Number of Households	Percent
1. Gentlemen, etc.	*4*	*4·1*
2. Clergy	*1*	*1·1*
3. Yeomen }1 4. Husbandmen	*17*	*17·3*
5. Craftsmen	*22*	*22·5*
6. Labourers	*18*	*18·5*
7. Paupers		
8. Others		
Not Stated ²	*36*	*37·0*
Total	*98*	*100·0*

Gentlemen, etc. include all nobility, baronets, knights, esquires, gents, persons called Mr. or Mrs., doctors, servants of the crown, etc. Widows go under Not Stated.   Others   include factory workers, if present.

Notes

1. *Neither term was in the 1676 list; households with servants and with no stated occupations are included here, (see table 1·1)*

2. *Includes two women described as 'single woman'*

Figure 5.3

tables is to make it immediately clear what is meant by a category which requires explanation. The investigator is left room at the bottom of the table to provide any further essential guidance, and in this case it was found necessary to explain who have been taken as yeomen and husbandmen in Clayworth in 1676. If other explanations had been needed to show what had been done to arrive at the figures put into the categories, they would have been added too. The table is complete only when the investigator is confident that his work on it could be reproduced by a successor with no further explanation from him.

Obviously this last principle is a difficult one to follow, and table 1 clearly raises at the outset of the series all the challenging issues which have just been referred to. Why these seven social categories, it may well be asked, these and not others? Is it justifiable to ask the investigator to classify every occupation in one or other of them? Where would families of merchants be classed, for example, or shopkeepers, or those intended by the intriguing description which appears in Gregory King's *Scheme* for 1688, 'Persons in Liberal Arts and Sciences'? The only answer we can give is that the categories in table 1 seem to us to be the smallest convenient number which fits the evidence we have so far surveyed. Classing the families of merchants with

Settlement *Clayworth* Date *1676* Population *401*

Table 1.1   Numbers and Classification of Occupations.

Occupation	Number of Households	Category in Table 1.	Occupation	Number of Households	Category in Table 1.
Bricklayer	1	5	Smith	3	5
Butcher	1	5	Singlewoman	2	not stated
Cooper	1	5	Tailor	2	5
Gentleman	4	1	Weaver	4	5
Yeoman & Husbandman ①	17	4.	Wright	3	5
Labourer	18	6			
Pindar	1	5	Total	64	
Rector	1	2			
Sheppard	4	5	Not Stated	34	
Shoemaker	1	5	Total Households	98	

All occupations must be listed. Where an individual within a household is given an occupation other than that of the head of household, this must be noted below.

Notes

① Neither term was used in the census list; households with servants and no stated occupations were included here: see table 1. One head of household stated "parish-clark" included here.

Figure 5.4

the gentlemen, for example, may be unexpected, but it is a fact that all merchants of standing had the title Mr which was a mark of gentry. Classing those in liberal arts, etc. (if ever we found families to correspond) and shopkeepers as craftsmen would also seem to correspond with contemporary usage.

But in any case the user can see exactly what has been done by referring to table 1.1, *Numbers and Classification of Occupations,* where every description found in the list is reproduced, and the category to which it was assigned in table 1 is indicated. It is appropriate that the classification adopted for table 1 should be designed for the rural settlements which account for nearly all those we have so far analysed. When we come to study the listings for London in the 1690s, we may have to introduce a further table, table 1.2, with a special set of categories. As we have already said, any investigator is at liberty to add what tables he pleases for his own special purposes, though it is important that he fill in those tables we suggest as far as his evidence allows, so that comparability can be maintained.

This is not the place to discuss the intricate problem of status, class and occupation, and we must now move to the second general subject covered by the tables, size of household. Table 2

Settlement *Clayworth* ate *1676* Pop. *401*

Table 2. Overall Size of Household.

Size:	Households		Persons	
	Number	Percent	Number	Percent
1 to 3	47	48·0	119	29·5
4 to 5	32	32·5	144	36·0
6 and over	19	19·5	138	34·5
Total	98	100·0	401	100·0

Mean size of Household: 4·09

Notes

Figure 5.5

198

presents in brief form what seems to us to be a very important feature of the social structure of every English community up to 1841, the mean size of household and the overall distribution of persons in small, medium and large households. It illustrates the extent to which the experience of a high proportion of individuals (in Clayworth in 1676 it will be seen to have been 34·5 per cent) was of living in large households, with six or more members, although a good majority of households (here over 80 per cent) were of smaller size than this, and the mean size rarely reached 5 (here 4·09). Once more the singling out of this feature as significant is a matter of judgment on our part, judgment of the social structure as a whole, as we have got to know it so far. The phenomenon under examination is the loss of

Settlement *Clayworth* Date *1676* Pop. *401*

Table 2.1   Size of Household and Social Status.

Number of Persons in Household:

Social Status:	1	2	3	4	5	6 and over
Gentlemen, etc.						*4*
Clergy			*1*			
Yeomen }① Husbandmen }			*2*	*3*	*1*	*11*
Craftsmen			*9*	*3*	*8*	*2*
Labourers		*4*	*7*	*4*	*2*	*1*
Paupers						
Others					*-*	
Not Stated	*6*	*6*	*13*	*5*	*5*	*1*
Total	*6*	*10*	*31*	*16*	*16*	*19*

Notes:

① For information concerning the use of these terms in the Clayworth census see Notes to Tables 1 and 1.1

Figure 5.6

199

persons going as servants from the humbler households to the more exalted ones. This exchange is presented in detail in table 2·1 where the categories of table 1 are used again, and the diminishing size of household down the social scale is illustrated. Not until table 3 (omitted here) are the details of household size presented, so that the user can see just how many people lived alone, how many in households of 2, 3 and 4 persons, and so on upwards.

With table 4 we begin the examination of the anatomy of the household, the kinship system, the propensity to marry, to lose spouses, to have children and keep servants, which is the main preoccupation of the whole series. Table 4 itself, as will be seen, merely registers how commonly the family and household in earlier times was, as now, usually headed by a married couple whose relationship provided the fundamental linkage for the whole domestic society. Earlier death, however, ensured that quite a proportion (here twenty-five per cent) were headed by widowed persons, and some of them, in our view exceptional

Settlement *Clayworth* Date *1676* Pop. *401*

Table 4. Marital Status of Heads of Household.

	Numbers	Percent
Married Couples	67	68·4
Widowers	7	7·1
Widows	18	18·5
Bachelors	4	4·1
Spinsters	2	2·0
Unspecified Men		
Unspecified Women		
Unclear*		
Total	98	100·0

*Describe where necessary.

Notes

Figure 5.7

200

ones, were headed by unmarried individuals. Table 5 (see page 193) is intended primarily to compare Gregory King's figures for the whole country in the 1690s with those we can prepare on this subject from the listing being examined. It is interesting and important, or so we believe, that King should introduce 'Servants' into this set of categories which corresponds roughly to what we think of as 'Marital Status', because it confirms the then universal association of the status of servants with the condition of celibacy. As we have said, King's estimated proportions often turn out to be very accurate for the communities we analyse, and his general proportion of servants (ten per cent) is of the right order too, as far as we can see.

Table 6 (not reproduced) is a first examination of the presence of kin in our ancestors' houses, testing the hypothesis that they were not more, but if anything less, liable to have their relatives living with them than we are. We are a little uncertain as yet

Settlement *Clayworth* Date *1676* Pop. *401*

Table 7. Composition of Households Headed by Married Couples.

Households composed of married couples and their:	Number	Percent
Offspring*, Relative(s), Servant(s).	2	3·0
Offspring, Relative(s).	2	3·0
Offspring, Servant(s)	17	25·0
Offspring only.	33	49·2
Relative(s), Servant(s).	1	1·5
Relative(s) only.	3	4·5
Servant(s) only.	4	6·0
Other Persons (including lodgers)		
Combinations of Above**		
Married couples living alone.	5	7·5
Total	67	100·0

*Offspring means resident offspring of whatever union and of whatever age, unmarried or married. Relatives means all other kin.

** Specify.

Notes

Figure 5.8

201

about the form of this table, and of all those up to number 12 which examine the composition of the household in detail. One of the difficulties is actually filling them in, though the use of the slip-sorting method already recommended makes them less tedious to work than might appear. Table 7 is the only one of this part of the series which we now present as an example. It will be seen from a glance at it that the dissection in tabular form of the composition of the household is an unwieldy business. But we have persisted in the process of trying to show what difference it made to the household if the head was widowed, or unmarried, and how often irregular households are found, because we believe that this has demographic value as well as social structural significance.

This is as far as it seems advisable to try the reader's patience with a commentary on the series whose headings are written out on pages 189–91 above. The remaining tables which we include here, numbers 14, 15, 20, 26 and 26.1 are, we believe, intelligible enough in themselves, at least with the hints which

Settlement ___Claywarth___ Date *1676* Pop. *401*

Table 14. Juveniles and Dependents* by Sex and as a Proportion of the Population.

	Number	Percent of Juveniles and Dependents	Percent of Population
Males	75	51·7	18·7
Females	70	48·3	17·4
Males and Females	145	100·0	36·1
Rest of Population	256		63·9
Total	401		100·0

*Includes all persons in offspring position in households, whether or not named as son or daughter, together with relatives of generation later than head of household (nephew, grandson, etc.), foster children, parish children etc., but not servants. Must be filled in where ages are given, even though persons in offspring position may have reached maturity.

Notes

Figure 5.9

202

Table 15. Proportion of Households with Resident Offspring.

Headed by:	Households with Offspring		Households without Offspring	
	Number	Percent of households	Number	Percent of Households
Married couples	54	55·1	13	13·3
Widowers	5	5·1	2	2·0
Widows	15	15·3	3	3·1
Bachelors			4	4·1
Spinsters			2	2·0
Unspecified males				
Unspecified females				
Total	74	75·5	24	24·5

Notes

Table 20. Servants by Sex as a Proportion of the Population.

	Number	Percent of Servants	Percent of Population
Males	43	64·2	10·7
Females	24	35·8	4·0
Males and Females	67	100·0	16·7
Rest of Pop.	334		83·3
Total	401		100·0

Notes

Figure 5.9

203

Table 26.   Composition of Population by Age and Sex.

Age	Male		Female		Total	
	Number	Percent	Number	Percent	Number	Percent
Under 1	7	3·1	5	2·6	12	2·8
1-4	22	9·7	16	8·1	38	8·9
5-9	23	10·0	19	9·7	42	9·7
10-14	31	13·5	25	12·7	56	13·2
15-19	30	13·1	16	8·1	46	10·8
20-24	13	5·7	32	16·2	45	10·6
25-29	18	7·9	12	6·1	30	7·0
30-34	21	9·2	11	5·6	32	7·5
35-39	8	3·5	14	7·1	22	5·2
40-44	14	6·1	8	4·1	22	5·2
45-49	2	·8	8	4·1	10	2·4
50-54	19	8·3	20	10·2	39	9·2
55-59	5	2·2	1	·5	6	1·4
60 and over.	16	7·0	10	5·1	26	6·1
Unknown						
Total	229	100·0	197	100·0	426	100·0

Notes

Settlement *Ealing* Date *1599* Pop.**426**

Table 26.1.   Means and Medians of Ages by Sex.

	Mean Age	Median Age	King
Males	25·5	20·3	
Females	26·1	23·2	
Total Population	25·8	21·8	27½ (mean)

Notes

Figure 5.9

204

have been given for earlier ones. It will be noticed that none of the set of seven tables and sub-tables numbered 24 and covering lodgers is presented. This is because we have so far found lodgers in sufficient numbers to make the tables worth tackling only in one place, and that is the city of London. There, not only individual lodgers, but lodging families, sometimes four lodging households to one landlord household, are a common feature. Some lodging families kept their own servants, but the listings ordinarily make it clear that the landlord was still master of the house. It will be noticed too that tables 25, 26 and 26.1 have not been filled up for Clayworth in 1676 as in the other examples we give, but for the village of Ealing in 1599. This, of course, is because William Sampson did not interest himself in the ages of his parishioners when he went the rounds with his church-wardens in April 1676, but the constables of Ealing did do so in 1599.

Tables 30 to 33 are somewhat different from the rest because they depend more directly than the others on the parish registers. They are included in the series as a check between the register and the listing as well as for the purposes of deciding matters of demographic importance, as in table 31 which attempts to re-cover the age of the mother at the birth of the first child of each marriage recorded in the listing. They are themselves checks on the reliability and consistency of the listing also, because it is not uncommon to find ages which are difficult to credit when the age of the first listed child is subtracted from the age of his mother. It is dubious, however, whether it will finally be advisable to retain these tables in the series at all.

Peter Laslett

NOTES

1 See H. Gill and E. L. Guilford, *The Rector's Book, Clayworth Notts.* (Nottingham 1911). Quotations here come from the original in the parish chest of Clayworth which shows that Sampson thought of his writing, which continued throughout his holding of the cure, as a *Register*. A full discussion of this document and of Sampson as a recorder of demographic evidence will be found in an article by Peter Laslett and John

205

Harrison, 'Clayworth & Cogenhoe' in *Historical Essays presented to David Ogg* (ed. H.E.Bell and R.L.Ollard: London 1962).

2 The listing of children not present in the family at the time of the census, might assist in the filling out of FRFs, for example. Preliminary, experimental attempts were made at Cambridge to reconstitute at Clayworth, and at Cogenhoe (see below), but, as was expected, the smallness of the parishes and the gaps in their registers made it unlikely that the results would have been of any value.

3 The initial object at Cambridge was to assemble lists from clearly pre-industrial times. But for the past year we have sought documents of any date up to 1841, and since the main text was completed our collection has grown rapidly. It now includes many places in Wiltshire and Westmorland. We would be glad to hear of any document which conforms to the description given in the text and we very much hope that any reader of this book who knows of the existence of such a list will let us know.

4 Sampson himself made it 411, the only numerical error we have found him in. See Laslett and Harrison, 'Clayworth & Cogenhoe', where the facts about turnover of population are analysed in some detail but only in a preliminary way.

5 Measured as a proportion of newcomers in the population at the end of the period; see Laslett and Harrison, 'Clayworth & Cogenhoe', where the figure is given as 52 per cent. Further work has been done on the Cogenhoe evidence by Mrs Susan Stewart. Her revised figure is higher than it would have been if the turnover at Cogenhoe between 1618 and 1628 had been the same as the turnover at Clayworth between 1676 and 1688.

6 Contained in J. Hutchins, *History of Dorset*, 4 vols., 2nd ed. (Gough and Nichols, 1796–1815). The exact date of this extraordinary document is not yet known, and the information it contains has yet to be studied.

7 This very valuable document was printed by K. J. Allison in the *Bulletin of the Institute of Historical Research*, xxxvi (1963). Since the above was written we have had notice of a listing of Poole in Dorset in 1575, also taken by the constables, and of another of parts of Coventry in 1520. We have become aware also that even earlier listings have survived for communities in other European countries.

8 Though Sampson did not actually make his return to his Archbishop until Thursday, April 20. The Compton census and its value for demographic history is being studied by Miss Ann

Whiteman, of Oxford, who discovered the Goodnestone document. See also C.W.Chalklin, 'The Compton Census of 1676: the Dioceses of Canterbury and Rochester', *Kent Records*, xvii, (Kent Arch. Soc.: Ashford 1960), 153–74.

9 See 'Clayworth & Cogenhoe' already quoted, translating a passage in Latin from J.S.Burn, *The History of Parish Registers in England* (1862), 212; the statement in the next sentence is from the same article. It has not been possible to trace the authority for Burn's quotation ('some old Rituals' is his phrase) since that article was written, but it is suspected that this was not, in fact, an English source, but a continental, Roman one. It is possible that Burn was using an English translation of a Roman ritual of some date after 1614, when, as I am informed by a great authority on these matters, Professor Mols of Louvain, the *Liber Status Animarum* was first prescribed. Some work has been done on such of these records as survive from parishes in Western Europe, particularly it would seem in Belgium, but none, as far as I know, on the lines laid down here. It is not clear that the practice was, in fact, confined to the period after 1614 in the continental Roman Church; indeed it seems more likely that it had been a custom for long before then, perhaps as is hinted in the text above an immemorial pastoral tradition, though varying from region to region, especially from diocese to diocese. This was certainly the case with the parish registers, which were part of the regulations of certain Western European dioceses for a very long time before they became the subjects of national legislation and of general ecclesiastical decree in the sixteenth and seventeenth centuries.

10 For example, the admirable guide by W.E.Tate, *The Parish Chest*, 3rd. printing, (Cambridge 1960) or John West, *Village Records* (London 1962).

11 For example, those of the huge Diocese of Lincoln; see C.W. Forster, *The State of the Church* (Lincoln Record Society: 1926); see also the Harleian Manuscripts in the British Museum, vol. 280, folios 157–72.

12 An example of such a set of returns for the Lincoln Diocese are those from the years 1706–21, published in *Speculum* 1, for the Diocese of London, one dating from 1723–48 is a set of documents in MS 9550 in the Guildhall Library. Lionel Munby's excellent pamphlet *Hertfordshire Population Statistics* (Herts. Local History Society: Hitchin 1964) lists these sources and is a remarkable demonstration of how unexpectedly plentiful demographic sources of this kind can be for a particular county.

13 L. M. Marshall, 'The Rural Population of Bedfordshire', *Publications of Bedfordshire Historical Record Society*, xvi (1934).

14 Original in the Staffordshire Record Office at Stafford, in the form of a copy made by William Salt.

15 See D.V.Glass, 'Gregory King and the Population of England and Wales at the end of the Seventeenth Century', *Eugenics Review*, xxxvii (1946) 170–83, and 'Gregory King's Estimate of the Population in England and Wales', *Pop. Stud.*, iii (1950) 338–74. His Victorian authority is R.E.Chester Waters, 'List of the Inhabitants of Melbourne, Derbyshire, 1695', *Journal of the Derbyshire Natural History Society*, vii (1885). It is typical of the difficulties over documents of this kind that the Melbourne listing should have disappeared since Waters discussed it.

16 This might imply that registration was looked upon as unreliable in the years before 1695, as it certainly implies that registration might be expected to improve afterwards. The various provisions respecting registration, etc., are too complicated to be summarised here.

17 The commonest defect is that family divisions are not made clear, as for Melbourne and Fenny Compton in Warwickshire, though some seem at first sight to be incomplete listings, as those for New Romney and for Donhead.

18 The originals are in the Kent Record Office and are commented upon by Chalklin in *Kent Records*, xvii. See also Glass in *Eugenics Review* (1946) and in *Pop. Stud.* (1950). For other work on the returns under the 1694 Act see especially P.E.Jones and A.V. Judges, 'London Population in the late Seventeenth Century', *Econ. Hist. Rev.*, vi (1935) 45–63.

19 Charles Davenant first published the *Scheme* in 1698, and George Chalmers the full treatise in 1801, but the only accessible version of the latter is that edited by G.E.Barnett in 1936 (printed at Baltimore; see the introduction for details of King's works). Much of King's valuable calculation and generalisation remains in manuscript. A detailed discussion of him as a theorist and examiner of social structure is in preparation.

20 The first edition of the form reproduced here does not allow of 'some' answers being given by checking under *d* and *g*: subsequent editions will do so.

6

SOCIAL STRUCTURE FROM THE EARLY CENSUS RETURNS

An Analysis of Enumerators' Books for
Censuses after 1841

THE FIRST THREE CENSUSES OF ENGLAND AND WALES

THE 1801–31 census volumes are important if somewhat frustrating sources for the economic and social historian. From them may be drawn information on the size of male and female populations of counties, hundreds, parishes and municipal boroughs (from 1801), along with dioceses (from 1831). There is data on occupations, although in a crude form. In 1801 enumerators were asked what number of persons in their parish or township were chiefly employed in agriculture; in trade, manufacture, or handicraft; and what number were not comprised in either of the two preceding classes. The results of this part of the census were thought to be a failure, since there was obviously scope for attributing women, children and servants to either the last category, or to that of the household head. Thus in 1811 the question was amended to an enquiry into the number of *families* employed in each class: the question was retained in this form in 1821, and the results of the enquiry were presented for every county, hundred, parish and township in the printed volumes. The scope of the occupational enquiry was extended in 1831. There were tables showing the division of families into the groupings of 1821, but additional columns split the males aged twenty and over into seven broad occupational categories (agriculture; manufacture; retail trade and handicraft; capitalists, bankers and professional men; non-agricultural labourers; male servants; and 'others'). Moreover a detailed list of the particular trades and handicrafts comprised in the third category was given for each county, together with the number of persons assigned to these trades in each county and its larger boroughs.

Age-structure was ill-catered for in the early censuses. Only the 1821 questionnaire included any provision for this, and the question was optional both to the enumerators and to the parties concerned. Nevertheless, perhaps surprisingly, about eighty-nine per cent of the population did state their ages. Age–sex structures were printed for counties, hundreds, and large towns and boroughs. It is noteworthy that in the case of some census areas, age enumeration was virtually complete.

There is also information on housing. The 1801 census asked enumerators to give the number of inhabited and uninhabited houses in their parish or township: in 1811 the question was extended to cover houses which were 'building and therefore not yet inhabited'. These questions were repeated in 1821 and 1831, and the printed volumes always gave details for all units from the parish upwards.

Finally, the parish register abstracts published along with the census volumes, merit mention. By the Population Act of 1800, which brought the first census into being, clergymen were to submit details of the number of males and females (a) baptised and (b) buried in each decennial year from 1700 to 1780, and in each year from 1781 to 1800. They were also to state the number of marriages in each year from 1754 to 1800. Summaries were printed for large cities, hundreds and counties. Similar information, covering the years 1801–10 and 1811–20, was required in 1811 and 1821. By slightly extending the questionnaire in 1831, information on the ages of deceased persons, 1813–30 was elicited, along with the number of illegitimate children born in each parish in the year 1830.

It is clear that there were many defects in early census procedure. As far as the population figures are concerned, we are unable to check their accuracy, and some modern writers have believed the 1801 census to be as much as five per cent deficient. We cannot say how accurate the age–sex distributions of 1821 may be. There was no clear definition of a house, which was left to the discretion of the enumerator. The degree of omission in the parish register abstract and the extent to which burials and baptisms may be equated with births and deaths are notoriously difficult questions, discussed elsewhere in this book. Finally, it is probable that most students will find directories to be more useful indications of local occupational distributions than any information given in the censuses, certainly before 1831.[1]

THE CENSUS MATERIAL FOR 1841–51

In 1841 a new method of compiling the decennial census was tried. To replace the simple tally-sheet methods of earlier years, each householder received an individual schedule, and was to fill it in prior to collection by the enumerator. The enumerator was obliged to copy down the details for each household into an 'enumerators' book', as, indeed, is still the regular practice. The original schedules no longer exist, but the enumerators' books have been preserved. Those of 1841, 1851 and 1861 have, under the hundred-year rule, become historic documents and have found their way to the Public Record Office where they have been carefully indexed and preserved in numbered boxes. We may expect a fresh set of data to be available to historians every tenth year, in 1971, etc.

The physical condition of the documents is good, on the whole. The entries in the 1841 books are in pencil, but are still quite legible. In 1851 the use of ink seems to have been obligatory. It would appear that the 1861 returns are not wholly complete, nor are they in such good condition.[2]

Though not so thorough in its coverage as the modern counterpart, the scope of the census questionnaire for 1841 was impressive. The householder had to record the address of the premises, the name, age, occupation and sex of each person who abode there on census night. In addition, he had to declare whether the birthplaces of his co-habitants were in the same county, elsewhere in England and Wales, in Scotland, Ireland or Foreign Parts. The 1851 and further successive censuses asked for the same details, but new precision was called for in the recording of birthplaces (parish and county of birth) and ages, which were no longer, as with over fifteens in 1841, to be given to the lowest term of five. Two valuable new requirements were that the relationship of each individual to the household head and his or her marital condition had to be recorded.

This mass of material remains an almost untapped reservoir of

211

City or Borough of *Southwark*

Parish or Township of *St Saviour*

PLACE.	HOUSES		NAMES of each Person who abode therein the preceding Night.	AGE and SEX.		PROFESSION, TRADE, EMPLOYMENT, or of INDEPENDENT MEANS.	Where Born	
	Uninhabited or Building.	Inhabited.		Males.	Females.		Whether Born in same County.	Whether Born in Scotland, Ireland, or Foreign Parts.
George Street		1	James Johnson	40		Chemist	Y.	
			Jane do.		35		N.	
			William do.	15		Shoem. Ap.	Y.	
			Anne do.		13		Y.	
			Edward Smith	30		Chemist's Sh.	N.	
			Sarah Roolins		45	F. S.		J.
do.	26	1	John Cox	60		Publican	N.	
do.	1 B		Mary do.		45		Y.	
do.	1 B		Ellen do.		20		N:	
			James Macpherson	25		M: S.		J.
			Henry Wilson	35		Army	N.	
			n. k.	above 20				
Extra Parochial Place, named The Close.		1	William Jones	50		Farmer	Y.	
			Elizabeth do.		40		Y.	
			William do.	15		Navy	Y.	
			Charlotte do.		8		Y.	
			n. k. do.	5 months			Y.	
			Richard Clerk	20		Ag. Lab.	N.	
do.	26	1	Robert Hall	45		Tailor	Y.	
			Martha do.		30		Y.	
			John Muller	25		Tailor J.		J.
			Ann Williams		20	F. S.	N.	
Chapel Row.		1	Edward Jackson	35		Ind.	N.	
			Charles do.	30		Cl.	N.	
			James Leary	20		M. S.		J.
TOTAL in Page	226 2B	5		15	10			

C b

Figure 6.1. Specimen page from an 1841 enumerator's book[3]

data on the social structure of Victorian Britain. A few writers have dipped into it from time to time to provide carefully selected illustrative material for urban histories.[4] Lawton has prepared a survey of the population of Liverpool in 1851 using samples drawn from different areas of that city.[5] Professor Beresford has discussed the nature of the material and its utility to biographers, geneaologists and those working on the history of institutions, communities, particular social groups, streets or areas.[6]

Lawton's study is without doubt the nearest approach to what one might term a scientific analysis of the data. In essence, he drew seventeen samples, from different districts within the Liverpool area, eight of these being within the Parliamentary Borough of Liverpool. In all, they covered 13,932 individuals out of a population of upwards of 375,955. The sample areas seem to have been selected with the intention of shedding light on local differences. 'Area 1 is representative of the crowded wards of the commercial centre . . . Scotland Road area (area VII) was associated primarily with a working-class population in fairly crowded conditions . . . Abercromby Square sample (area III) consisted of spacious residences of merchants . . .' etc. He went on to analyse the occupational groupings, birthplaces of the inhabitants, age and sex-structure in the sample areas. He concluded that 'in the Liverpool of 1851 there was a well-marked zoning . . . certain distinctive districts can be distinguished not only in terms of the period and type of development of their buildings . . . but also in respect of population structure. This has been viewed from a number of points which are, however, intimately related to one another.'

With certain exceptions, such as his attempt to relate birth-places to certain occupational groups, we are, however, left to form impressions about the relationships of these variables to one another. Apart from the fact that the writer does not give full information on exactly how his samples were selected, our major quibble is likely to be that the relationships between variables are not quantitatively evaluated and measured by statistical techniques, and it is especially important to do this if we are to be able to produce comparable results from comparative surveys. One such study of the social structure of York, 1841–51, is in the course of preparation by myself as a doctoral thesis. A study on similar lines will shortly be commenced on Nottingham, an old county town which, unlike York, had been much altered by the Industrial Revolution. Comparable studies of towns of a different type, such as the newer industrial towns, the ports, centres of conspicuous consumption, and indeed rural areas, would have great value, and our knowledge of the social structure of mid-Victorian England would, it is clear, be much enhanced.[7]

This paper will discuss some of the difficulties presented by the raw data (with the methods of circumventing them that may be adopted), and will generally describe the methods used in taking samples and presenting results worked out in connection with the York survey mentioned above.

DELIMITATION OF A POPULATION, AND BOUNDARY PROBLEMS

It is possible either to take a sample from a given population or take it in entirety, but in both cases it is important to be clear about the size of that population and about precisely which of the enumerators' books relate to it.

The obvious first step is to examine the way in which population units were constituted in the printed volumes of the censuses. In 1841 the census was operated through the newly created body of registration officials. The Poor Law Amendment Act of 1834 had created the union as the general unit of Poor Law administration, and this new subdivision was adopted first for registration of births, deaths and marriages (from 1836) and then for the census.

The country was divided, for the purposes of taking the 1841 census, into enumeration districts of a limited size, the boundaries of which were strictly defined. Although the unit of enumeration was now based on Registration Districts, old 'fundamental subdivisions' of the counties were retained in the printed volumes, i.e. the counties were divided into hundreds, wapentakes (in the north), or rapes and lathes (in certain southern counties). Within these divisions the data for the various parishes was presented. Throughout the printed volumes the municipal boroughs are to be found within their respective counties, and particulars of parliamentary boroughs are given in an appendix. The enumerators' books are also boxed according to this plan. Each parish has at least one separate book, and a hundred, or wapentake, etc., will be found to be covered by the contents of two, three or four boxes of documents, according to its size. All the various units of population, down to individual parishes and hamlets, have been indexed at the Public Record Office. It may be added that an identification page at the beginning of each enumerators' book shows not only the name of the parish, its hundred, the municipality of which it formed a part (if any), and its Parliamentary Constituency, but also notes the name of the registration area of which it formed a part.

In 1851 the 'fundamental divisions' of the counties were ignored, and the data were now presented in the printed volumes under the headings of (a) Registration District or Poor Law Union, (b) Subdistrict, (c) Parish or Township. Each individual entry in the Population Tables has its reference number, e.g. St Helen Stonegate parish, York, is numbered No. 11 parish in No. 2 Subdistrict (Bootham) of Registration District No. 515 (York). Similarly, Sprowston parish (Norfolk) is numbered No. 10 Parish in No. 2 (Sprowston) Subdistrict within Registration District No. 233 (St Faiths).[8] One or two enumerators' books will cover a single parish and normally one box at the Public Record Office will cover all the Parishes and Townships within a Subdistrict. Several boxes, according to the number of Subdistricts, will thus enclose the complete enumeration of a particular registration district in 1851.

The Registration District (normally coterminous with the Poor Law Union) may for some purposes be an ideal unit of study. Where this is so, there is the added advantage that the birth, death and marriage totals for that unit appear in the annual reports of the Registrar-General. However, one may be interested in a particular part of a registration district, e.g. an urban nucleus at the centre which one wishes to separate out; or conceivably one may be interested in a unit of study which is comprised within several subdistricts or even more than one union. The urban agglomeration of York, for instance, lay in three subdistricts, each of which also contained some purely rural parishes quite outside the urban limits, however defined. The most convenient unit of study will probably be the town, and, since this will not normally be synonymous with a Registration District, a further decision will have to be taken as to whether the municipal or Parliamentary borough boundaries of the town are the best limits to take. Very often the Parliamentary boundary will encompass a larger area and a greater population than that of the municipal borough and it is sound practice to try to include all physical suburban extensions to the town whenever possible. In the case of York, such physical extensions spilt well over the Municipal Borough boundary and yet were neatly contained within the Parliamentary Borough limits, thus making these obviously the best to take. How general this may be it is difficult to say, but an examination of a series of maps drawn up for the Municipal Boundaries Commission of the 1830s suggests that the Parliamentary borough limits will often be suitable.[9] Incidentally, the three published volumes of the Commission may be of some considerable assistance in identifying the boundaries of a town, though in cases where Ordnance Survey maps were prepared during the 1840s and 1850s, still more valuable plans exist. York, for instance, was surveyed in the late 1840s and maps of the city were prepared on the six inch and very generous five feet to the mile scales.[10]

From the late 1830s onwards then, there is normally no difficulty in locating the boundaries of an urban unit from maps, and it is unlikely, moreover, that investigators will have difficulty in deciding which of the enumerators' books within a particular box at the Public Record Office relate to his chosen population unit. At the head of each page of each book, the enumerator was to enter the parish name, the name of the municipality and that of the Parliamentary area of which it formed a part. That municipal and Parliamentary boundaries often cut across parish boundaries presents no difficulty, for where 'part of' a particular parish lay in a town and part of it lay outside this, separate books were normally used. In the experience of the present writer, there has been no great difficulty in connection with the York region. The Municipal Borough contained twenty-seven whole and eight 'parts' of parishes. The Parliamentary Borough contained all these, with the addition of part of the parish of St Olaves, Marygate, and parts of the townships of Clifton, Heworth and Fulford. In all cases save that of Heworth in 1841, it proved to be possible to separate out the York part of

216

the township or parish from that which definitely was not. In the case of Heworth, the enumerator had neglected to identify clearly the York and non-York parts of the township and had not properly completed the entries on the first page. Such cases, one would imagine, are rare. In this instance, it was decided to include all of Heworth township as being within the borough, since there were in any case only 395 persons in the whole township. If it is necessary to resort to such a procedure in the case of the data from one census, say 1841, it must be remembered that if comparisons are to be drawn with the data of 1851 and successive years, the modified boundary must be retained, even if in later census years the constituent parts of the area are readily identifiable.

Indeed, as a general principle, it is clear that inter-censal comparisons over lengthy periods will be invalidated unless cognizance is taken of boundary changes which may have taken place in the meantime.

THE DRAWING OF SAMPLES

The sheer bulk of the census data ensures that (except for a small area or a particular social group) it will be necessary to take samples. Having identified the enumerators' books which cover the area of study, sampling is not a difficult task. It is necessary to decide on an appropriate sampling fraction, the size of which should depend on three things: (a) the number of units (households) in the total population, and (b) what exactly the investigator wishes to say about them, and (c) the amount of time the investigator has at his disposal. To illustrate these points it is clear that one cannot generalise with confidence about the measurable characteristics of a population of four households if one random case is taken, even though this is a 25 per cent sample. There is a distinct likelihood that an extreme case has been taken. On the other hand a 1 per cent sample may be quite adequate if one is asking certain broad questions about a very large population; such a fraction has been used to provide preliminary results in the 1 per cent sample tables of the censuses of 1951 and 1961.

A 10 per cent sampling fraction, on a household basis, was in fact chosen for York, a city of about thirty thousand persons in 1841, forty thousand in 1851. It was guessed that such a sample would contain 7–800 households and 3–4,000 persons, which it seemed feasible to attempt to record, as indeed it proved to be. On that basis, it was possible to use the characteristics of the sample as measures of population parameters in respect of such variables as household and family size, birthplaces (in suitable groups), ages (in groups), classes (groups of occupations), proportion of sharing households, proportion of households with domestic servants and with lodgers, etc. What was more important, the variables could be related within certain limits and the results appraised by the careful use of tests of significance of difference which are essential once resort has been had to the techniques of sampling.[11] It was possible to say, within a measurable range of error, on the basis of the 1851 York sample, what was the proportion of native-born heads with more than four children, or the mean family size of that group. Or, to take other examples, how the mean birth-spacings varied by class and area;[12] how age-groups were related to birthplaces; how social class was related to having domestic servants or having lodgers, or sharing a house. Many examples could be given, but it is clear that for broad practical purposes, such questions can be answered from a sampling proportion of the order of 10 per cent on a city as big as York at this period. On the other hand, it would not be wise to press such correlations too far and attempt to state categorically the birthplace distribution of billiard-table makers if there were twenty in the whole population and two in the sample. Nor would it be wise, to press the argument to absurdity, to take multiple correlations to the point of asking what proportion of Irish heads aged 20–39, who were in a given social class and had at least two relatives living in, had four or more children. In the first case, the margins of error involved, which can be calculated, would be so large as to make the argument worthless, and in the second case, there would be a continual squaring of the range of error involved with the introduction of each new variable.

Finally, on the question of size of sampling fraction, it is worth adding that one should not blindly take as large a proportion of the items in the population as is humanly possible to record in the time available. Statisticians point out that it is necessary to quadruple the size of a sample in order to double its accuracy (i.e. halve the standard error). In point of fact, it is essential that the historian who has had either little or no training in statistics should take skilled advice on the size of the sampling fraction to be employed in his particular case. The 10 per cent fraction, used in the York case, will probably be found to be generally useful however.

The sampling fraction having been decided upon, one may proceed to the Public Record Office in order to record the sample. One should carry three sets of notebooks, the first to record the most important details of the households in the sample, the second to give ancillary information on these households and for use in keeping a record of precisely *which* households were used in the first notebook; the third for recording details of institutions, etc. These will be referred to as the sample, ancillary, and institutional notebooks respectively.

We may first consider how households should be chosen for the sample, and how they may conveniently be recorded in the first or 'sample' notebooks. It is necessary to obtain an unbiassed random sample (i.e. households should be selected as they come up in random fashion, without reference to any particular characteristics which they possess). Such a sample may best be drawn by working through the pages of the enumerators' books in a mechanical fashion, recording the relevant details of every tenth household (in the case of a 10 per cent sample) in the manner shown below. In most cases, details of institutions such as hospitals, workhouses, barracks, prisons, etc. will be given in separate enumerators' books and may be safely ignored at this stage. Quasi-institutional households, such as small boarding schools and common lodging houses of considerable size will often be found among the main body of households in the normal enumerators' books however. It is likely that the inclusion of such 'households' would bias and distort some of the quantitative results which are required in respect of family structure and institutions; they should therefore be left out of the sample. In the York case, all obvious boarding schools, etc., and all households having more than ten non-members of the head's family were omitted.[13] Instead the very next household was substituted and was followed by the recording of the *ninth* following household in order to preserve the original sequence. It was considered that any important minority groups of households which were suffering from systematic exclusion in this manner could be studied by means of sub-samples. The only such group in York was that of the Irish, who, as elsewhere, did tend to congregate in large numbers in lodging houses. The main samples were deficient in the proportion of Irish persons as compared with the known proportion in the city as a whole. To make up for this, all the Irish in one particular parish were recorded elsewhere, for separate study.

Each tenth household then, subject to the above qualification of the procedure, was recorded in the sample notebooks. In the York case it was intended to process the data on eighty-column punched cards of the Hollerith or I.B.M. type, each column having up to twelve punching positions, so that it was convenient to use sample notebooks which had also been ruled into eighty columns.[14] In relation to the 1851 data, the characteristics of each household, running across one page of a notebook were recorded as follows:

Columns		
1, 2		Serial number of the Parish or Township
3, 4, 5		Serial number of the household
6, 7		Number of persons in the household
8, 9		Number of persons in the head's family
10		Type of household, i.e. whether head (first listed person) is a married, single or widowed male: or whether a married, single or widowed female
11		Birthplace of head
12		Age of head
13, 14		Occupation of head
15		Age of wife, where appropriate
16		Birthplace of wife
17		Occupation of wife, if stated as other than 'housewife' etc.
18		Number of children of head
19		Age of first (eldest) child
20		Birthplace of first child
21–38		Ages and birthplaces, alternately, of other children of head

220

39	Whether the head's family is sharing the residence with another family unit (defined for this purpose as another married couple or a male or female person with at least one child)
40	Number of lodgers in the household, including any family groups defined as under 39
41	Birthplace of first lodger
42	Occupation of first lodger
43	Industrial grouping of first lodger
44–70	Spaces for recording similar facts about up to nine other lodgers
71	Number of domestic servants
72–78	Spaces for recording the numbers of domestic servants born in up to seven geographical areas
79	Number of identifiable relatives living in household, not already recorded
80	Number of visitors

Such a notebook arrangement is suitable for recording data from the Census of 1851. Small re-arrangements are necessary for dealing with the data of 1841, but it is unnecessary to detail these. There is nothing sacrosanct about the system outlined above; in any case, even in 1851, *ad hoc* alterations will have to be made to suit the needs of each investigation. For instance, serial numbers running to four digits might be needed for larger samples than the York ones: again, one may wish to record details of more than ten lodgers (I did not, see above) and may consequently be prepared to sacrifice some data on domestic servants, visitors or relatives, in order to allow further space for lodgers. It must be borne in mind, however, that whatever arrangement suits the individual operator, he cannot have more than eighty columns because of the limitations of the punched card machinery, although he may of course have less.

The second, or ancillary notebook should be filled at the time of recording. In it can be noted the serial number, parish, page number and head's surname for each of the households incorporated into the sample (e.g. 398, St Helen Stonegate, 24,

Fox). One can also record minor details such as ages and sexes of domestic servants, lodger's ages, etc., which are given in the enumerators' books but which have not been recorded in the eighty-column sample notebooks for reasons of space.

The third, or 'institutional', notebook may be used for recording details of hospitals, workhouses, barracks, prisons, etc., which have been set on one side and do not form part of the main sample. Obviously it is neither necessary nor desirable to lose this data, which provides us with valuable information on the proportion of paupers, the proportion in hospitals, and other information relating to the magnitude of social problems and the arrangements for relief. This notebook may also be used for giving details of interesting quasi-institutions or for recording details of any minority groups of households which have been systematically excluded in the process of taking the main sample (e.g. the Irish in York, referred to above).

It will be appreciated that once the sample notebooks are filled, they contain information on each household which is partly in numerical form (number of children, number of relatives, etc. and all ages) and probably an equal amount that is not, e.g. birthplaces, occupations, etc. Such information must be reduced to numerical form, capable of being dealt with by the machine. Having spent several weeks recording the data on, say, 800 households one may expect to spend at least as long in grouping the data and reducing it to numerical form. Using new sheets or notebooks, again ruled into eighty columns, all ages of heads and wives should be reduced into up to ten groups (15–, 20–, 25–, 30–, 35–, 40–, 45–, 50–, 60– and 70–), and codified 0–9 respectively. The ages of children may be similarly reduced to eleven groups, 0–, 1–, 2–, 3–, 4–, 5–6, 7–9, 10–12, 13–14, 15–, 25–, and coded 0–10 respectively, although the true ages in the original notebooks should be preserved for other uses. Again, we cannot possibly hope to indicate individual birthplace parishes or even counties and further classification will be necessary here. York birthplaces were divided into: (a) born in York (punched 1 in the appropriate columns), (b) born in the agricultural East and North Ridings (punched 2), (c) industrial West Riding (3), (d) contiguous Northern counties (4), (e) elsewhere in England and Wales (5), (f) Scotland (6), (g) Ireland (7), and (h) Foreign Parts (8).

Again, the multifarious occupations of the household heads may be used as the basis of dividing the heads into social classes and industrial groupings, for while there is little interest in the distinctions between butcher, baker, greengrocer, shoemaker, etc., the differences between these people as a group and, perhaps, unskilled workpeople on the one hand and professional classes on the other will probably be important.[15] However, interest may also be focused on certain particular occupations (in the York case, railwaymen, labourers, agricultural labourers and building workers) and such groups, while being subsumed under social classes (col. 13) and industrial groups (col. 14), may still be distinguished by using a double entry (e.g. 4/7) in the social class column, which would enable one to see in a glance at the notebook that the individual was not only in Class IV, but was also an agricultural labourer. Similarly 3/6 might mean that here was an individual in class 3 (skilled workman) and also a railwayman. Such double entries may be placed on the cards in turn without difficulty by double-punching the appropriate column (see below). Finally, each parish or township within the sample population will have to have its name replaced by a number, and descriptive terms such as whether sharing, marital status of household head, etc., will be given code numbers.

During this period of preparing the sample for placing on punched cards, a map of the county is very useful, together with a gazetteer (lists of all parishes, townships and hamlets were published along with the printed volumes of nineteenth-century censuses). It may well be necessary to re-examine the data for certain households in the enumerators' books, having discovered a few errors of omission or that some highly improbable entries occur in the recorded data. The ancillary notebook will facilitate finding the appropriate household anew. During this part of the preparation, immense patience must be exercised and tests on the accuracy of the recording of data should be carried out. For instance, it is useful to check on the total number of individuals in the population as implied by adding up all the figures for household size and family size, and then to compare these with the recorded numbers of heads, wives, children, lodgers, domestic servants, relatives and visitors. One should also check that the code-numbers used are consistent and that

223

the allocations to class, birthplace and age groupings are correct.

Further statistical tests to ensure that the sample is a fair representation of the population should be carried out at this stage, before embarking on the labour involved in committing the sample to punched cards. I extracted an age distribution for the population for the municipal borough part of my sample; a sex distribution; a birthplace distribution; and the number of males over twenty employed in certain occupations (those occupations, in fact, which employed more than 100 males over twenty years of age). The distributions obtained from the sample were compared with the distributions relating to the Municipal Borough of York as a whole (obtained from the printed volumes of the Census), and tests of significance of difference were carried out on them. The tests generally showed that there was no significant difference between the age, sex, occupational and birthplace distributions in the sample and in the original population, and that it could be reasonably regarded as representative.[16]

The sample having proved to be satisfactory, one may proceed to the transference of the data from sheets to standard eighty-column punched cards of the Hollerith or I.B.M. type. One household, now represented by a string of figures along the horizontal line of the sheets, can be placed on each card. Let us take an actual example of a York household and show how, by the various processes of extraction, recording, codifying, and punching, it became one of the punched cards.

On the reproduction of a page of one of the York enumerators' books (figure 6.2), the reader will observe the household of Joseph Kimber, a grocer. After recording this household in the sample notebook as outlined above, our entry, reading horizontally and using the column headings outlined above, took the form shown in figure 6.3. After further codification and classification the entry – on new sheets – appeared as in figure 6.4. Finally, figure 6.5 shows the punched card on which the same data has been codified.

The actual preparation of punched cards is not difficult. The necessary machinery will often be available on university sites, usually in the hands of departments other than History; the proprietors of such machinery will often allow their machinery

No. of Houses	Name of Street, Place, or Road, and Name or No. of House	Name and Surname of each Person who abode in the house, on the Night of the 30th March, 1851	Relation to Head of Family	Condition	Age of Males	Age of Females	Rank, Profession, or Occupation	Where Born	Whether Blind, or Deaf-and-Dumb
		Mary A. Speck	Daur	U		12	Scholar at home	York City	
		William do	Son		11		do "	do do	
		Robert do	Son		10		do "	do do	
		Elizabeth do	Daur			6		do do	
		John do	Son		4			do do	✓
		Mary Ann Neesam	Assistant	U		12	Dressmaker (Assistant)	Loughborough, Leicester	✓
		Elizabeth Buckley	do	U		14	William do	Yorkshire, Pontefract	✓
		Sarah A. Orssrd	do	U		16	do	do, Pottington	✓
		Hannah Roth	Servt	U		19	General Servt	do, Nonstion	✓
	37 King's Square	Joseph Kimber	Head	Mar	52		Grocer	York City	
		Ann do	Wife			40		do do	
		Mary J. do	Daur	U		12	Scholar	do do	
		Joseph do	Son		9			do do	
		Henry Guy	App	U	17		Grocer (App)	do do	✓
		Jos. Lynd	App	U	14		do	do do	✓
		Jane Smith	Servt	U		20	General Servt	Yorkshire, Ripon	✓
	3d King's Square	John Marsh	Head		36		Furniture Broker	Middlesex, London	✓
		Charlotte Marsh	Wife			35		Yorkshire, Pontefract	✓
		Sarah Anne Marsh	Daur			4		York City	
		Elizabeth Wilmshurst	Servant	U		17	General Servt	do do	
		Total of Persons...			8	12			

Figure 6.2

225

1	2	3	4	5	6	7	8	9	10	11	12	13	14	15	16	17	18	19	20
HT	KC	3	4	7	0	7	0	4	Mar. M	York	52	Grocer (Emp. 2)		40	York		2	12	York
21	22	23	24	25	26	27	28	29	30	31	32	33	34	35	36	37	38	39	40
9	York																	NO	2
41	42	43	44	45	46	47	48	49	50	51	52	53	54	55	56	57	58	59	60
York	Grocer (App.)		Yorks Riccall	Grocer (App.)															
61	62	63	64	65	66	67	68	69	70	71	72	73	74	75	76	77	78	79	80
										1	b.	Bulmer		(Yorks)				0	0

Figure 6.3

1	2	3	4	5	6	7	8	9	10	11	12	13	14	15	16	17	18	19	20
1	8	3	4	7	0	7	0	4	0	1	7	2	4	5	1		2	7	1

21	22	23	24	25	26	27	28	29	30	31	32	33	34	35	36	37	38	39	40
6	1																	0	2

41	42	43	44	45	46	47	48	49	50	51	52	53	54	55	56	57	58	59	60
1	3	4	2	3	4														

61	62	63	64	65	66	67	68	69	70	71	72	73	74	75	76	77	78	79	80
										1		1						0	0

Figure 6.4

to be used and may even give help in the form of an assistant to do the actual punching. If the investigator finds that he himself is allowed access to the electric punching machine, he will probably find that he can soon prepare between one and two hundred cards in the course of an evening's work. The finished cards then have to be verified, i.e. each card has to be put through a similar machine which will indicate errors of transposition of data from record sheet to punched card.

At the stage now reached, the investigator will be ready to begin work analysing the data on the cards. Before we go on to consider this last aspect of the exercise, however, it should be pointed out that the description of the taking and preparing of samples has been given in terms of what may be done with the 1851 material. The foregoing description of the methods used may also be applied to 1861 and further successive censuses, but has to be modified in the case of samples from the 1841 enumerators' books.

Certain modifications of the notebook and card layout will probably be made to suit individual needs. What is a much more important problem, however, is that a certain amount of difficulty will probably be experienced (in some parishes) in identifying the beginnings and ends of households in the enumerators' books. In the 1851 books this is clear enough – a ruled line in ink is drawn across the page at the end of each household in the enumerators' books. In 1841, however, small

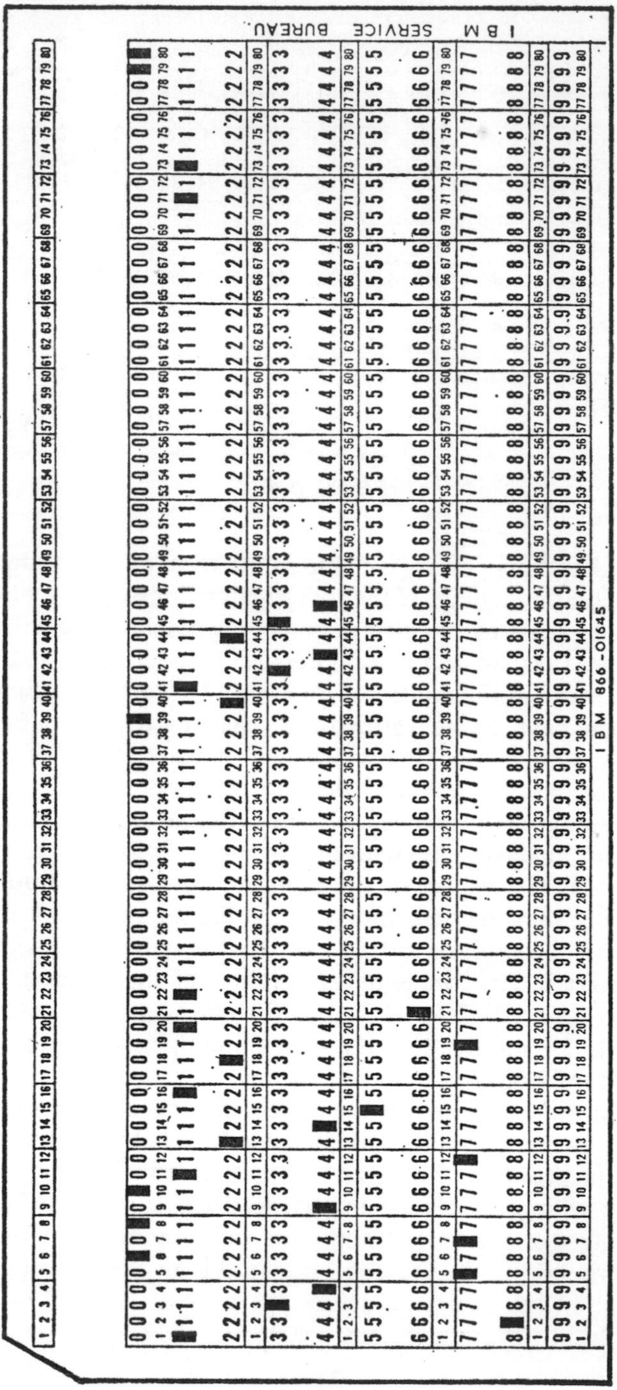

Figure 6.5

228

strokes are used to indicate the end of the family (/) and household respectively (//).[17] Obviously, after such a double-stroke, a new house should be inserted in the third column. Sometimes the marks will be confused and // used to end the family, with / to end the household. Alternatively, a new house will often be credited, without the previous household having been ended in the proper manner; or the double-stroke will be used with no new house indicated. Clearly, some sort of rule needed to be developed for the purpose of counting the households, and after consideration, it seemed best to decide that both the double-stroke and the appearance of a new house credited in the appropriate column should mark the point where one household ended and another began.

A further major difficulty in connection with the 1841 data will arise from the fact that relationships to the head of the household are not stated. In the York case, it was assumed that the first listed person was the head and to allocate other individuals as wife, child or relative of the head, a fairly complex set of rules had to be drawn up and adhered to. To allocate persons *of the same surname*, the rules were as follows:

(a) The first listed female within 15 years of the head's age was assumed to be his wife. Other females, provided that (from consideration of their ages) they were born when the head and wife (where applicable) were aged not below 15 and not over 50, were assumed to be daughters. Any further females were treated as relatives.

(b) Males: the other males bearing the same name were regarded as sons, provided that they too were born when the head and his wife were aged not less than 15 and not more than 50. Other males were regarded as relatives.[18]

Further rules had to be made to cover the allocation of those *not bearing the head's surname.*

Domestic servants were taken as being all those so described in the occupation column, unless they bore the same name as the head (in which case they were taken to be children or relatives) or unless the head of the household was also by occupation (as occasionally happened) described as a servant (whereupon they were credited to the lodgers).

Lodgers: in the 1851 case, this category had consisted solely of persons so described. In the 1841 sample, this category was rather swollen, being residual in character and containing all persons not covered by the above rules. In it were, no doubt, true lodgers but also visitors and some relatives of the head who could not be identified since they did not bear his surname.

An example may be given of how the inmates of a household might be placed under such rules. In the example on page 212 is the household of James Johnson, a chemist. Of those bearing his surname Jane would be treated as his wife, being aged five years less. William and Anne were presumably born when both James and Jane were aged between 15 and 50, since their respective ages are 15 and 13. Sarah Robins would be classified as a domestic servant from the evidence of the occupations column, and Edward Smith as a lodger. Looking to the household of Edward Jackson, it will be observed that the first listed male of the same name would obviously not qualify as a son – he would be treated as a relative.

It is clear that while the rules are probably as good a method as any of deciding upon relationships to heads, there are nevertheless elements of doubt which are not present with 1851 and subsequent data. Much caution must therefore be used if it is desired to draw inter-censal comparisons between family sizes, number of children, relatives and lodgers, etc. On the other hand, comparisons of the orders of magnitude of, say, inter-class differences in these respects might still be made over the 1841–51 period.

Finally, it is necessary to point out one further difficulty which will arise in connection with the 1841 data. In the occupations column, there is no evidence of the status of, for example, a 'comb manufacturer', 'linen manufacturer', etc. The instructions to the enumerator were that an individual must be assumed to be a 'master', unless the letter J (journeyman) was placed there. Few 'J's are to be found in the York books and the distinction is useless, one fears. In 1851, there was information on how many men an entrepreneur employed, but this was not given ten years before. Hence it will be found that to place household heads into classes, one must rely partially on the retaining of domestic servants as a criterion of social class. For comparative purposes (as in the York case), it will not normally be difficult to modify the 1851 social classes (see Appendix D).

In conclusion, it may be added that throughout any survey which incorporates samples from both the 1841 and 1851 data, it is advisable to work to the following general principles.

(a) The student should attempt to extract all possible results from the superior data of 1851 and subsequent censuses.

(b) He should then attempt the same with the inferior 1841 data.

(c) Then, and only then, the categories and classifications used in 1851 may be modified into the forms needed to draw comparisons with the earlier 1841 material.

THE ANALYSIS AND PREPARATION OF RESULTS

Having carried out all the preceding steps, one is now in a position to begin to draw out preliminary results, which can be conveniently recorded in tabular form. New notebooks with the appropriate columns must be prepared and the punched cards taken to a card-sorting machine. This may be set to sort on a particular column, and will sort (and count) the cards according to the punched holes that have been made in that column. The machine 'reads' the cards by means of electrical contact and throws the cards into numbered pockets. This it will do at the rate of about 600 cards a minute. It is worth mentioning that if one were dividing the whole mass of cards into, say household size, it would be necessary to sort two columns (6 and 7) because two digits are involved. Again, it should be pointed out that sorting machines of this type 'reject' by throwing into an appropriate pocket cards which are not punched at all on the column which is being sorted. It is also possible to blank off certain punching positions, which is useful in connection with columns that have been double-punched. For instance, if the social classes had been punched 1–5 in column 13, one could cut out the machine's ability to cover punching positions 6–10 which may have been (in the York case *were*) used for other purposes, such as singling out particular occupations.

By successively altering the column setting device on the machine, it is possible to produce tables of related variables without difficulty and in a very short time. What sort of tables ought one to try to produce? In principle, any of the variables recorded on the cards could be related to any other. If the cards contain the information detailed, it is possible for example to relate birthplaces of all third lodgers to ages of the fourth children of household heads (by sorting on column 25 and then re-sorting the cards on column 47). We can sort serial numbers of parishes against serial numbers of households. Such exercises would tell us absolutely nothing about social structure, and it may be useful to list some of the more important and significant tabulations that could be drawn from cards which had been processed in the manner described on pages 220–7.

1 Distribution of household size
2 Distribution of family size
3 Distribution of children of household heads
4 Distribution of domestic servants
5 Distribution of lodgers
(All these would be performed by simply sorting on columns 6 and 7, 8 and 9, 18, 71 and 40 respectively.)

More importantly, the following *relationships* might be drawn out.

1 Head's social class to birthplace of head (columns 13 and 11)
2 Head's social class to age groups (13 and 12)
3 Head's social class to number of domestic servants (13 and 71)
4 Head's social class to number of lodgers (13 and 40)
5 Head's social class to whether sharing (13 and 39)
6 Head's social class to number of relatives living in (13 and 79)
7 Head's social class to marital status of head (13 and 10)
8 Head's social class to Parish serial no. (13 and 1–2)
9 Head's social class to number of children (13 and 18)
10 Head's social class to wife's birthplace (13 and 16)
11 Marital status of head to his age-group (10 and 12)
12 Marital status of head to his birthplace (10 and 11)
13 Marital status of head to his number of children (10 and 18)
14 Marital status of head to whether sharing (10 and 39)
15 Marital status of head to number of lodgers (10 and 40)
16 Marital status of head to number of relatives (10 and 79)
17 Birthplace of head to number of children (11 and 18)

18 Birthplace of head to age group (11 and 12)
19 Birthplace of head to birthplace of wife (11 and 16)
20 Birthplace of head to whether sharing (11 and 39)
21 Birthplace of head to number of lodgers (11 and 40)
22 Birthplace of head to number of domestic servants (11 and 71)
23 Birthplace of head to number of relatives (11 and 79)
24 Age of head to age of wife (12 and 15)
25 Age of head to birthplace of wife (12 and 16)
26 Age of head to number of children (12 and 18)
27 Age of wife to number of children (15 and 18)
28 Age of wife to birthplace of wife (15 and 16)
29 Birthplace of wife to number of children (16 and 18)
30 Birthplace of wife to number of relatives (16 and 79)
31 Number of children to whether sharing (18 and 39)
32 Number of children to number of lodgers (18 and 40)
33 Number of children to number of domestic servants (18 and 71)

Obviously this is not an exhaustive list, but simply a selection of tables which might prove to be illuminating. Sometimes it might be appropriate to have further breakdowns. For example, while the tabulations 27 (Age of wife to number of children), and 33 (Number of children to number of domestic servants) would be useful, even more interesting facts might emerge if social class were taken into consideration. This could easily be done by simply sorting the cards on column 13 *before* the commencement of the operations on columns 15 and 18: and 18 and 40 respectively. Again in the case of tabulation 18 (Birthplace of head to age of head), we could, if desired, restrict this to male heads simply by previously sorting on column 10, which would enable us to extract any female heads.

Sometimes the tabulated results will appear very much in the form we want them. Such a case is that of the relationship between social class of household head and the number of domestic servants (York 1851, see figure 6.6).

In such a case, one may simply take the results a stage further and prepare a new table showing that 81 per cent of Class I heads had one or more domestic servants: 53 per cent had two or more, and so on for the other classes. The differences in this

Social Class of Household Head

Number of domestic servants	I	II	III	IV	V	All classes
0	11	45	351	97	98	602
1	17	48	25	5	0	95
2	13	12	8	0	0	33
3	9	1	2	0	0	12
4	6	0	0	0	0	6
5	2	1	0	1	0	4
6	0	0	0	0	0	0
7	1	0	0	0	0	1
	59	107	386	103	98	753

Figure 6.6

case are so marked that tests of significance of difference would hardly seem necessary, although they should always be performed, since one is working from a sample.

Not all the tables derived from the punched cards will be so straightforward to interpret, however. Another example from the York survey (1851 sample) was recorded as follows after machine analysis. It relates social class of head to birthplace.

Social Class of Head

Birthplace	I	II	III	IV	V	'X' (not placed)	all classes
York	24	32	146	29	29	9	269
East & North Ridings	10	29	100	41	32	9	221
West Riding	10	26	72	19	20	5	152
Northern Counties	7	8	31	6	3	1	56
Rest of England and Wales	5	9	19	0	5	1	39
Scotland	1	0	10	2	1	0	14
Ireland	1	1	6	6	8	3	25
Foreign Parts	1	1	1	0	0	0	3
Unknown, illegible, etc.	0	1	1	0	0	0	2
	59	107	386	103	98	28	781

Figure 6.7

After conversion to percentage terms, one would be looking for statistically significant relationships between the variables. After conversion (I have not here drawn up a further table), it would appear among other features, that York-born citizens were less likely to be in classes IV and V, than were immigrants from the agricultural Ridings or from Ireland. 21·6 per cent of York-born heads were in these classes, while 33·0 per cent of the East and North Riding heads were so placed, and 44·0 per cent of the Irish. On the other hand, immigrants from the surrounding Northern Counties and the rest of England tended to have a higher proportion in classes I and II (26·8 per cent and 35·9 per cent) than the natives of the city (20·8 per cent) which may suggest a relationship between degree of skill and distance people were willing to move (always excepting the rather special Irish case). However, it would certainly be necessary to carry out tests of significance of difference before assertions based on such a table were incorporated into a finished work.

In point of fact, it may be said that it is at this point where the tasks of historical interpretation begin. The type of exercise described within these pages can provide a skeletal statistical framework unobtainable from other sources. Statistical evaluation of the results and tabulations is of fundamental importance, but in order to understand and explain his own results, the student will need to have recourse to a whole range of sources on nineteenth century local history. Local newspapers, city council and guardians' minute books are of immense value where they survive. Parliamentary papers of all types (including particularly the Annual Reports of the Registrar-General, Factory Inspectors, Education, etc.) should be thoroughly combed. A discussion of such sources in detail would fill another chapter, however, and cannot be attempted here.[19]

W. A. Armstrong

NOTES

1 The methods and procedures used in taking nineteenth century censuses are described in the reports themselves. They have also been traced in two modern works of great value.

   Interdepartmental Committee on Social and Economic Research: Guides to Official Sources, no. 2, *Census Reports of Great Britain, 1801–1931* (H.M.S.O., 1951); and A. J. Taylor,

'The Taking of the Census, 1801–1951', *British Medical Journal* (7 April 1951).

2 M.W.Beresford, 'The unprinted Census Returns of 1841, 1851, 1861 for England and Wales', *Amateur Historian*, v (1963), 266. I have not used the data for the 1861 census.

3 Note that the abbreviations 'Y' and 'N' in the penultimate column mean yes and no in answer to the question whether the individual was born within the same county. Similarly 'S', 'I' and 'F' in the last column refer to Scotland, Ireland or Foreign Parts. 'MS', 'FS', 'J' and 'CL' were authorised abbreviations for male servants, female servants, journeymen and clerks.

On 225 below an illustration of an actual page from the 1851 return for York is shown (Public Record Office reference number H.O. 107/2353). The letter is Crown copyright material and is reproduced by permission of the Controller of H.M. Stationery Office.

4 E.g. E.M.Sigsworth in *Victoria County History. A History of the County of York. The City of York* (ed. P.M.Tillott: London 1961), 272 and 282. W.H.Chaloner, *Social and Economic Development of Crewe* (Manchester, 1950), 38 and 59. T.C. Barker and J.R.Harris, *A Merseyside Town in the Industrial Revolution: St Helens 1751–1900* (London 1959), 281.

5 R.Lawton, 'The Population of Liverpool in the mid-Nineteenth Century', *Trans. Hist. Soc. Lancs. & Ches.*, cvii (1955), 89–120.

6 Beresford, *Amateur Historian*, v.

7 As Professor Ashton and others have noted, we know a great deal about the social pathology of nineteenth century England, due to the fact that historians have made perhaps too much uncritical use of the Parliamentary Blue Books. See *Capitalism and the Historians* (ed. F.A.Hayek: London 1954), 35. What we lack are studies of the 'normal' communities and classes, which did not seem to present problems to contemporaries.

8 Census, 1851, *Population Tables*, Pt I, II, Yorks Div., 48; and I, Eastern Div., 44.

9 Municipal Borough Boundaries, *R. Comm. Rep.* (1837), xxvi–xxviii.

10 There is an extremely useful article on nineteenth-century town plans by J.B.Harley, 'A Guide to Ordnance Survey Maps as Historical Sources. IV, The Town Plans and Small-Scale Maps of England and Wales', *Amateur Historian*, v (1963), 251–9.

11 For worked examples see Appendix E. The principle and practice of such tests is lucidly explained in R.G.D.Allen, *Statistics for Economists* (London 1949), chap. 9.

12 Naturally the historian's difficulties do not end when he has found how mean birth-spacings varied between class and class, or between area and area. He ought to attempt to solve the question of whether the observed variations reflect primarily differential fertility or differential infant mortality. Judgment can only be made after reference to other sources of information. For example, his local sources of evidence (such as newspapers) are likely to single out certain areas as being notoriously unhealthy from time to time. In York, the Walmgate district was considered to be bad in the 1840s. As late as 1888 infant death rates in that district were 338 per thousand, as compared with 283 per thousand for the city as a whole. *V.C.H., City of York,* 284.

13 The head's family was defined as himself (or herself), wife (if any) and their children (including any step-children). The definition excluded mothers, mothers-in-law, uncles and aunts, nephews, nieces, brothers, sisters, etc., of the head, who were treated as relatives.

14 The following description of how recording notebooks may be prepared with economy of effort is not exactly the same as that used in the York work. It represents what seems likely to be generally useful after much trial and error.

15 See Appendix D for a discussion of the subsuming of occupational groups under social classes and industrial groupings.

16 See Appendix E.

17 See facsimile reproduced as figure 6.1 above.

18 While it is true that some males must have fathered children when they were over fifty, it was assumed that any such 'sons' or 'daughters' were, on the whole, more likely to have been relatives.

19 I wish to record my grateful thanks to Mr Prior and the staff of the punched card section at the University of Birmingham, and to members of the Department of Social Science at the University of Nottingham. Statisticians who have helped me at various times include Mr Morris of Birmingham and Dr Granger of Nottingham. Above all, however, my debt is to Dr D.E.C. Eversley of Birmingham who had the original idea of sampling from the enumerators' books and who has given me immense help and stimulus at all times.

NOTE. See Appendix D for a classification of occupations; Appendix E for statistical tests.

A BIBLIOGRAPHY OF BRITISH
DEMOGRAPHIC HISTORY

THIS work is intended to cover the period from the beginning of the sixteenth century to the end of the nineteenth century. Some articles may go further than these limits but have been included where they deal with material for the period required.

The bibliography is divided into two parts. The first part, 'General and Introductory Works', incorporates works on sources, general studies of the problems of population history and population estimates, studies of death rates, studies of marriage, fertility and birth rates, and studies of internal migration. The second part is subdivided into groups of counties for the sake of convenience of reference and because this method demonstrates the areas where little or no demographic research has been done.

The material is arranged alphabetically within each section, and the bibliography follows the limitations of the book in excluding references to the problems of pre-1500 demographic history, to Irish population problems and to emigration.

ABBREVIATIONS

Amateur Hist.	*Amateur Historian*
Am. Hist. Rev.	*American Historical Review*
Arch. Camb.	*Archaeologica Cambriensis*
Brit. J. Soc. Med.	*British Journal of Social Medicine*
Bull. Bd. Celtic St.	*Bulletin of the Board of Celtic Studies, University of Wales*
Camb. Hist. J.	*Cambridge Historical Journal*
Chesh. Hist.	*Cheshire Historian*
Comp. St. Soc. Hist.	*Compartive Studies in Society and History*
Ealing Loc. Hist. Soc.	*Ealing Local History Society*
East Mid. Geog.	*East Midland Geographer*
Econ. Geog.	*Economic Geography*
Econ. Hist.	*Economic History*

Bibliography

Econ. Hist. J.	*Economic History Journal*
Econ. Hist. Rev.	*Economic History Review*
Econ. J.	*Economic Journal*
Eng. Hist. Rev.	*English Historical Review*
Eug. Rev.	*Eugenics Review*
Field St.	*Field Studies*
Flints. Hist. Rec. Soc.	*Flintshire Historical Record Society*
Geog.	*Geography*
Geog. J.	*Geographical Journal*
Halifax Antiqu. Soc.	*Halifax Antiquarian Society*
Hist.	*History*
Irish Geog.	*Irish Geography*
Irish Hist. St.	*Irish Historical Studies*
J. Chester North Wales Arch. Archaeol. Hist. Soc.	*Journal of the Chester and North Wales Architectural, Archaeological and Historic Society*
J. Derby. Archaeol. Nat. Hist. Soc.	*Journal of the Derbyshire Archaeological and Natural History Society*
J. Econ. Hist.	*Journal of Economic History*
J. Hist. Soc. Church in Wales	*Journal of the Historic Society of the Church in Wales*
J. Inst. Act.	*Journal of the Institute of Actuaries*
J. Merioneth Hist. Rec. Soc.	*Journal of the Merioneth Historical Record Society*
J. Roy. Soc. Arts	*Journal of the Royal Society of Arts*
J. Roy. Stat. Soc.	*Journal of the Royal Statistical Society*
Jewish Soc. St.	*Jewish Social Studies*
Lincs. Hist.	*Lincolnshire Historian*
Lincs. Notes Queries	*Lincolnshire Notes and Queries*
Manch. Sch. Econ. Soc. St.	*Manchester School of Economic and Social Studies*
Pop. St.	*Population Studies*
Proc. Roy. Soc. Med.	*Proceedings of the Royal Society of Medicine*
Pub. Beds. Hist. Rec. Soc.	*Publications of the Bedfordshire Historical Record Society*
Pub. Hlth. (Camb.)	*Public Health, Cambridge*
Rec. Bucks.	*Records of Buckinghamshire*
Rep. Trans. Devon. Assoc.	*Reports and Transactions of the Devonshire Association*
Scot. Geog. Mag.	*Scottish Geographical Magazine*
Scot. Hist. Rev.	*Scottish Historical Review*
Scot. J. Pol. Econ.	*Scottish Journal of Political Economy*

239

Scot. Med. J.	*Scottish Medical Journal*
Scot. St.	*Scottish Studies*
Sociol. Rev.	*Sociological Review*
Surrey Rec. Soc.	*Surrey Record Society*
Sussex Archaeol. Coll.	*Sussex Archaeological Collections*
Thoresby Soc.	*Thoresby Society*
Trans. Anglesey Antiqu. Soc.	*Transactions of the Anglesey Antiquarian Society*
Trans. Cumb. West. Antiqu. Archaeol. Soc.	*Transactions of the Cumberland and Westmorland Antiquarian and Archaeological Society*
Trans. Hist. Soc. Lancs. Chesh.	*Transactions of the Historic Society of Lancashire and Cheshire*
Trans. Hon. Soc. Cymmrodorion	*Transactions of the Honourable Society of Cymmrodorion*
Trans. Lancs. Chesh. Antiqu. Soc.	*Transactions of the Lancashire and Cheshire Antiquarian Society*
Trans. Leics. Archaeol. Soc.	*Transactions of the Leicestershire Archaeological Society*
Trans. London Middx. Archaeol. Soc.	*Transactions of the London and Middlesex Archaeological Society*
Trans. Newbury Dist. Field Club	*Transactions of the Newbury and District Field Club*
Trans. Pap. Inst. Brit. Geog.	*Transactions and Papers of the Institute of British Geographers*
Trans. Roy. Hist. Soc.	*Transactions of the Royal Historical Society*
Trans. Thoroton Soc.	*Transactions of the Thoroton Society*
Trans. Woolhope Nat. Field Club	*Transactions of the Woolhope Naturalist and Field Club*
Univ. B'ham Hist. J.	*University of Birmingham Historical Society*
Wilts. Archaeol. J.	*Wiltshire Archaeological Journal*

Bibliography

PART 1: GENERAL AND INTRODUCTORY WORKS

Sources

BELLAMY, J., 'A Note on the Occupation Statistics in British Censuses', *Pop. St.*, vi (1952–3), 306–8.
An article drawing attention to certain omissions in the censuses with regard to occupation data for the purposes of comparative studies.

BRETT-JAMES, N.G., 'The London Bills of Mortality in the Seventeenth Century', *Trans. Lond. Middx. Archaeol. Soc.*, vi (1933), 284–309.
A history of the bills from the fifteenth to the seventeenth centuries, discussing how and why they were made, and considering their accuracy, with an appendix of extant bills and details of where these are kept.

BURKE, A.M., *Key to the Ancient Parish Registers of England and Wales* (London 1908).
A history of parish registers from the Act of 1538 to the establishment of civil registration in 1837, with an annotated index of every parish and the date of the earliest entry in the register.

BURN, J.S., *The History of Parish Registers in England* (London 1829).
A history of the registers, with an account of their contents, also discussing the registers of dissenters and of ambassadors' chapels.

COX, J.C., *The Parish Registers of England* (London 1910).

ELDRIDGE, H.T., *The Materials of Demography. A Selected and Annotated Bibliography*, Columbia University Press (New York 1951).
A bibliography of secondary works on the problems, methods of analysis and studies of demography.

ELSAS, M., 'Parish Records', *J. Hist. Soc. Church in Wales*, ix, no. 9 (1954), 5–13.
A brief article describing various parish records, such as registers, wardens' rate books and account books, constables' records, etc., in relation to Wales.

GLASS, D.V., 'Gregory King's Estimate of the Population in England and Wales, 1695', *Pop. St.*, iii (1949–50), 338–74.
A study of the accuracy and validity of King's estimate, concluding that it is fairly reliable for age composition and total population.

GLASS, D.V., 'Graunt's Life Table', *J. Inst. Act.*, lxxvi (1950), 60–4.
An analysis of the statistical methods of one of the first demographers.

241

GLASS, D.V., 'A Note on the Under-Registration of Births in the Nineteenth Century', *Pop. St.*, v (1951–2), 70–88.
An analysis of the completeness of birth registration.

GLASS, D.V., 'Some Aspects of the Development of Demography', *J. Roy. Soc. Arts*, civ (1955–6), 854–69.
A survey of the development of demography from the pioneer days of Graunt to the first censuses and the work of William Farr and to the later development of statistical methods for the study of fertility, etc.

HECTOR, L.C., 'Hints on Interpreting the Public Records. The Census Returns of 1841 and 1851', *Amateur Hist.*, i (1953), 174–8.
A brief history of the censuses before 1841, with a description of the method of collection and the contents of the censuses of 1841 and 1851.

Interdepartmental Committee on Social and Economic Research, *Guides to Official Sources, No. 2. The Census Reports of Great Britain, 1810–1931*, H.M.S.O. (London 1951).
A history tracing developments and changes.

MARSHALL, L.M., 'The Levying of the Hearth Tax, 1662–88', *Eng. Hist. Rev.*, li (1936), 628–46.
An account of the administrative and financial background to the tax, with a description of popular reactions.

MITCHELL, B.R. and DEANE, P., *Abstract of British Historical Statistics* (Cambridge 1962).
This valuable collection of statistics includes population data, such as birth and death rates, statistics of sex and age groups, marital conditions, etc.

SCOTT, J.A., 'The London Bills of Mortality', *Report of the County Medical Officer of Health and the Principal School Medical Officer for the Year 1957*, L.C.C. (London 1958).
A study of the bills considering the difficulties of their interpretation such as the area covered, inaccuracies and problem of medical nomenclature, etc. This article also considers the population estimates of Graunt and Rickman, discussing their accuracy and the demographic trends shown.

TAYLOR, A.J., 'The Taking of the Census, 1801–1951', *Brit. Med. J.*, i (1951), 715–20.
A short history of the census, with a description of its machinery, forms of enquiry, and an assessment of its accuracy.

THIRSK, J., 'The Contents and Sources of English Agrarian History after 1500 with special reference to Lincolnshire', *Lincs. Hist.*, ii (1955), 31–44.
Although this describes mainly agricultural material, many of

the sources listed (such as the Archdeacons Returns of 1563 and 1603, the Muster Returns of 1558–88, the Hearth Tax Returns, the Compton Census, etc.) can be used to study the population.

THIRSK, J., 'Sources of Information on Population', *Amateur Hist.*, iv, nos. 4 and 5 (1959), 129–33 and 182–5.
A summary of the problems of studying demographic history for the period 1500–1760 and particularly for the years 1640–1700, stressing local variations and assessing the sources such as parish registers, the subsidy assessments of 1524 and 1525, the Chantry Certificates of 1547, the census returns of 1563 and 1603, the Protestation Returns of 1641–2, and the Hearth Tax Returns.
WRIGLEY, E.A., 'Parish Registers and Population History', *Amateur Hist.*, vi, Nos. 5 and 6 (1964–5), 146–151 and 198–203.

General studies dealing with population estimates, social and economic questions, review articles, etc.

BUER, M., *Health, Wealth and Population in Eighteenth Century England* (London 1926).
CHAMBERS, J.D., 'Enclosure and Labour Supply in the Industrial Revolution', *Econ. Hist. Rev.*, v (1953), 319–43.
A study of enclosure and its effects on population, labour supply, marriage rates, etc.
EVERSLEY, D.E.C., 'Population and Economic Growth in England before the "Take-Off". Some notes on methodology and the objects of future research', *First International Conference of Economic History, Contributions and Communications* (Stockholm 1960).
A study of the various possible explanations for eighteenth century population growth, such as a decline in mortality due to immunity, or to a decline in the virility of certain diseases, or to improvements in diet, etc.; or to a rise in the birth rate due to increased fertility, as a result of earlier marriage, the demand for labour, etc., and suggesting lines of future research.
GLASS, D.V., 'Gregory King and the Population of England and Wales at the end of the Seventeenth Century', *Eug. Rev.*, xxxvii (1946), 170–83.
A study of the methods and materials used by King.
GLASS, D.V., 'The Population Controversy in Eighteenth Century England, Part 1. The Background', *Pop. St.*, vi (1952–3), 69–91.
An account of the background to the contemporary discussion as to whether the population was rising or falling, considering the state of knowledge and views on the question of population decline, and of proposals to improve available statistics.

GLASS, D.V., 'Population and Population Movements in England and Wales, 1700–1850', in *Population in History*, ed. D. V. Glass and D. E. C. Eversley (London 1965).
A critical survey of literature and statistics available before the establishment of the census and the Registrar General's office.

GONNER, E.C.K., 'The Population of England in the Eighteenth Century', *J. Roy. Stat. Soc.*, lxxvi (1913), 261–303.
A discussion of various sources for the study of population in the eighteenth century, considering their reliability and with an attempt to calculate the total population using particularly Gregory King's estimate.

GRIFFITH, G.T., *Population Problems of the Age of Malthus* (Cambridge 1926).
The first study of the problem of population rise in the eighteenth century, estimating birth, death and marriage rates and discussing the influencing factors, such as medical and nutritional improvements.

HABAKKUK, H.J., 'English Population in the Eighteenth Century', *Econ. Hist. Rev.*, vi (1953), 117–33.
An article reviewing the accepted thesis that the increase in population in the eighteenth century was due to a fall in the death rate as a result of medical improvements, challenging these assumptions, and suggesting that the birth rate was the determining factor.

HABAKKUK, H.J., 'The Economic History of Modern Britain', *J. Econ. Hist.*, xviii (1958), 486–501.
A summary of the unsolved problems and the literature to date, with suggestions for further study and possible hypotheses, among these the explanation of the development of industry in terms of the growth of population.

HAMMOND, J.L., 'The Movement of Population during the Industrial Revolution', *Hist.*, xii (1927), 146–8.
A summary of the various theses and the state of knowledge explaining population rise.

HOLLINGSWORTH, T.H., 'A Demographic Study of the British Ducal Families', *Pop. St.*, xi (1957–8), 4–26.
A study of fertility and marriage rates of the highest social class, from the eighteenth century.

HOLLINGSWORTH, T.H., 'The Demography of the British Peerage', supp. *Pop. St.*, xviii, no. 2 (1964).

KRAUSE, J.T., 'Some Implications of Recent Work in Historical Demography', *Comp. St. Soc. Hist.*, i (1958), 164–88.

A critical study of the evidence for the hypothesis that the birth rate was the major determinant of population growth in the pre-industrial west, with a study of recent research on fertility and mortality.

LANGER, W.L., 'Europe's Initial Population Explosion', *Am. Hist. Rev.*, lxix (1963), 1–17.
A study of the problem, discussing particularly the influence of disease and diet, forwarding the thesis that improved diet was the main reason for the rise in population.

MARSHALL, T.H., 'The Population Problem during the Industrial Revolution', *Econ. Hist. Rev.*, i (1926–9), 429–56.

MARSHALL, T.H., 'The Population of England and Wales from the Industrial Revolution to the World War', *Econ. Hist. Rev.*, v (1934), 65–78.
A historical revision, discussing the work so far done in this field.

PHELPS BROWN, E.H., and HOPKINS, S.V., 'Wage Rates and Prices: Evidence for Population Pressure in the Sixteenth Century', *Economica*, xxiv (1957), 289–306.
A study using indices of retail prices and wage rates for unskilled labourers, which indicate a rise in the population during the sixteenth century followed by a decline in the seventeenth century due to plague, famine, etc.

RICH, E.E., 'The Population of Elizabethan England', *Econ. Hist. Rev.*, ii (1949–50), 247–65.
A study of the sources considering their accuracy, with estimates of the population for the years of the subsidies, also analysing population trends and migration, etc.

TUCKER, G.S.L., 'English Pre-Industrial Population Trends', *Econ. Hist. Rev.*, xvi (1963), 205–18.
A re-examination of the problem, questioning the exact date when the population began to increase.

WELTON, T.A., *England's Recent Progress. An Investigation of the Statistics of Migrations, Mortality, etc. from 1881–1901* (London 1911).
A large statistical study analysing migratory movements, their age structure, marriages and deaths, etc.

Studies of death rates

BROWNLEE, J., 'The History of the Birth and Death Rates in England and Wales, taken as a whole from 1570 to the present time', *Pub. Hlth. (Camb.)*, xxix (1915–16), 211–22, 228–38.

ELDERTON, W.P. and OGBORN, M.E., 'The Mortality of Adult Males since the middle of the Eighteenth Century, as shown by the experience of Life Assurance Companies', *J. Roy. Stat. Soc.*, cvi (1943), 1–30.
A study of the statistics of insurance companies and a comparison of the mortality rates of the general population, with tables and a discussion of the article.

EVERSLEY, D.E.C., 'Mortality in Britain in the Eighteenth Century; Problems and Prospects', *Conference on Historical Demography*, Paper 20 (Liège 1963).
A resumé of theories of the causes of population growth in the eighteenth century, discussing the problems of sources, the figures now collected and analysed and their implications.

HAMMOND, B.L., 'Urban Death Rates in the Early Nineteenth Century', *Econ. Hist.*, i (1926–9), 419–28.
A study of death rates, particularly in Manchester, concluding that the death rate did not decline.

LOGAN, W.P.D., 'Mortality in England and Wales from 1848–1947', *Pop. St.*, iv (1950–1), 132–78.
A survey of the changing causes of death, with tables of death rates by sex, age and cause of death for six periods.

MCKEOWN, T., and BROWN, R.G., 'Medical Evidence related to English Population Change in the Eighteenth Century', *Pop. St.*, ix (1955–6), 119–41.
An analysis of the influence of medical improvements, the traditional explanation of the rise in population, suggesting that these had little effect on the death rate, and concluding that the increase in population was more probably due to a rise in the birth rate than to a decline in the death rate.

MCKEOWN, T., and RECORD, R.G., 'Reasons for the Decline of Mortality in England and Wales during the Nineteenth Century', *Pop. St.*, xvi (1962–3), 94–122.
A study of the disease groups which account for the reduction in mortality from 1851 to 1900, discussing the possible influences and concluding that a rising standard of living was a more likely cause than medical therapy or changes in the relationship between the infectious organisms and the human host.

TAYLOR, W., 'Changing Mortality from 1841–1947, measured by the Life Table', *Brit. J. Soc. Med.*, v (1951), 162–76.
A history of life tables and a discussion of techniques.

Bibliography

Studies of marriage, fertility and birth rates

BLACKMORE, J.S., and MELLONIE, F.C., 'Family Endowment and the Birth Rate in the Early Nineteenth Century', *Econ. Hist.*, i (1926–9), 205–13, 412–18.

A study of the thesis that family allowances through parish relief and the Speenhamland System were a factor in decreasing the birth rate.

GLASS, D.V., 'Marriage Frequency and Economic Fluctuations in England and Wales 1851–1934', in *Political Arithmetic*, ed. L Hogben (London 1938).

A study of methods of analysing marriage rates.

GLASS, D.V., 'Changes in Fertility in England and Wales, 1851–1931,' in *Political Arithmetic*, ed. L. Hogben (London 1938).

A study of reproduction rates and fertility changes between the census years to throw some light on the marked fall in fertility.

GOODE, J.W., 'Marriage among the English Nobility in the Sixteenth and Seventeenth Centuries: A Comment', *Comp. St. Soc. Hist.*, iii (1960–1), 182–206.

A study of the aims and financial aspects of marriage.

HABAKKUK, H.J., 'Marriage Settlements in the Eighteenth Century', *Trans. Roy. Hist. Soc.*, xxxii (1950), 15–30.

A study of marriage arrangements of the aristocracy and gentry, and the social and legal devices to protect estates, etc.

KRAUSE, J.T., 'Changes in English Fertility and Mortality, 1781–1850', *Econ. Hist. Rev.*, xi (1958–9), 52–70.

A reconsideration of available evidence and demographic statistics, discussing under-registration of births and deaths in parish registers.

STEVENSON, T.H.C., 'The Fertility of Various Social Classes in England and Wales from the middle of the Nineteenth Century to 1911', *J. Roy. Stat. Soc.*, lxxxiii (1920), 401–44.

An analysis of fertility since 1876, by social class, occupation and place of residence.

Studies of internal migration and settlement

BUCKATZSCH, E.J., 'The Constancy of Local Populations and Migrations in England before 1800', *Pop. St.*, v (1951–2), 62–9.

A study of the possible statistical sources and methods for testing the constancy of populations and of migration at different dates, with summaries of results already obtained.

247

BOWLEY, A.L., 'Rural Population in England and Wales; a study of the Changes of Density, Occupation and Ages', *J. Roy. Stat. Soc.*, lxxvii (1914), 597–645.

A comprehensive study of rural population, with much statistical data including the numbers of persons in each registration district for the years 1861, 1901 and 1911, and estimates of weekly wages by counties from 1861.

CAIRNCROSS, A.K., 'Internal Migration in Victorian England', *Man. Sch. Econ. Soc. St.*, xvii (1949), 67–81.

A study of migration for the decennial periods from 1841 to 1911, also analysing the causes of migration into and from particular areas.

CUNNINGHAM, W., *Alien Immigrants to England* (London 1897).

A social study of immigrants to England from the time of the Norman Invasion to the French Revolution.

GARTNER, LLOYD P., 'Notes on the Statistics of Jewish Immigration to England, 1870–1914', *Jewish Soc. St.*, xxii (1960), 97–102.

HANDLEY, J.E., *The Irish in Scotland, 1798–1845* (Cork 1945).

A study of Irish immigration to Scotland, discussing seasonal migration, the occupations followed, areas of settlement, effects on Scottish institutions, etc.

HANDLEY, J.E., *The Irish in Modern Scotland* (Cork 1947).

A sequel to the above work.

KERR, B.M., 'Irish Seasonal Migration to Great Britain, 1800–38', *Irish Hist. St.*, iii (1942), 365–80.

A study of the reasons for and of the reactions to harvesting migration, in Ireland and England, and of its effects.

LAWTON, R., 'Irish Immigration to England and Wales in the Mid-Nineteenth Century', *Irish Geog.*, iv (1959), 35–54.

A comprehensive study of the features of Irish immigration, its importance and effect on England and Wales, with a detailed study of the Irish community in Liverpool in 1851.

NEWTON, M.P., and JEFFREY, J.R., *Internal Migration*. General Register Office, Studies on Medical and Population Subjects, No. 5, H.M.S.O. (London 1951).

A study of migration and changes in population distribution since the Industrial Revolution, and particularly for the period 1947–50, with detailed statistics for special areas, of the size and direction of migrant streams, age and sex composition, etc.

REDFORD, A., *Labour Migration in England, 1800–50* (2nd ed., Manchester 1964).

A study of internal migration, showing that the bulk of the movement was short-distance; with a revised bibliography.

Bibliography

SAVILLE, J., *Rural Depopulation in England and Wales, 1851–1951* London 1957).
 A study of the causes, patterns and effects of migration from rural to urban areas, with a detailed analysis of the South Hams district of South Devon.

SMITH, C.T., 'The Movement of Population in England and Wales in 1851 and 1861', *Geog. J.*, cxvii (1951), 200–10.
 A consideration of the censuses and particularly of the enumerators' notebooks as source material for the study of migration, relating this to the economic conditions of different areas and indicating the main areas of population loss and gain.

WELTON, T.A., 'Population Movements in England and Wales, 1881–1901', *Spectator*, ci (1906), 692–3.
 A study of internal migration to industrial centres, colliery districts, military and naval depots, considering the areas of greatest immigration and emigration.

PART 2: LOCAL STUDIES OF DEMOGRAPHIC HISTORY

Scotland

ADAM, M.I., 'The Causes of the Highland Emigrations of 1783–1803', *Scot. Hist. Rev.*, xvii (1920), 73–89.
 Arguing that over-population was the determining cause.

CROWE, P.R., 'The Population of the Scottish Lowlands', *Scot. Geog. Mag.*, xliii (1927), 147–67.
 A geographical description with accounts of population densities and changes for periods from 1810 to 1921.

DEWDNEY, J.C., 'Changes in Population Distribution in the County of Fife', *Scot. Geog. Mag.*, lxxi (1955), 27–42.
 A study of the population in various parishes, related to natural resources, agriculture, climate, industry, etc.

DUNLOP, J.C., 'The Fertility of Marriage in Scotland; a Census Study', *J. Roy. Stat. Soc.*, lxxvii (1914), 259–88.
 A study of fertility considering the influence of age at marriage, occupation, etc., with statistical data from 1861.

FERGUSON, T., 'Mortality in Shetland a Hundred Years Ago', *Scot. Med. J.*, v (1960), 107–12.
 A study of the causes of death and of the age at death from death certificates.

GAILEY, R.A., 'Settlement and Population in Kyntyre, 1750–1800', *Scot. Geog. Mag.*, lxxvi (1960), 99–107.
 A reconstruction of the population using estate papers and two estate censuses of 1779 and 1792, analysing the areas of settlement, age and sex structure, and social status.

249

GAULD, W.A., 'Agriculture and Population in Galloway', *Scot. Geog. Mag.*, xxxviii (1922), 232–42.
A survey of types of agriculture and population statistics from parish sources from 1775.

KYD, J.G., 'Scotland's Population', *Scot. Hist. Rev.*, xxviii (1949), 97–107.
A survey of demographic trends since Webster's census of 1755, with tables for the decennial census periods.

KYD, J.G., *Scottish Population Statistics, including Webster's Analysis of Population, 1755* (Edinburgh 1952).
A copy of Webster's Census, which gives the total population divided into protestants and papists and the number of 'fighting men' for all parishes; with an introduction giving the background and information on earlier estimates, and appendixes of civil census material and intercensal increases and decreases.

LEARMOUTH, A.T.A., 'The Population of the Isle of Skye', *Scot. Geog. Mag.*, lxvi (1950), 77–103.
A non-statistical study of population, considering the influence of environmental factors, agriculture and industry.

MACDONALD, D.F., *Scotland's Shifting Population, 1770–1850* (Glasgow 1937).
A study of population, considering changes, rural depopulation, industrial and urban concentration, Irish immigration, etc.

MCINTOSH, N.A., 'Changing Population Distribution in the Cart Basin in the Eighteenth and Early Nineteenth Centuries', *Trans. Pap. Inst. Brit. Geog.*, Pub. No. 22 (1956,) 139–57.
A study of an area within the county of Renfrewshire, from the time of the Poll Tax of 1695 to the nineteenth century, considering changes in distribution related to the decline in agriculture and the development of industries.

O'DELL, A.C., 'The Population of Scotland, 1755–1931. A General Survey', *Scot. Geog. Mag.*, xlviii (1932), 282–90.
A reconstruction of the population using Webster's census and the public censuses, with diagrams showing densities, natural increases, etc.

O'DELL, A.C., 'Population Changes', in *The North East of Scotland* ed. A.C.O'Dell and J.MacKintosh (Aberdeen 1963).
A brief study of population trends in the Aberdeen area, since Webster's analysis.

OSBORNE, R.H., 'Scottish Migration Statistics: A Note', *Scot. Geog. Mag.*, lxxii (1956), 153–9.

Bibliography

A study of the period 1855 to 1954, analysing the redistribution of the population, natural increase and migration, by counties.

OSBORNE, R.H., 'The Movements of People in Scotland, 1851–1951', *Scot. St.*, ii (1958), 1–46.
A study of internal migration, immigration and natural increase, related to agricultural and industrial changes.

REHFISCH, F., 'Marriage and the Elementary Family among the Scottish Tinkers', *Scot. St.*, v (1961), 121–48.
A description of the marriage customs and family life of a minority group.

WALTON, K., 'The Distribution of Population in Aberdeenshire, 1696', *Scot. Geog. Mag.*, lxvi (1950), 17–26.
A discussion of population densities and agricultural settlement, from a poll tax which gives the name, status, place of residence and occupation, of all over the age of sixteen and not a pauper.

WALTON, K., 'Climate and Famines in North-East Scotland', *Scot. Geog. Mag.*, lxviii (1952), 13–24.
A general and non-statistical study of harvests and famines in the eighteenth century.

WALTON, K.,'Population Changes in the North East of Scotland, 1696–1951', *Scot. St.*, v (1961), 149–80.
A study of the changes, rates of increase and decline of the population with a consideration of the background to them.

WALTON, K.,'Regional Settlement', in *The North East of Scotland*, ed. A.C. O'Dell and J. Mackintosh (Aberdeen 1963).
A study of settlement and migration from the eighteenth to the twentieth centuries.

YOUNGSON, A., 'Alexander Webster and his "Account of the Number of People in Scotland in the Year 1755"', *Pop. St.*, xv (1961–2), 198–200.
An account of the making and contents of the census.

Wales

DAVIES, V.C., 'Some Geographical Aspects of the Decline in the Rural Population of Wales with special reference to Merioneth', *J. Merioneth Hist. Rec. Soc.*, ii (1953), 58–65.
An analysis of the places of migration from Merioneth for the period 1851–1911, with tables and maps for the census years.

GILPIN, M.C., 'Population Changes round the Shores of Milford Haven from 1800 to the Present Day', *Field St.*, i (1960), 23–36.
A study of changes in population totals and distribution for five periods – 1801–41, 1841–91, 1891–1931, 1931–51 and 1951–60.

251

HODGES, T.M., 'The Peopling of the Hinterland and the Port of Cardiff', *Econ. Hist. Rev.*, xvii (1947), 62–72.
A study of migration into South Wales from England from 1801 to 1914.

LEWIS, E.D., 'Population, Immigration, the Welsh Language', in *The Rhondda Valleys* (London 1959).

MINCHINTON, W.E., 'The Place of Brecknock in the Industrialisation of South Wales', *Brycheiniog*, vii (1961), 1–70.
A study of population growth and particularly of immigration, analysing the character and places of origin of immigrants from the year 1801.

OWEN, L., 'The Population of Wales in the Sixteenth and Seventeenth Centuries', *Trans. Hon. Soc. Cymmrodorion*, 1959, 99–113.
A reconstruction of the population of Wales for the period 1550 to 1563 and 1664 to 1670, from Hearth Tax returns, with an estimate of the increase in population by counties and by hundreds.

OWEN, L., 'The Growth of Population in Anglesey, 1563–1801', *Trans. Anglesey Antiqu. Soc. Field Club* (1960), 26–38.
A reconstruction of figures of total population in the parishes of Anglesey for the years 1563, 1670 and 1801.

PARRY, O., 'The Hearth Tax of 1662 in Merioneth', *J. Merioneth Hist. Rec. Soc.*, ii (1953), 16–38.
A description and history of the tax, with a copy of the part relating to Merioneth with notes.

PHILLIPS, Rev.J., 'The Oldest Parish Registers in Pembrokeshire', *Arch. Camb.*, ii (1902), 115–27; iii (1903), 298–318; v (1905), 38–61.
A study of the registers of St Mary's Haverfordwest, relating points of interest such as the state of the documents, families, years of high death rates, etc.

SYLVESTER, D., 'Settlement Patterns in Anglesey', *Trans. Anglesey Antiqu. Soc. Field Club* (1949), 1–24.
A study of settlement divided into five periods from the Tudor period to the twentieth century.

SYLVESTER, D., 'Settlement Patterns in Rural Flintshire', *Flints. Hist. Rec. Soc. Pub.*, xv (1954–5), 6–42.
A study of the border area from the Early English settlement to the nineteenth century, considering geographical factors and agricultural influences.

THOMAS, B., 'Wales and the Atlantic Economy', *Scot. J. Pol. Econ.*, vi (1959), 169–92.
A general study paying particular attention to a comparison of migration characteristics of England and Wales.

Bibliography

THOMAS, B., 'The Migration of Labour into the Glamorganshire Coalfield, 1861–1911', *Economica*, x (1930), 275–94.
A statistical study of population, immigration and economic activity in the South Wales coalfield.

WILLIAMS, D., 'A Note on the Population of Wales, 1536–1801', *Bull. Bd. Celtic St.*, viii (1935), 359–63.
A consideration of the reliability of the sources with tables of population totals.

WILLIAMS, M.I., 'Seasonal Migration of Cardiganshire Harvest Groups to the Vale of Glamorgan in the Nineteenth Century', *Ceredigon*, iii (1957), No. 2.

Northern England, comprising the counties of Northumberland, Cumberland, Westmorland nad Durham

BAINBRIDGE, T.H., 'Cumberland Population Movements, 1871–81', *Geog. J.*, cviii (1946), 80–4.
A study of the population and industrial growth of the area, during a decade of great local prosperity, considering the role of migration from rural to industrial areas, and from outside the country.

BAINBRIDGE, T.H., 'Population Changes over the West Cumberland Coalfield', *Econ. Geog.*, xxv (1949), 128–33.
A study of population increase and decrease from 1801 to 1931, discussing the trends and factors in the parishes of the area.

HOUSE, J.W., 'North-Eastern England; Population Movements and the Landscape since the early nineteenth century', *Research Ser., No. 1, Dept. Geog. Univ. Durham* (Durham 1954).
A study of population, employment and migration from the first official figures to 1951.

JAMES, F.G., 'The Population of the Diocese of Carlisle in 1676', *Trans. Cumb. West. Antiqu. Archaeol. Soc.*, li (1952), 137–41.
A copy of a document, probably compiled from returns of local clergy, listing the parishes, the number of communicants, Catholics, Quakers and Dissenters.

JONES, G.P., 'The Population of Broughton-in-Furness in the Eighteenth Century', *Trans. Cumb. West. Antiqu. Archaeol. Soc.*, liii (1954), 136–48.
An attempt to estimate the population of the district, using parish registers and the census of 1801, and analysing the influences of a rising birth rate, of an apparently declining death rate and of immigration into the area.

JONES, G.P., 'Some Population Problems relating to Cumberland and Westmorland in the Eighteenth Century', *Trans. Cumb. West. Antiqu. Archaeol. Soc.*, lviii (1959), 123–39.

A reconstruction of the population, using Rickman's estimate, an estimate by Denton on Carlisle and parish registers, and assessing the environmental factors behind the population increase.

SMAILES, A.E., 'Population Changes in the Colliery Districts of Northumberland and Durham', *Geog. J.*, xci (1938), 220–32.

Yorkshire

BECKWITH, F., 'The Population of Leeds during the Industrial Revolution', *Thoresby Soc.*, xli (1948), 118–96 and 401.

A study using parish registers, the figures from visitations and private estimates, analysing marriage, birth and death rates, the causes of death, migration, etc., with appendixes giving population totals from the registers and the bills of mortality.

BRETTON, R., 'Settlement Certificates and Removal Orders', *Halifax Antiqu. Soc.*, (1959), 9–26.

Copies of certificates and orders for the late seventeenth century and the eighteenth century, with a descriptive introduction.

BUCKATZSCH, E.J., 'Occupations in the Parish Registers of Sheffield, 1655–1719', *Econ. Hist. Rev.*, i (1948–9), 145–50.

A study of the parish registers to make tentative deductions as to the distribution of the working class among the occupations, which shows the importance of the cutlery trade.

BUCKATZSCH, E.J., 'The Places of Origin of a Group of Immigrants into Sheffield, 1624–1799', *Econ. Hist. Rev.*, ii (1949–50), 303–6.

A study of labour migration from the lists of indentures of the Cutler's Company, showing that there was not much increase in the distance travelled.

DRAKE, M., 'An Elementary Exercise in Parish Register Demography', *Econ. Hist. Rev.*, xiv (1961–2), 427–45.

A study of sixteenth and seventeenth centuries parish registers for three Yorkshire wapentakes, analysing demographic trends, with tables of annual baptisms, burials and marriages.

FARRER, J.A., 'Mortality: Changing Pattern', *Lancet*, i (1957), 365–7.

A study of the ages at death and the causes of death from the parish registers of rural parishes from the year 1804.

Bibliography

SHEPPARD, J.A., 'Rural Population Changes Since 1851. Three Sample Studies', *Social Rev.*, x (1962), 81–95.
An analysis of depopulation in terms of labour requirements, different types of farming, etc., in three Yorkshire parishes.

Derbyshire, Lancashire and Cheshire

COUZENS, F.C., 'Distribution of Population of the Mid-Derwent Basin since the Industrial Revolution', *Geog.*, xxvi (1941), 31–8.
A study of population and industry.

GODFREY, W.E., 'The Plague of Chesterfield, 1586–7', *J. Derby. Archaeol. Nat. Hist. Soc.*, lxxiv (1954), 32–42.
A study of plague related to the state of the economy, with the information on deaths apparently compiled from parish registers.

HOWSON, W.G., 'Plague, Poverty and Population in parts of north-west England, 1580 1720', *Trans. Hist. Soc. Lancs. and Chesh.*, cxii (1961), 29–57.
A medical-statistical study of plague in a number of Lancashire villages and of the recovery in the post-plague period.

LAWTON, R., 'The Population of Liverpool in the mid-nineteenth century', *Trans. Hist. Soc. Lancs. and Chesh.*, cvii (1955), 89–120.
An analysis of the population considering occupations, age and sex structure, Irish immigration, etc., with maps, diagrams and statistics.

MARSHALL, J.D., 'The Lancashire Rural Labourer in the Early Nineteenth Century', *Trans. Lancs. Chesh. Antiqu. Soc.*, lxxi (1961), 90–128.
A study of the standard of living, wages, employment, etc., of the rural working class for the period 1812 to 1833, and of the factors influencing migration to the industrial areas.

MORRISON, E.J.D., 'The Hearth Tax in Chester', *J. Chester North Wales Arch. Archaeol. Hist. Soc.*, xxvi (1947), 31–43.
An analysis of the Hearth Tax, dealing mainly with the size of houses and the occupations of those assessed.

SYLVESTER, D., 'Rural Settlement in Cheshire; Some Problems of Origin and Classification', *Trans. Hist. Soc. Lancs. Chesh.*, ci (1949), 1–34.
A study of settlement and population from the Domesday Survey to the nineteenth century.

WATERS, R.E. CHESTER, 'A Statutory List of the Inhabitants of Melbourne, Derbyshire, in 1695', *J. Derby. Archaeol. Nat. Hist. Soc.*, vii (1885), 4–30.
A copy of a tax assessment with a reconstruction of the population, households and occupations.

West Midlands, comprising the counties of Staffordshire, Shropshire, Herefordshire, Worcestershire and Warwickshire

EVERSLEY, D.E.C., 'A Survey of Population in an Area of Worcestershire from 1660–1850, on the Basis of Parish Records', *Pop. St.*, x (1956–7), 253–79.
   An attempt to reconstruct total population and birth, death and marriage rates, using parish registers.

JACKSON, J.N., 'Thoughts on the Distribution of the Rural Population in Herefordshire at the beginning of the nineteenth century', *Trans. Woolhope Nat. Field Club*, xxxiv (1952–4), 178–94.
   A study of parish populations, relating these to geological conditions, communications, agricultural and cultural influences, to explain the low density of population in the nineteenth century.

LAWTON, R., 'Population Movements in the West Midlands, 1841–61', *Geog.*, xliii (1958), 164–77.
   A study of migration and population loss and gain, using census birth place data for the West Midlands.

REDMILL, C.E., 'The Growth of Population in the East Warwickshire Coalfield', *Geog.*, xvi (1931), 125–40.
   A study of population density and changes from 1801, discussing the influence of mining and industry.

SOGNER, S., 'Aspects of the Demographic Situation in Seventeen Parishes in Shropshire, 1711–60. An Exercise Based on Parish Registers', *Pop. St.*, xvii (1963), 126–46.
   A study from the parish registers of the Coalbrookdale area of birth, death and marriage rates, with an attempt to establish total population, using calculated birth and death rates.

STYLES, P.H., 'A Census of a Warwickshire Village in 1698', *Univ. B'ham. Hist. J.*, iii (1951–2), 33–51.
   A reconstruction from a surviving manuscript of the 'Marriage Duties Tax' for Fenny Compton for the year 1698, showing fertility and death rates and using comparisons with the Hearth Tax returns to establish social structure, wealth and migration.

STYLES, P.H., 'The Evolution of the Law of Settlement', *Univ. B'ham. Hist. J.*, ix (1963), 9–63.
   A study of the law and its administration from the records of Warwickshire villages.

WALKER, M., *Warwickshire County Records: Hearth Tax Returns, Vol. 1. Hemlingford Hundred: Tamworth and Athelstone Divisions.* With an introduction to the Warwickshire Hearth Tax Records by P.H. Styles (Warwick 1957).

Bibliography

A copy of the records, with an introduction considering the history of the assessment and analysing the returns.

WISE, M.J., 'Some Notes on the Growth of Population in the Cannock Chase Coalfield', *Geog.*, xxxvi (1951), 235–48.

An investigation of the characteristics of the population structure, demonstrating that many demographic problems originated in the rapid development of the area after 1850, describing the growth of population, the age and sex structure, etc.

East Midlands, comprising the counties of Huntingdonshire, Leicestershire, Lincolnshire, Northamptonshire, Nottinghamshire and Rutland

CHAMBERS, J.D., 'The Vale of Trent, 1670–1800. A Regional Study of Economic Change', *Econ. Hist. Rev.*, Supp. 3 (1951).

A study of industrial development and population trends.

CHAMBERS, J.D., 'Population Change in a Provincial Town, Nottingham, 1700–1800', in *Studies in the Industrial Revolution*, ed. L.S. Pressnell (London 1960).

A study of Nottingham, demonstrating the nature of the link between industry and demographic forces, and reconstructing birth and death rates, with quinquennial tables of various demographic data.

CLARKE, A.B., 'Melton Mowbray Lay Subsidy, 1548', *Trans. Leics. Archaeol. Soc.*, xviii (1934–5), 196–201.

A copy of the subsidy, with an introduction and notes on the population.

CONSTANT, A., 'The Geographical Background of Inter-Village Population Movements in Northamptonshire and Huntingdonshire, 1754–1943', *Geog.*, xxxiii (1948), 78–88.

A study of population movement from parish registers, for the periods 1754–1844 and 1844–1943, analysing the direction, extent and causes of movement.

CORNWALL, C.E., 'The People of Rutland in 1522', *Trans. Leics. Archaeol. Soc.*, xxxvii (1961–2), 7–28.

A study from a muster return, examining the system of land tenure, the distribution of wealth and population.

CORNWALL, J., 'An Elizabethan Census', *Rec. Bucks.*, xvi (1956), 258–73.

An attempt to reconstruct the population from a survey of men and harness made in 1522, of which only fragments survive, and from an ecclesiastical survey of 1562–3, of the diocese of Lincoln.

GOULD, J.D., 'The Inquisition of Depopulation of 1607 in Lincolnshire', *Eng. Hist. Rev.*, lxvii (1952), 392–6.

A short study of depopulation and emigration, showing that both were great in Lincolnshire.

GUILFORD, E. L., 'Nottinghamshire in 1676', *Trans. Thoroton Soc.*, xxviii (1924), 106–13.

A copy of a manuscript of a religious census which enables an estimate of the total adult population to be made.

HOSFORD, W. H., 'Scopwickiana. A Lincolnshire Village in 1838', *Lincs. Hist.*, ii, No. 7 (1960), 29–37.

A study of the village of Scopwick from a descriptive book published in 1838, with a section on population, enumerating occupations, ages, sex, etc.

HOSKINS, W. G., 'Wigston Magna Lay Subsidies, 1327–1599', *Trans. Leics. Archaeol. Soc.*, xx (1938–9), 55–64.

A study of the subsidies, giving the population in families for the years 1524–5, 1564 and 1605, indicating a rapid rise in population during the sixteenth century, with copies of the subsidies.

HOSKINS, W. G., 'The Population of an English Village, 1086–1801', *Trans. Leics. Archaeol. Soc.*, xxxiii (1957), 15–35.

An analysis of population trends, particularly for the period 1524–1801, with an introduction describing the source material for each period.

LANGLEY, A. S., 'A Religious Census of 1676, A.D.', *Lincs. Notes Queries*, xvi (1920–1), 33–51.

A copy of the sections of the Compton Census relating to Lincolnshire with an introduction.

LASLETT, P., and HARRISON, J., 'Clayworth and Cogenhoe', in *Historical Essays 1600–1750, presented to D. Ogg*, ed. H. E. Bell and R. L. Ollard (London 1962)

MILLS, D. R., 'The Poor Laws and the Distribution of Population *c.*1600–1800, with special reference to Lincolnshire', *Pub. Inst. Brit. Geog.*, xxvi (1959), 185–95.

A description of the Elizabethan Poor Law, the Law of Settlement and the Poor Law Reform Act of 1834, with a discussion of a method of assessing the effects of the Poor Laws on the distribution of population and a description of this in certain parts of Lincolnshire.

MORLEY, C. D., 'Population of Northampton and the Ise Valley, 1801–1951', *East Mid. Geog.*, No. 11 (1959), 20–9.

A study of population trends in a country dominated by the development of one town and by a group of smaller towns on the River Ise.

PARKER, L. A., 'The Depopulation Returns for Leicestershire in 1607', *Trans. Leics. Archaeol. Soc.*, xxii (1947), 229–93.

A study of enclosures in Leicestershire, with a copy of the commission's returns, followed by tables analysing the distribution of enclosures among the social classes.

PEYTON, S.A., 'The Village Population in the Tudor Lay Subsidy Rolls', *Eng. Hist. Rev.*, xxx (1915), 234–50.
A discussion of the status of those paying this tax, and an attempt to reconstruct the population from a comparison of the rolls for Nottinghamshire.

WOOD, A.C., 'A Note on the Population of Nottingham in the Seventeenth Century', *Trans. Thoroton Soc.*, xl (1936), 109–13.
An attempt to estimate population changes and the death rate from the records of three Anglican churches of the town, concluding that the sharp increase in population in the 1730s was due to immigration.

WOOD, A.C., 'A Note on the Population of Six Notts. Towns in the Seventeenth Century', *Trans. Thoroton Soc.*, xli (1937), 18–26.
A study of Worksop, Mansfield, Newark, East Retford, Southwell and Tuxford, using statistics of burials and annual death rates to estimate total population for various periods from the late sixteenth century to the mid-eighteenth century.

East Anglia, comprising the counties of Norfolk, Suffolk and Cambridgeshire

BROOKES, P.F., 'The Pattern of Settlement in East Anglia', *Chesh. Hist.*, No. 8 (1957), 13–20.
A study of settlements from those of the Early English to the nineteenth century, as influenced by geographical and agricultural conditions.

DARBY, H.C., 'The Movement of Population to and from Cambridgeshire between 1851 and 1861', *Geog. J.*, ci (1943), 118–25.
A consideration of the thesis of short distance migration using census material, concluding that for this decade at least migration to London and to the industrial areas of Lancashire and Yorkshire was as strong as short distance movement.

DICKINSON, R.E., 'The Distribution and Functions of the Smaller Urban Settlements in East Anglia', *Geog.*, xvii (1932), 19–31.
A study of urban settlements in a rural area, considering their origins, size, amenities, etc.

Home Counties, comprising the counties of Bedfordshire, Berkshire, Buckinghamshire, Essex, Middlesex, Oxfordshire and Surrey

ALLISON, K.J., 'An Elizabethan "Census" of Ealing', *Ealing Loc. Hist. Soc.*, Members' Papers, No. 2 (1962).

A copy of a list of inhabitants made in 1599, which gives the names, ages and occupations of the population, divided into households, with an introduction and suggestions as to its use.

CANNAN, E., *Notes on the Population of Oxford* (London 1901).

A short study with a section on nineteenth-century changes, dealing only with totals and population per room as in the 1891 census.

MARSHALL, L.M., 'The Rural Population of Bedfordshire, 1671– 1921', *Pub. Beds. Hist. Rec. Soc.*, xvi (1934), 2–198.

An investigation particularly of the increase and decline in the population of the parishes of Bedfordshire, based on the Hearth Tax return of 1671 and on the censuses of 1801 and 1921.

MEEKINGS, C.A.F., 'Surrey Hearth Tax, 1664', *Surrey Rec. Soc.*, xvii (1940).

A copy of the tax, with an introduction and tables of population structure.

MELVILLE, R., 'Records of Apprenticeship and Settlement in a Berkshire Village in the Eighteenth Century', *Trans. Newbury Dist. Field Club*, x (1954), 32–43.

A study of settlements in the parish of Blewbury, with extracts from the Poor Law papers and a list of those paupers who received settlements in the parish for the years 1697–1801.

MUNBY, L., *Hertfordshire Population Statistics, 1563-1801* (Hitchin 1964).

Copies of figures of population from ecclesiastical sources, with and introduction on their use and on population trends.

London

BROWNLEE, J., 'The Health of London in the Eighteenth Century', *Proc. Roy. Soc. Med.*, xviii (1924–5), Sect. Epidem. State Med., 73–85.

Estimates of the death rate by age and by disease from the London Bills of Mortality.

GEORGE, M.D., 'Some Causes of the Increase of the Population in the Eighteenth Century as illustrated by London', *Econ. J.*, xxxii (1922), 325–52.

An examination of the London Bills of Mortality, and a consideration of the influence of gin, Hanway's Act and medical improvements as causes of the decline in the death rate in eighteenth-century London.

JONES, P.E., and JUDGES, A.V., 'London Population in the Late Seventeenth Century', *Econ. Hist. Rev.*, vi (1935), 45–63.

A study and comparison of King's estimate and of the authors' estimate of the population, compiled from the returns of the tax on baptisms, marriages and burials in 1695.

KORZYBSKI, S., 'Le Peuplement des grandes agglomérations urbaines. Londres et Paris aux XIXᵉ et XXᵉ Siecles', *Population,* vii (1952), 485–520.

SHANNON, H. A., 'Migration and the Growth of London, 1841–91', *Econ. Hist. Rev.,* v, pt. 2 (1934), 79–86.
A study of the increase in population, considering whether this was due to natural increase or to immigration, and also considering the places of origin of immigrants.

South-East England, comprising the counties of Hampshire, Kent and Sussex

CHALKLIN, C. W., 'The Compton Census of 1676: The Dioceses of Canterbury and Rochester', in Kent Records, A Seventeenth Century Miscellany, *Kent Archaeol. Soc., Records Publication Committee,* xvii (1960), 153–74.
A copy of the census with an attempt to reconstruct the population.

KENYON, G. H., 'Kirdford Inventories, 1611–1776', *Sussex Archaeol. Coll.,* xciii (1955), 78–156.
A study of agriculture, with information about numbers of population, occupations and prosperity in a large parish.

JOHNSTON, G.D., 'Wisborough Green Population in 1831', *Sussex Notes Queries,* xiii (1953), 254–5.
A copy of the enumerator's draft of 1831.

South-West England, comprising the counties of Gloucestershire, Wiltshire, Dorset and Somerset

DAWE, P. N., 'A Dorset Lay Subsidy Roll, 1525', *Somerset Dorset Notes Queries,* xxvi (1954), 204–13, 225–30; xxvii (1955), 25–30, 54–7.
A copy of the Roll with notes, mainly dealing with the distribution of wealth.

MEEKINGS, C.A.F., *Dorset Hearth Tax Assessments, 1662-1664* (Dorchester 1951).
A copy of the tax, with an introduction dealing with the history of the source and its use in population reconstruction.

SHANNON, H.A., and GREBENIK, E., *The Population of Bristol* (Cambridge 1943).
A study of population trends, with a historical survey from 1861.

SMITH, M. WEAVER, 'Snap – a Modern Example of Depopulation', *Wilts, Archaeol. J.*, lvii (1958–60), 386–90.

A study of a settlement which was completely depopulated as a result of the decline in farming at the end of the nineteenth century.

TAWNEY, A.J., and TAWNEY, R.H., 'An Occupational Census of the Seventeenth Century', *Econ. Hist. Rev.*, v (1934), 25–64.

An analysis of a census relating to Gloucestershire men in the year 1608, describing their occupations and the distribution of industries.

Western England, comprising the counties of Devon and Cornwall

CHOPE, R. PEARSE, 'The Early History of the Manor of Hartland', *Rep. Trans. Devon. Assoc.*, xxxiv (1902), 418–54.

A manorial history, also considering the evidence for the existence of free tenents, particularly for the years 1301 and 1566.

HOSKINS, W.G., 'Population', in *Devon* (London 1954).

A general survey of the population of the county from the Domesday Survey to the twentieth century.

PICKARD, R., *Population and Epidemics of Exeter in Pre-Census Times* (Exeter 1947).

A reconstruction of the population and epidemics, using parish registers, wills and bishops' registers.

POUNDS, N.J.G., 'Population Movement in Cornwall and the Rise of Mining in the Eighteenth Century', *Geog.*, xxviii (1943), 37–46.

An attempt to assess migration using ecclesiastical lists of total population or of the number of families in each parish.

The Isle of Man and The Scilly Isles

DURY, G.H., 'The Population of Guernsey: An Essay in Historical Geography', *Geog.*, xxxiii (1948), 61–9.

A study of population from 1600, with maps of distribution from the mid-eighteenth century to 1931, and tables of parish population for the years 1615, 1651, 1727 and the decennial censuses.

HARRISON, W., 'A List of the Householders in the Town of Douglas, Isle of Man, with their names, 1730', *Manx Soc.*, xxx (1880), No. 3.

A copy of a record giving the names of residents, with the number of children, servants and lodgers, with an introduction giving information on population for two other eighteenth century sources.

Bibliography

MOORE, W., *A History of the Isle of Man* (London 1900).
Population figures and some analysis for the period 1765–1900
are given in Vol. 1, 412–3 and in Vol. 2, 572–4; and tables of
population for the main towns and villages for certain years in
the eighteenth century and for the census years in Vol. 2, 646–7.

ROBIN, A.C., 'Notes on the Population of Guernsey', *Trans. La
Société Guernesiase*, xiv (1946–9), 181–94.
A survey of the changes in numbers, the age and sex structure
and the distribution of the population from the early nineteenth
century to 1931.

PART 3: PRINCIPAL SERIES OF PRINTED PARISH
REGISTER TRANSCRIPTS

Bedfordshire Parish Register (Bedford 1931–)
Cumberland and Westmorland Antiquarian and Archaeological
   Society – Parish Register Section (1912–)
Devon and Cornwall Record Society (Exeter 1910–)
Durham and Northumberland Parish Register Society (Sunderland,
   Newcastle-upon-Tyne 1898–1926)
Dwelly's Parish Records (Herne Bay 1913–26)
Harleian Society – Registers of London Parishes (London 1877–)
Lancashire Parish Register Society (Rochdale, etc. 1898–)
Lincoln Record Society – Parish Register Section (Lincoln 1914–25)
Parish Register Society (London 1896–)
Shropshire Parish Register Society (1900–)
Staffordshire Parish Register Society (London 1902–)
Sussex Record Society (Lewes 1911–)
Worcestershire Parish Register Society (Worcester 1913–)
Yorkshire Parish Register Society (Leeds 1899–)

Phillimore Series of Marriage Registers (ed. successively by W. P. W.
   Phillimore, T. M. Blagg, and C. H. Ridge from 1897) for the
   counties of Berkshire, Buckingham, Cambridge, Cheshire,
   Cornwall, Cumberland, Derby, Dorset, Essex, Gloucester,
   Hampshire, Hertford, Huntingdon, Kent, Leicester, Lincoln,
   Middlesex, Norfolk, Northampton, Nottingham, Oxford, Somerset,
   Suffolk, Warwick, Wiltshire, Worcester and York.

Lynda Ovenall

APPENDIX A

A METHOD OF DETERMINING A BASE POPULATION
FOR AN INTERMEDIATE PERIOD BETWEEN
CENSUS YEARS. (*Based on S. Sogner's paper*)[1]

THE basis of this method is the assumption that although it is unlikely that any given population will exhibit a steady growth rate, it is plausible to assume that birth rates (as measured by quinquinnial averages) do not exhibit very considerable variations at any rate before 1800.

We then ask: what birth rate would produce the natural increase shown in the registers? From existing work in this field, it seems that in general rates are between thirty and forty per thousand. Therefore the extreme limits of the population at a given time are those which would yield, with the observed baptisms, rates within those limits.

In fact we calculate the base population in the following manner: *Multiply* the average annual baptisms of the *second* base period by a thousand and divide by x (indicating birthrate). *Subtract* average annual baptisms of the *first* base period multiplied by a thousand and divide by x. The result should equal the observed natural increase between the two periods. From this, we can calculate x – the birthrate.

Example: Average baptisms 1756–60   712·2
Average baptisms 1711–15   407·2
Natural increase (Burials – baptisms) 1711–60
=8,615

Then $$\frac{712·2 \times 1,000}{x} - \frac{407·2 \times 1,000}{x} = 8,615 \qquad x = 35·4$$

Therefore   population $1711 = \frac{407·2}{35·4} \times 1,000 = 11,563$

,, $1760 = \frac{712·2}{35·4} \times 1,000 = 20,118$

264

Appendix A

From these base figures we calculate annual totals (forwards from 1711 and backwards from 1760) and the determined intermediate *rates* by the normal process.

This method has the disadvantage that it gives inaccurate results if the average baptisms of the base period represent abnormal years. Moreover, if there has been a change in the birthrate circular reasoning distorts the results. If, for instance, the observed natural increase is the result of a birthrate of 30 in 1711, and 32 in 1760, the net increase resulting would be the same, and the same is true if other possible combinations. Nevertheless, it may be claimed that this method does produce plausible base populations in what might otherwise be a vacuum, and the method is particularly suitable where there are no continuous series between say, the Hearth Tax or the Compton Census and the Census of 1801. Moreover, although the absolute rates are not reliable, their relative behaviour gives a better guide. But then this consideration applies to almost any model growth curve we may devise.

D. E. C. Eversley

1 S. Sogner, 'Aspects of the Demographic situation in Seventeen Parishes in Shropshire, 1711–60. An Exercise based on Parish Registers', *Pop. Stud.*, xvii (1963).

APPENDIX B

POPULATION GROWTH CURVES

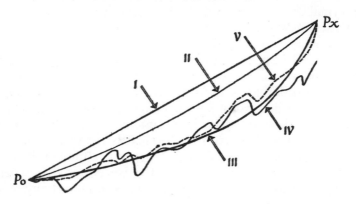

THE following general models may be considered for growth curves.

1. Curve I. The straight line connecting two known populations (enumeration dates). This implies, of course, a steadily decreasing rate of growth – unlikely in the eighteenth century when most of the increase took place in the last third of the century, but more acceptable for, say, the period 1550–1650, since in many parts of England during this period the rate of growth was higher in the earlier decades than in the later.

2. Curve II. The constant rate of growth, or 'compound interest model', based on the assumption that the rate of growth was the same throughout the period. For our purposes, this means that an equal percentage increase is added, notionally, annually. The actual population P_x, x years from the beginning of the period when the known population was P_0, is given by:

$$P_x = P_0(1 + r)^x$$

where r is the annual rate of increase.

266

Appendix B

For a large number of years or when the annual rate of increase is small this approximates to exponential growth with the formula:

$$P_x = P_0\, e^{rx}$$

where e is the constant of exponential function.

To ascertain r using the compound interest formula:

$$(1 + r)^n = \frac{P^n}{P_0}$$

$$1 + r = \sqrt[n]{\left(\frac{P^n}{P_0}\right)}$$

$$r = \sqrt[n]{\left(\frac{P^n}{P_0}\right)} - 1 = Y - 1$$

where P_n is the known population at the end of the period which is n years long [to calculate Y, subtract $\log P_0$ from $\log P_n$, divide the answer by n and antilog.].

3. Curve III. It may be assumed that the rate of growth accelerated throughout the period. This leads to a very complex formula even in the simplest case where the rate of acceleration is a constant, say, F:

$$P_x = P_0\, e^{\frac{r_1(e^{Fx} - 1)}{e^F - 1}}$$

where r, is the rate of growth between year 0 and year 1.

This curve is indeterminate since a large number of combinations of initial growth rates and rates of acceleration could give the same end result (in more mathematical terms, there are two unknowns r and F, even when $x = n$ and so P_n is known, and with only one equation it is impossible to calculate them both simultaneously).

4. Curve IV. This is a curve which might result from adding baptisms and subtracting burials from a known starting population, P_0. Populations, especially small populations, in pre-industrial times did not follow smooth growth curves. Theirs was a switchback motion.

267

5. Curve V. This is a 'true' curve, related of course to curve IV, but incorporating changes due to migration and free from the defects arising from under-registration.[1]

1 I am indebted to Peter and Valerie Jackson, Gillian Lee and Margaret Line for their help with the statistical argument of this appendix.

D. E. C. Eversley

APPENDIX C

THE QUESTION OF SAMPLING

IN France, there has been a good deal of discussion of whether any useful contribution to regional demographic studies can be made by taking a sample of parish registers and investigating these fully. The method was first proposed by M. Henry[1] and his colleagues and an enquiry is now in progress. M. Baehrel,[2] on the other hand, has attacked this scheme on a number of grounds. This debate has no particular relevance to British conditions, but we wish to discuss briefly what could be gained from a national sample enquiry for England.

The problem may be divided into two sections: the usefulness of an enquiry using aggregative methods, and on the other hand, using reconstitution. Taking the first method, which is the concern of chapter 3, we could draw samples of parishes by a number of methods: (a) a random sample nationally on the basis of a complete list of parishes, which contains an alphabetical list of all places mentioned in the census, mostly parishes, from which a predetermined fraction could be drawn;[3] (b) by broad economic regions; (c) by choosing a number of parishes out of each county. As for the national sample, this is certainly feasible. There would have to be strict rules about replacement of parishes rejected because on inspection their registers turned out to be unsuitable by any of our tests, and judging by past experience, this would very frequently be the case. The question then arises whether those parishes eventually included in the sample because they satisfied minimum conditions, would in some way be biased: because the procedure would tend to exclude urban parishes, or very small parishes, or those with a strong Nonconformist element – in other words, precisely those in which we might be most interested from an economic and social point of view.

Even if we were satisfied that no such bias existed, we should still be faced with the fact that the answers we should obtain would be strictly national ones – in other words, they might give us a better idea than Rickman's decennial summaries of the ups and downs of baptisms, burials and marriages in the country

269

as a whole, but hardly enough to recognise regional variations. Nevertheless, this would be a valuable procedure, and consideration should be given to some such scheme so as to enable us to pin-point more accurately for the country as a whole the main turning points in demographic history.

The second method of sampling, by regions, is much more feasible, especially in those areas which remained predominantly rural (whether or not they include areas of rural industry, as in Nottinghamshire). One can identify tracts of homogeneous economic structure, cutting across county boundaries, each containing some hundreds of parishes, from which a 10 per cent or even 5 per cent sample might be drawn with a fair prospect of obtaining a representative cross-section, though it must be remembered that it would be difficult to devise any objective statistical tests to know how good the sample is – there are no global statistics against which one might check the totals (though one could, as a matter of interest, check total events for the years collected by Rickman against those published by him).

The third method, by county, really seems to have little to commend it, as opposed to choosing an area containing a dozen or so contiguous parishes within a county for intensive investigation. However, there would be much to be said for a national scheme whereby through regional centres of research it was ensured that such a trial area were selected in each county, thus producing a sample stratified by availability of registers and ease of identification, rather than a random one, but this might be all to the good. We already possess such studies for quite a number of counties, and the scheme might be extended.

When we turn to the reconstitution method, the difficulties of sampling are even greater. As Dr Wrigley makes clear, even fewer single parish registers will meet the stringent tests required to make his method practicable, and therefore a random sample could only be drawn with so many rounds of substitution that one might as well start at the other end by surveying all parish registers in the country, selecting all those which offer useful information, and then choosing from this much shorter list a sample which is geographically and economically stratified in such a way as to offer some hope of useful conclusions.

Appendix C

It has also been suggested that sampling might be carried out by checking on single years, or decades, with a large number of registers, or, more easily, taking random pages from registers. The latter method would involve producing regional (or national aggregates) by entering on common tabulations data from hundreds or even thousands of parishes. The theory of this has not been worked out, but it has been suggested that one could in this way achieve chronological or regional stratification by a method of quotas which would be gradually filled: e.g. it might be decided that we need data from 1,000 parishes for the years 1701–10, 1731–40 and so on, or from single years randomly chosen within a decade, and information would then be aggregated until the 1,000-parish quota was complete. These 1,000 parishes would also be stratified, geographically so that 100 might be 'rural south-western', 100 'upland fringe areas', 100 'coastal belt', 300 'industrial north' and so on.

However, the resources and degree of co-operation between different research centres demanded by such a scheme might at the moment make this impracticable in England, though the possibility ought to be borne in mind.

D. E. C. Eversley

1 M. Fleury et L. Henry, 'Pour connaître la population de la France depuis Louis xiv. Plan de travaux par sondage', *Population* (1958), 663–86.

J. N. Biraben, M. Fleury et L. Henry, 'Inventaire par sondage des registres paroissiaux de France', *Population* (1960), 25–58.

2 R. Baehrel, 'Sur des communes échantillons', *Annales* (1960), 702–41.

3 E.g. John Gorton: *Population of Great Britain according to the returns made to Parliament in 1831* (London 1832).

APPENDIX D

THE CLASSIFICATION OF OCCUPATIONS

AN attempt is here made to subsume household heads under different social classes on the basis of their stated occupations. In view of the nature of the data, it was thought unwise to attempt a classification more refined than that of the Registrar-General. The Registrar-General's Social Classes consist of the following:

 I Capitalists, manufacturers, professional, etc.
 II Small shopkeepers, lower professional, farmers, etc.
III Skilled labour.
 IV Semi-skilled labour.
 V Unskilled labour.

His five classes are fundamentally defined in terms of social status, for the classes are based on 'general standing within the community'. However, and perhaps more particularly for the nineteenth century, they may be regarded as groups of persons having similar standards of life and probably, in general, similar incomes with which to maintain such standards.

Broadly speaking, the conventions of the Registrar-General's 1950 volume, *The Social Classification of Occupations* was used, with slight modifications. These included the attribution of all persons employing 25 or more to Class I; the upgrading of those otherwise in Class III to Class II if they employed 1 to 24 persons; small shopkeepers who employed no-one were demoted to Class III; certain minor anachronisms were eliminated; and those described as 'Independent', 'House and Land Proprietor', 'Pauper', etc., were placed under Classes I, I and V respectively. Other heads were not classifiable at all, e.g. 'Spinster', 'Husband away', 'Housewife'.

Such was the social classification of the heads used in the 1851 sample. It is dependent in part on the fact that employers stated how many men they employed. Lacking this information for 1841, an alternative scheme was used as follows:

272

Class I. As in 1851 sample, but less the handful of large entrepreneurs, not now identifiable.
Class II. Those who would have come in either Class II or III in 1851, but only if they employed domestic servants.
Class III. The same, but not employing domestic servants.
Classes IV and V. As for 1851.

It should be noted that if comparisons are to be drawn between the social classes at the two dates, those of 1851 will have to be modified to suit those of 1841.

Industrial Classification

No attempt was made to ascertain the industries in which people worked by the census authorities until 1911. The York heads were divided into:

I   Professional.
II   Administrative (local and central govt., and managers).
III   Manufacturing industry.
IV   Distribution, Personal Services, Transport and Building.
V   Agriculture and ancillary trades.
VI   Residual (the retired, Armed Forces, annuitants, etc.).

I refrain from giving further details of this here. In the York study it contributed little of value to the survey, probably because the economy of the city did not permit of proper distinctions being drawn between manufacturing industry and services, etc. At the same time I should be pleased to provide lists of occupations ascribed to the various classes and industrial groupings to any serious enquirer. It is especially important that comparability should be preserved in future studies.

W. A. Armstrong

APPENDIX E

As was pointed out on page 218, once recourse has been had to sampling, tests of significance of difference become obligatory. In the first instance, they are necessary for the purpose of testing whether the sample is representative of the total population. The 1851 York sample was tested in respect of birthplaces, age and sex distributions, and major occupational groups. We may take the first as an example.

Birthplaces of the Population of York Municipal Borough, 1851

Percentage born in	In sample	In census, printed volumes
York	47·3	46·1
East and North Ridings } West Riding	37·1	36·5
Northern Counties	6·0	5·3
Rest of England and Wales	4·5	5·1
Scotland	1·1	1·3
Ireland	3·5	5·3
Foreign Parts	0·3	0·3

There were 3,317 persons in the sample.

We are about to test whether the actual sample of 47·3 per cent (p) for persons born in York could reasonably have arisen by the processes of random sampling, given that the proportion in the whole was 46·1 per cent. In fact 95 per cent of all values of p will lie in the range $\pi \pm 1{\cdot}96\sqrt{\dfrac{(1 - \pi)}{n}}$ where p is the sample proportion, π the known population proportion, and n the number of items (in this case persons), in the sample. In only five cases out of 100 will p lie outside the range given by the formula; if it does, it is probable that there has been some systematic bias in recording.

274

Substituting the appropriate figures, our formula now reads:

$$0.461 \pm 1.96 \sqrt{\frac{0.461\,(1 - 0.461)}{3,317}} = 0.461 \pm 0.017$$

The value of p should thus lie in the range 0·478 to 0·444. Our sample value for p is 0·473, so that we are justified in concluding that the sample is representative of the city as a whole in respect of the proportion born in the city. Similar tests should be carried out on the other values, and the method may be applied to age, sex and occupational distributions in the same manner. The investigator should expect his sample to fail the test every twentieth time or so, and should not conclude that his sample is a poor one unless there are more frequent failures.

The test that has been described is based upon the normal theory of distribution, which in different forms, has various applications that are useful and indeed essential to us. Let us examine a further type of test. In the table relating York birthplaces to Social Class, it will be seen that 269 out of 781 household heads (0·344) were born in the city. But while only 0·216 of all York-born heads were in Classes IV and V, no less than 0·330 of the 221 heads born in the agricultural East and North Ridings were so placed. The question to be solved is whether this represents a true difference in the populations, or whether it merely arises as a result of sampling error.

To test this, we set up the proposition that in fact both populations, the York-born and the E. and N.R.-born had in fact a similar proportion, π, in Classes IV and V, and we have to try to demolish this hypothesis. However, we do not know what π might be, and our best estimate is to be obtained from pooling the two sample proportions, using the formula: $\dfrac{n_1 p_1 + n_2 p_2}{n_1 + n_2}$ where p_1 and p_2 are the proportions with the given character (i.e. in low social classes) in the two samples, and n_1 and n_2 are the number of items (persons) in the two samples. Substituting the necessary figures, our formula reads (with a little rounding),

$$\frac{(269 \times 0.22) + (221 \times 0.33)}{269 + 221} = 0.27.$$

The standard error of the difference between p_1 and p_2 is given by the formula $\sqrt{\left(\pi(1 - \pi) \left(\dfrac{1}{n_1} + \dfrac{1}{n_2} \right) \right)}$

And, substituting our calculated values, the equation now reads: $\sqrt{\left[(0\cdot27)(0\cdot73)\left(\dfrac{1}{269} + \dfrac{1}{221} \right) \right]} = 0\cdot04$.

The actual difference between the proportions p_1 and p_2 is $0\cdot11$, i.e. $0\cdot33 - 0\cdot22$, which is considerably more than $1\cdot96$ times the calculated standard error of $0\cdot04$, and thus, according to the normal theory, we would be justified in concluding (with a 5 per cent chance of error) that there is a significant difference between the two proportions. York-born persons did in fact figure less in the low social classes than did agricultural Yorkshire migrants. The historian in us now has to explain this, for the statistics tell us no more.

Obviously, even using the one table of raw data, there are many hypotheses which could be investigated and tested, but the use of a desk calculator will make relatively light work of what would otherwise be very laborious calculations. The statistical tests described in this appendix are the most generally useful ones: in cases which involve very small proportions of samples which are themselves very small, in absolute terms, different types of tests would be preferable from a statistical point of view, e.g. the use of Poisson probability paper in cases where λ is less than 20 ($\lambda = np$, where n is the sample size, p is the proportion of the original population with the given attribute).

W. A. Armstrong

INDEX

Age
  at marriage, 5–6, 8, 33, 34,
    71–3 *passim*, 99, 110, 111
  at death, 61, 104, 110
  structure in early censuses,
    210, 211
Aggregation, 44, 97, 111
  quinquennial and decennial
    aggregates, 29, 65, 75
  derived statistics, 73, 74–6
  calculation of rates, 76–81
  tests of rates, 81–3
  correction factors, 84–5
  calculation of base
    populations, 85–6
  calculation of population
    curves, 57, 76, 85–6, 266–8
  interpretation of crude rates,
    86
  time required, 88
  practical aids, 89
  see also Parish registers,
    Nonconformity, Rates

Baptisms, 25, 26, 55–6, 71–6
  passim, 82–8 *passim*, 164–5
  under-registration of, 26,
    83–4
  to determine base population,
    264
  slips in family reconstitution,
    125–8, 132–4
Baptism rates, 48–52
  crude, 87–8 *passim*
  of Clayworth, 165
Baptism registers, 61–2, 102–3,
    105, 108, 114

Births, 74–6 *passim*, 54–6
    passim
  illegitimate, 62
  stillbirths, 61
  under-registration of, 61
  see also Illegitimacy;
    Baptisms
Birth rates, 33–7 *passim*
  importance of age-specific
    fertility to, 33
  interpretation of crude, 87–8
    passim
  plausibility of, 55–6
Bishops' Transcripts, 46, 107,
    116, 117–18
Burials, 25, 81–8 *passim*, 97,
    99, 100, 103, 114, 121,
    164–5
  under-registration of, 83, 87
  slips in family
    reconstitution, 128–32
Burial rates, 48, 52
  of Clayworth, 165
  plausibility of, 55–6
Burial registers, 62, 103, 105,
    114, 116

Calendar
  problems of, 65–6, 114,
    118–20
  see also Harvest year
Census, 4, 25, 36, 77–8
    passim, 265
  of 1801 to 1831, 102, 209–11
  of 1801 and 1811, 80
  of 1831, 45
  of 1841, 111
  of 1841 and 1851, 211–14, 221

Census—*cont.*
use of, for social structure,
212
see also, York, Nottingham,
Liverpool, Enumerators'
books
Chapelries, 48–9, 106, 114, 116
Chilvers Coton, listing of
inhabitants of, 162, 173
Clayworth
listing of inhabitants in,
160–1, 179, 180, 186, 196,
205
defects of, 162, 164, 169
second listing of, 165
use of, by ecclesiastical and
economic historians, 172–3
Climate, 14, 15, 39, 101, 153
winters of 1709–10, 1740–41,
29
Cogenhoe
listings of inhabitants in,
171, 187
Colyton, 4, 97, 105
aggregative study of, 97–100,
111–17
Community Listing Forms,
178–82
supplementary information
for, 181
Compton Census, 79, 169–70,
171, 265
Contraceptives, 5, 28, 29
Crulai, 4, 30, 110, 111
Culture
comparative studies of, 8
literacy, 9
oral, 9
see also Literacy

Deaths
see Burials, Burial rates,
Burial registers, Mortality

Decrease
see Increase
Demography, historical
significance of, 4, 11, 14
and social structure, 6, 10,
160–205 *passim*
need for comparative and
international studies of, 8,
19
value to social and economic
history, 10, 15, 101–2, 153
and national history, 14–15,
18
in relation to local history,
6–7, 38–9
need for standardisation, 19,
44
choice of groups, 20–9
problems in study of single
places, 21
problems in study of regions,
21, 23–4, 26
problems of migration, 24–5
study of minority groups,
28
problems of time scale,
29–31
arrangement of data, 29–31
techniques of interpolation
and extrapolation, 32, 37
basic rules, 38–9
sampling, 269–71
see also, Aggregation,
Enumerators' books,
Family reconstitution,
Listings of inhabitants

Ealing
listings of inhabitants in,
162, 169, 173, 205
Enclosure
effect of, on population, 26,
38

Enumerators' books, 80,
118, 172, 211, 215
problem of boundaries, 214–
217
sampling fractions, 217–19
random sample, 219–20
tests of samples, 224,
274–6
analysis by sample notebook,
220
by ancillary notebook, 221,
223
by institutional notebook,
222
difficulties of 1841 data,
229–31
preparation of tables of
variables, 232–4
interpretation of results, 235
see also Census, Punched
cards
Epidemics, 14, 18, 45, 98
cholera, 15, 29
effect of, on minority groups,
28
influenza, 29
Expectation of life, 14, 36
see Mortality

Family reconstitution, 5, 33
disadvantages of, 44
definition of, 96
value of, 100
sources for, 102–4
problems of sources, 106–9
size of unit, 104–6
in France, 153
use of, in measurement of
migration, 152
use of, in measurement of
literacy, 152
summary of method, 111

analysis of registers, 112
transfer of register data,
117–21
sorting of slips, 121–3
calculations, 144–6, 149–51
derivation of rates, 146–8
use of other records, 152
see also Family
Reconstitution Forms,
Nonconformity, Parish
registers, Quakers,
Migration, Literacy,
Burial, Baptism and
Marriage registers
Family Reconstitution Forms,
111, 123–53 *passim*
baptism slips, 125–8
burial slips, 128–32
baptism and marriage slips,
132–4
marriage recall slips, 134–8
widows, widowers and
remarriages, 138–42
checks, 143
calculations from, 144–6,
149–51
derivation of rates, 146–8
see also Family
reconstitution
Farr, William, 61, 83
Fertility, 29, 45, 54, 57, 76,
87–8 *passim*, 99, 100, 111,
148, 153
Fertility rates
derived from FRFs, 146, 148
age-specific, 33–7 *passim*,
100, 140

Goodnestone
listing of inhabitants in,
168, 169
Graunt, J., 1

Harvest year, 4, 31, 97, 112
Henry, L.
  methods of, 4, 5, 17, 30,
    110–11, 182
Household
  problem of multiplier, 78,
    178
  tables of analysis of, 195–6
  size of, 199
  composition of, 195,
    201–4
  see also Lodgers, Servants
Hundreds, 23–24, 72, 214, 215

Illegitimacy, 45, 62, 88
  record of in family
    reconstitution, 125–7, 131
Increase, natural, 12, 33, 36,
    58, 74, 87, 99
  by immigration, 12
  causes of, 16
  see also Expectation of life,
    Baptisms, Burials

King, Gregory, 1, 2, 77, 176–8,
    197
  listings as a check to work
    of, 192, 201

Lathes, 214
Legislation
  health and welfare, 14
  corn laws, 15–16
  Settlement Act, 20, 64
  licensing of Nonconformist
    places of worship, 52
  Hardwicke's Marriage Act
    of 1753, 63, 121, 152
  Poor Laws, 64, 214
  Marriage Duty Act, 174–6,
    177

Population Act 1801, 210
  see also Taxes
Liber Status Animarum,
    170–2 *passim*
Listings of inhabitants, 79–80,
    163–4, 165
  aims of analysis, 192
  requirements of, 14, 163
  uses of, 164–5
  types of, 169–77
  ecclesiastical lists, 171–2
  state lists, 173–7
  Community Listing Forms,
    178–82
  analysis tables, 183, 189–205
  supplementary information,
    181, 183–5, 187–8, 205
  presumptive answers, 185
  see also Chilvers Coton,
    Clayworth, Compton
    Census, Goodnestone,
    Ealing, Household,
    Liber Status Animarum,
    Occupations, Parish
    registers
Literacy, 9
  measurement of, from
    parish registers, 121, 152
Liverpool, 27
  study of, from census
    material, 213
Local history
  and parish registers, 7
  as a framework for
    population history, 6–7,
    19, 235
  local units, 27
  see also Enclosure,
    Epidemics, Legislation,
    Speenhamland, Wars
Lodgers
  in listings, 205
  in Enumerators' books, 221,
    222, 230

London, 22, 149, 163, 175
  growth of, 12
  Jews in, 53
  listings of, 165
  lodgers in, 205

Malthus, Robert, 1
Maps
  use of, 216, 223
Marriage, 35, 74–6 *passim*, 97,
  99, 100, 103, 114, 121,
  164–5
  movement of partners, 22
  determinants of, 34
  length of, from FRFs, 145
Marriage rates, 33–7 *passim*,
  52
  of Clayworth, 165
  see also Age, at marriage
Marriage registers, 63–74
  in family reconstitution,
    103, 105, 107, 114
  slips in family
    reconstitution, 123–5,
    132–4
Marx, Karl, 1
Methodism, 50, 51, 53
Migration, 44, 45, 104–5, 117,
  165–6
  Irish, 16
  regional, 17–19, 22
  character of migrants, 20
  long-distance before 1800,
    22
  problems of, 24–5, 44
  statistical implications of,
    60, 81
  problems of, in family
    reconstitution, 147–9
  analysis from family
    reconstitution material,
    152

illustrated by Clayworth
  listing, 167
Mortality, 4, 29, 33–7 *passim*,
  76, 87–9 *passim*, 98, 99,
  111, 148, 149, 153
  infant, 4, 29, 36, 71–3
    passim, 76, 87, 99, 110,
    149, 151
  different features of, in
    different groups, 28
  causes of, 61
Mortality rates, 55–6
  interpretation of crude, 87,
    88, 100
  age-specific, 100, 148
  mechanism of recovering
    from high, 89
  derived from FRFs, 146
  see also Burial rates

Nicholson, Francis, 168–71
  passim, 176
  see also Goodnestone
Nonconformity, 23, 26, 44,
  49–53, 81, 82, 84, 108, 116,
  170
  lists of registers, 50, 52
  licences, 52
  Abstracts of, 51–2
  tests to measure strength of,
    52–3
  burial grounds, 81
  family reconstitution from
    registers, 153
  see also Quakers, Methodism
Nottingham
  study of, from census
    material, 214
Nuptiality, 27, 76, 87–9 *passim*,
  99, 111, 153
  see also Marriage,
    Marriage rates, Marriage
    registers

Occupations, 61, 63–4 *passim*
analysis of from listings,
197–8
in early censuses, 209, 211
categories, 209, 223, 231,
272–3
in family reconstitution,
120, 152

Parish registers, 3, 100, 102–11
passim
of towns, 106
and local historian, 7
quality of, 45
inquiry of 1831 into, 45
transcripts of 117–18
custody of, 46–7
tests of 47–53, 54–6
problems of, in family
reconstitution, 45, 106–9
continuity of, 47–53
less reliable after 1780, 53,
60
content of, 61–4
French, 3, 110
use of, with listings, 181,
183–5, 187–8, 205
Abstract of 1833, 47
see also Under-
registration, Baptism
registers, Burial registers,
Marriage registers,
Chapelries, Non-
conformists, Quakers,
Bishops' Transcripts
Parliamentary constituencies,
216
Petty, W., 1
Protestation Returns, 100
Punched cards
use of, in family
reconstitution, 151
use of, in analysis, 182

use of, in census analysis,
220, 221, 226–7
transference of data, 222–4
sorting machine, 231

Quakers, 28, 29
registers, 50
registers of births, 61
and dating, 66
reconstitution of families,
153

Rapes, 24, 214
Rates
basic, as a test of registers,
54–6 *passim*
calculation of crude, 76, 86
crude, 100
derivation of, from family reconstitution, 146–51
see also Baptism rates,
Birth rates, Burial rates,
Mortality rates, Marriage
rates
Registration, civil, 52, 83
Districts, 214, 215
see also Under-
registration
Roman Catholics, 29, 52, 53,
153, 170, 171

Sampling, 217–20, 223–4,
269–71, 274–6
Sampson, William, 160–4
passim, 165–8 *passim*,
170, 172, 178
see also Clayworth
Servants, 201, 203, 205, 221,
222, 229, 230
Speenhamland system, 14, 15

Taxes
  uses of, 173
  Hearth, 77, 79–80, 100,
    173–7 *passim*, 265
  Poll, 173
  Window, 79, 173
  Land, 174

Under-registration, 32, 37,
  55, 61, 81, 87, 114, 268
  of baptisms, 26, 83–4
  of births, 61
  of burials, 83, 87
  see also Registration

Wapentakes, 24, 214, 215
Wars, effect of
  on population, 26, 29
  on migration, 18, 22
  on special groups, 28
  Civil War, 30, 38, 98
  on sex structure, 34
Weather,
  see Climate

York
  study of, from census material,
    213–24 *passim*, 219, 230,
    233–5, 274